It's So French!

VANESSA R. SCHWARTZ

VANESSA R. SCHWARTZ is professor of history, art history, and cultural studies at the University of Southern California.

The University of Chicago Press, Chicago 60637
The University of Chicago Press, Ltd., London
© 2007 by The University of Chicago
All rights reserved. Published 2007
Printed in the United States of America

16 15 14 13 12 11 10 09 08 07   1 2 3 4 5

ISBN-13: 978-0-226-74242-7   (cloth)
ISBN-13: 978-0-226-74243-4   (paper)
ISBN-10: 0-226-74242-3   (cloth)
ISBN-10: 0-226-74243-1   (paper)

Library of Congress Cataloging-in-Publication Data

Schwartz, Vanessa R.
    It's So French! : Hollywood, Paris, and the making of cosmopolitan film culture / Vanessa R. Schwartz.
        p. cm.
    Includes bibliographical references and index.
    ISBN-13: 978-0-226-74242-7 (cloth : alk. paper)
    ISBN-10: 0-226-74242-3 (cloth : alk. paper)
    ISBN-13: 978-0-226-74243-4 (pbk. : alk. paper)
    ISBN-10: 0-226-74243-1 (pbk. : alk. paper)
    1. Motion pictures—France. 2. Motion pictures—United States. 3. France—In motion pictures. I. Title.
    PN1993.5.F7S34 2007
    791.430944—dc22

2007019033

♾ The paper used in this publication meets the minimum requirements of the American National Standard for Information Sciences—Permanence of Paper for Printed Library Materials, ANSI Z39.48-1992.

To my three R's:

RON, REBECCA, & RACHEL

Contents

Illustrations

Acknowledgments

IN THE CONCLUSION of my last book, I considered the differences between Paris and Los Angeles as a meaningful way to understand the distinctions between cultural production and urbanism in the late nineteenth and the late twentieth centuries. I did not expect that soon thereafter, I would begin the twenty-first century living in Los Angeles, but I am thoroughly delighted that I have. As a child growing up in New York in the late 1960s and 1970s, both Paris and Los Angeles played potent roles in my imaginative horizon. To the French people who educated me, Paris functioned as the central cultural and historical reference point. But that made sense. They were French. My mother and her friends concurred, and so they sent their children off to learn the French language and made French culture a frame of reference for education. Thus, like many books, this one has a small and personal question behind it. Mine was simple: why did my parents send me to French school? Although I cannot speak for her friends, I can attest that my mother's interest in France was shaped by the movies—especially the colorful and spectacular 1950s Hollywood musicals that I watched over and over with her when I was a child, lying at the foot of my parents' bed. And so, this book, whose research I began in Paris as my mother lay dying in a hospital bed in New York, has tried to answer that question since she is no longer here to answer it herself. Oddly, my mother never actually visited either Paris or Los Angeles. My mother's fantasy places have become my reality and I have lots of people to thank in both places.

Before I do that, I must acknowledge my editors at the University of Chicago Press, Doug Mitchell and Tim McGovern, who accepted a book that they knew would be difficult and expensive to publish. Mara Naselli and Matt Avery produced it. I appreciate their expertise, support, and commitment to scholarship.

This book began as part of the Media and Nations seminar at the Humanities Research Institute (HRI) at University of California, Irvine. I thank Tony Kaes, the group convener, who invited me and Patricia O'Brien, the director who supported me as an "outside visitor" to the HRI. I also thank Dean Betty T. Bennett of American University for making it easy for me to go, and my fellow group members Ed Dimendberg, Susan Larsen, Roland Marchand, Hamid Naficy, Mark Poster, Rick Rentschler, and Sarah Banet-Weiser for making me think my interest in French Can-Can Barbie might be worthwhile.

I have used many archives and libraries in this project. Sometimes that has been easy and at other times difficult. The Bibliothèque de Film (BIFI) has become a genuinely exciting new research institution in Paris. I thank its former director Marc Vernet, and especially Régis Robert, who sat alone supervising me while I used the archives during a library strike and has since helped me in countless ways. I cannot claim the same enthusiasm for the new Bibliothèque Nationale de France, but within it I want to extend my thanks to the Inathèque and Madame Christine Barbier-Bouvet, who helped me get tapes of television reports about the Cannes Film Festival. The staffs of the Archives of the Minister of Foreign Affairs in Paris, the Minister of Foreign Affairs Archives in Nantes, the Municipal Archives in Cannes, and the Departmental Archives in Nice were of much help. In the United States, the National Archives in College Park, the Film Division at the Library of Congress, Jim D'Arc at the L. Tom Perry Special Collections Library at Brigham Young University, Barbara Hall and Faye Thompson and the staff at the Margaret Herrick Library of the Academy of Motion Picture Arts and Science in Los Angeles, and Ned Comstock at the University of Southern California's Special Collections in the Cinema Library have offered enthusiastic help.

It's been a long ride pioneering the field of "Gigi Studies" as Michal Ginsburg once called it. I would like to thank Michal for inviting me to present this work at Northwestern, and to acknowledge my debt to those people in the many places I have visited in the last six years where conversations have shaped this project. One of my favorite moments in this project was when I gave a lecture at the National Gallery of Art in Washington before a screening of *Gigi* during an exhibition of art nouveau. I thank my graduate students, Linda Downs, and the late Stel Sandris for arranging that. Others I would like to thank include but are not limited to Lynn Spigel and Dana Polan, then at USC's CNTV School; Christof Mauch and Heide Fehrenbach and the German Historical Institute; Jeff Ravel at MIT; Ed Berenson at New York University's French Studies Institute; the Film and History group at the Charles Henry Warren Center at Harvard; J. P. Daughton and the Bay Area French Studies Group; Margaret Cohen and the Stanford Center for the Study of the Novel; Janis Bergman-Carton at Southern Methodist University; David Prochaska at University of Illinois at Urbana-Champaign; Virginia Wright Wexman and Mary Beth Rose at University of Illinois at Chicago; Anne Higonnet at Columbia University; Judith Walkowitz and David Bell at Johns Hopkins University; and now, closer to home, Lynn Hunt and the Europe Seminar at the University of California, Los Angeles. In Europe, I would like to acknowledge the hospitality of Marlite Halbertsma of Erasmus University, Rotterdam; Julia Noordegraaf at the University of Amsterdam; Renée Kistemaker of the Amsterdam Historical Museum; and Judith Thissen and Andre Van der Velden of the University of Utrecht. In Paris, Antoine de Baecque; Christophe Prochasson, and Jean-Fréderic Schaub at the Ecole des Hautes Etudes en Sciences Sociales; Dominique Kalifa of Paris I; and Emanuelle Loyer of Sciences Po. I owe an especially large debt of gratitude to Pierre Billard who acted as the godfather to this project in relation to the Cannes Film Festival. He is a busy and important person, yet he and his late wife Ginette took pity on me and went out of their way to help me. I am glad to count them among my friends.

There are a number of people with whom I have collaborated closely on several other projects over the years and I am grateful they have been willing to work with me. Christian Delage (Paris VII) and Vincent Guigueno (Ecole des Ponts et Chausées) have shared an interest in *ciné-histoire*; Jeannene Przyblyski (San Francisco Art Institute) on the *Visual Culture Reader*; Phil Ethington (USC) and the Urban Icons gang, especially Jeffrey Wasserstrom (UC Irvine). They are as much friends as colleagues.

As peripatetic as I have been in order to do this book, it has been my pleasure to call USC my institutional home and to make Santa Monica my residence. At USC, the former provost, Lloyd Armstrong, and the former dean of the College, Joseph Aoun, were as supportive as I could have imagined anyone could be (and their Francophilia an added bonus). Dean Michael Quick has generously supported my research and this publication. The Center for

Interdisciplinary Research fellows and Neal Sullivan offered an important means to speak across disciplines. My colleagues, the staff, especially Lori Rogers, and students in the USC History Department are owed thanks. I want to most especially acknowledge my research assistants Megan Kendrick, Laura Kalba, Liz Willis-Tropea, Ryan Linkof, Jennifer Miller, Marcelo Sousa, Katie Kirchberg, and Rachel Schwartz. Dean Sally Pratt and the faculty and graduate students that have participated in the Literary, Visual, and Material Cultures Initiative and in my Modernity and Its Visual Cultures seminar have also helped shaped this book. I am especially glad to have the wisdom and good cheer of Nancy Troy, Richard Meyer, and Anne Friedberg as fellow travelers in Visual Studies at USC.

This manuscript has benefited from very intelligent readers who are also my friends and who generously improved it along the way. Elinor Accampo, Michael Bess, Deborah Cohen, Margaret Cohen, Ed Dimendberg, Phil Ethington, Richard Fox, Lynn Hunt, Michael Kazin, and Steve Ross, are owed enormous thanks. I am lucky to say that three people who read my first book are still as dear to me now as they were when I was writing my dissertation. The long-term conversations and far-flung friendships I have had with Leo Charney, Sarah Farmer, and Sharon Marcus have sustained me through the years.

My friends who have not read the book: Lenny Berlanstein; Beth Horowitz; Nydia Lysman-Pieczanski; Marcy Wilder; Aurie Hall; Steve Byrnes; Jamie Mandelbaum, Samantha and Lizzy Byrnes-Mandelbaum; Winnie Wechsler; Jeffrey, Alice, and Jacob Wasserman; Jon Wiener; Judy Fiskin; Linda Kent; Lisa Selin; and Ana Escobar have been central to my life during the writing of this project. Good times, good times.

To my family, I give the pride of place at the end of the acknowledgements. Our cousins, the Hoffman-Oppenheims, gave us family nearby. Ernie Isaacs and Edith Isaacs are wonderful in-laws and grandparents. Sid and Edith Posel opened their homes to me with great generosity. They have also shared their love of France in ways abstract and concrete. If it were not for the apartment on the rue des Archives, I am not sure when I would have finished this book. Ruth Haase and my sister Allison and her family have been practicing medicine without a license for years and we are still alive. I speak to my father Ron Schwartz almost every day. This is just one measure of the touchstone he has been for me. His generosity has always far exceeded anything I could have expected. I only hope I can be as good a parent to my child as he has been to me. My partner, Rebecca Isaacs, and our daughter, Rachel Schwartz, have accepted Frenchness as part of their lives. Rachel can't remember a time when I wasn't writing this book. She even believes France is important and goes to musicals with me. Rebecca has listened to war stories, offered critical advice, given warm baths and massages, taught me what support really means, and offered it in abundance. For this and more, I am grateful.

ANNOUNCING: THE 1957 TELEVISION AWARDS

LOOK

20¢ JANUARY 7, 1958

IKE'S
SECOND TERM
TRAGEDY

The mixed-up
Democrats

GM's 50 years
of men, money
and motors

Brigitte Bardot
conquers America

0.1 Triptych photo on the cover of *Look* Magazine, January 7, 1958.

Introduction

In the first week of January 1958, *Look,* a popular middle-brow American weekly, featured a triptych of three photographs on its cover (fig. 0.1). In the center, one sees an almost abstract high-tech image doctored with an overlay of saturated colors (identified within the magazine as an "electric induction furnace" essential to the fabrication of car radios). That image is linked to an article about General Motors' fifty-year history. Flanking this industrial image are two portraits. On the left, one of President Dwight Eisenhower is tied to a story about his "second term tragedy." The other, a glossy still of the French actress Brigitte Bardot pressed up against a wall, shoulders bared, pouting mouth, and eyes directly facing the viewer, is attached to the headline "Brigitte Bardot Conquers America." The president of the United States, cars, and a French movie star.

Let us reconsider the image and its accompanying text. Eisenhower's health problems, the unpopular school integration in Little Rock, and the Soviet achievements of Sputnik had dampened public enthusiasm for the president midway through his second term. That this subject should headline *Look*'s first issue for the year seems like business as usual. Yet, alongside the tale of GM's triumph and Eisenhower's tragedy, the magazine headlined Bardot's "conquest of America." This juxtaposition is particularly disarming since we have come to think of seduction rather than conquest as the apt term for the operations of mass culture on an uncritical audience. Richard Kuisel's influential book about the Americanization of France, *Seducing the French,* and Victoria de Grazia's more recent study, *Irresistible Empire: America's Advance through Twentieth-Century Europe,* both emphasize mass culture's power of persuasion and the lure of consumption as soft forms of power, which facilitated the lop-sided transatlantic exchange known as Americanization.[1] Was the use of the word "conquest" a joke, and a sexist one at that? Surely, but it was also more. Although the study of the Americanization of Europe has left us with a strong sense of domination of the Old World affected by the flow of mass culture from America to Europe, the *Look* headline suggests that mass culture traveled in a two-way exchange.

Like many an ephemeral item from everyday life in the past, the *Look* cover presents us with a world that is both remote from our own experience and also speaks to the present. *Look* magazine's striking cover images provoked me to ask a number of questions: if America was so powerful, how could a French movie star, a commercial import, have "conquered" it? Wasn't it true that the only movies that mattered were American movies? Weren't French films at best an elite art-house genre for the intellectual crowd? Although countless books have been dedicated to explaining Hollywood's conquest of the world film market, the magazine cover took for granted the power of a French movie star in a way that would be impossible today. It suggests that more than ten years after the end of World War II, French mass culture could "matter" in America.

How far we have come since the days of Bardot's conquest of America! It is hard to be an American historian who studies the history of modern France without feeling the effects of the contemporary rising tide of French anti-Americanism on the one hand and American dislike and disdain for a culture and nation we once held in very high esteem. The mutual admiration between the longtime allies the United States and France has been jolted out of its centuries-old state of bliss by changed post–Cold War political circumstances: French culture has declined in its power and prestige, and France and the United States have clashed over their very different approaches to migrating populations and resulting multiethnic societies. Our most recent memory of cultural conflict with the French has eclipsed a much longer history of close and peaceful relations. French wine poured literally and figuratively through the streets of midwestern towns where "freedom fries" were born as the French government criticized the recent American-led Iraq War. In rural France, Ronald McDonald and his fries fell under physical attack as activists resisted the "Americanization" of such essential forms of French culture as food.[2]

These now familiar clichés have replaced a longstanding history of shared interest and appreciation. From the early exploration in the sixteenth century to the subsequent colonial settlements of the next, the French king and Church had a keen interest in the North American continent. During the eighteenth century, which saw both the French Revolution and the independence of certain British colonies, intellectual life in Paris played an important role in shaping the ideas of revolutionary figures such as Thomas Paine, Benjamin Franklin, and Thomas Jefferson. France offered invaluable military support to the insurgent colonists (who can forget the exploits of General Lafayette?), and Alexis de Tocqueville provided one of the most enduring and insightful descriptions of the young American republic ever written.

Americans have literally followed in these footsteps ever since. France has always served as the favored destination of privileged American travelers. When world tourism expanded in the mid-twentieth century, France became the primary stop for American tourists crossing the Atlantic for the first time.[3] Because a comparatively small numbers of French immigrants lived in the United States relative to the Irish, Italians, Chinese, Germans and Jewish Russians and Poles, France avoided association with the despised and huddled masses on the shores of the New World. Unlike other major European nations, France remained a fantasy world of culture and civilization.

Recent scholarship has begun to rewrite the history of Franco-American relations. The earlier portrait of mutual aid and admiration between the two "sister republics" has given way to a surge of studies that outline enmity, disdain, and rivalry.[4] Philippe Roger's *The American Enemy* stands at the apex of this literature—a vast intellectual history of French anti-Americanism from the eighteenth century until today. He paints an unflattering portrait of French ethnocentrism in which anti-Americanism has served as a glue that helped bind French identity, especially since the Spanish-American War at the end of the nineteenth century. Roger's history of French rhetoric about America is, of course, a portrait of a nation seen through a distorted mirror. This book instead presents a more dynamic narrative of the history of transnational cultural circulation. It is an interactive model of Franco-American relations in a particularly important moment in the history of the Atlantic world: the 1950s and early 1960s.

Culture has, of course, played an important role in Franco-American histories in the twentieth century. Scholars have revealed the difficulties the French had coming to grips with becoming a consumer society, a process exacerbated by the arrival of American mass culture and products in the French market. Culture became the domain in which an anxious France would have to be compelled to modernize and join the century that was almost half over by the 1950s. In a variety of ways, historians have portrayed France as receiving rather than producing mass culture. That story then ends with the inevitable, although not always peaceful, French adoption of "American-style mass culture" by the late twentieth century.[5] Disneyland has built its own castle (inspired by Chambord) on the outskirts of Paris and the French countryside has enough plastic Ronald McDonald statues to make toppling one a meaningful form of cultural resistance.

Much French cultural history has reinforced the idea that mass culture is somehow "not French." We know about French painters and sculptors, haute couture and haute cuisine, artisanal chocolatiers and skilled furniture craftsmen. Historians have focused on French artisanal values, small-scale luxury production, and discourses that attempted to disavow mass taste by speaking of cultural fads as "chic." In short, studies have even claimed that the French managed to turn mass production into art.[6] My interest, beginning with *Spectacular Realities,* has been to restore the rightful if disavowed place of France—and Paris in particular—in developing consumerism and mass cultural entertainments.[7] French devotion to technology in the twentieth century shows that they have been active "modernizers." From the Eiffel Tower to high-speed trains, the supersonic transport plane, the Minitel, and nuclear energy, to high-tech glass and metal aesthetics in the renovation of Paris in the 1980s and 1990s, France has distinguished itself among those countries that embrace leading-edge technology.[8] In contrast, "culture" (literature, art, and music) in France has been seen as the "classical" French culture of Racine and Molière only improved by the complexity of Proust; it has been associated with the painters that defined modern art such as Courbet, Manet, and Renoir; it bears the matrix of high theory and philosophy from Descartes to Sartre, Derrida, and Foucault. Nonelite culture has been celebrated in the form of a rich "popular" culture of the peasantry and their folktales and carnivals.[9] Yet French "modernizers" existed in the cultural sphere as well. In particular, in the sphere of technologically reproducible image-making from lithography to posters and from photography to film, French people (especially in Paris) have innovated and disseminated mass culture and thus created a functioning mass society.[10]

Of the mass visual media that emerged in the late nineteenth century, no form has been as singularly influential as film. Although film developed almost simultaneously in France, England, Germany, and America, the first film screening proper happened in Paris in December 1895 in the Salon Indien of the Grand Café on the bustling boulevard des Capucines, near the Paris Opéra. That story itself involves a complex back and forth between France and America as Thomas Edison visited the Paris Exposition in 1889 and saw Etienne-Jules Marey's "chronophotographe," which helped him develop the Kinetoscope; the Kinetoscope helped lead the Lumière brothers to their own innovations—the Cinématographe they put on display in Paris in late 1895. In the medium's first twenty years, French companies, including Gaumont but especially Pathé, dominated the world market. Richard Abel has rightly spoken of how cinema was made "American" as a response to French domination.[11] But this had long been forgotten in the wake of World War I. A reversal in relative cultural and economic strength enabled the American film industry to dominate the world's silent screens. Ever since, Hollywood has been seen as the great harbinger of Americanization around the world.

Film may have been a key vector of Americanization, but its far greater and more enduring contribution has been to the globalization of culture. As this book will show, "Americanization" has had neither a clear nor functional definition, even during the 1950s to the mid-1960s.[12] Instead, what emerged was a "cosmopolitan" cinema in the twenty years after World War II. This term denotes multinational production teams making films that represented subjects, themes, and plots that underscored a transnational cultural experience and perspective rather than a discrete national experience of culture that contributed to separate national identities and rivalries.

Although we now often speak of "global media" culture we do not have a sufficiently textured sense of how it came to be. This book offers a history of that culture that is neither determinist (it is all in the technology) nor fatalistic (it is really about American domination), but rather shows just how contingent the story of global media is when approached as a historical problem. Historians of international relations such as Akira Iriye have suggested "globalization was a more pervasive force than the geopolitical realities during the 1950s, producing a number of developments outside the drama of the Cold War."[13] This study tries to capture one aspect of that connectedness during the height of the Cold War: the development of film culture.

When David Held and Anthony McGrew argue that corporations, not countries, are driving globalization, they are describing a situation that has been made possible by many factors, including the creation of a society connected by images, first cinematic and now delivered by television and the Internet.[14] Benedict Anderson's notion of "imagined communities" has shown the way national communities were forged through print culture, but the Euro-American image culture of the twentieth century is different from what Anderson describes. Thus, we need to ask whether the communities imagined in the twentieth century were exclusively "national" ones. Global identity has been forged in part through film culture and its images. But the global culture does not simply "replace" national or local culture. Instead, global culture becomes an idiom through which an additional identity is formed, one whose very definition is based on the knowledge that it is being simultaneously consumed around the world. In that way, of course, film has always been global.

This book presents one strand of that larger history of the globalization of film. Although my focus is France and America as an axis of cultural transfer, there are other ways of tracking the historical exchange of film culture that might be equally interesting.[15] While diplomatic historians have long worked in archives in different countries and intellectual historians write about international "republics of letters," cultural historians have shied away from both comparative and transnational history. It seemed easier to understand culture as a "local" expression and, famously in French studies circles, culture became a mechanism for understanding essential notions of nationality and national character.[16] Film as a cultural form, however, is best understood within the context of transnational cultural transfers and circulation.

Looking at France and America and their interaction in film is particularly important for several reasons. First, at different moments in time, each country claimed global hegemony of film production and distribution. Second, film played a central role as a commercial and cultural formation in both countries. Last, this study claims that looking at French and American film in the 1950s and early 1960s provides a critical axis of analysis. A close look at this period will help us better understand the developments of film history in relation to today's global media culture.[17]

Hollywood and Paris performed a pas-de-deux in the increasingly global production and distribution of films as the marketing of "Frenchness" became a fundamental element in the globalization of film culture. This book describes that interaction by looking at the extravagant Frenchness films of the 1950s, the creation of both a world stage for the presentation of films and an international marketplace of distribution at the Cannes Film Festival, Brigitte Bardot's meteoric career and the simultaneous interest in foreign-language film in America, the rise of the cosmopolitan films exemplified by *Around the World in Eighty Days,* and the growth of big-budget, English-language films shot on location all over the world.

The foregrounding of French and American film culture underscores another argument of the book: that "cosmopolitanism" emerged in film during the late 1950s and early 1960s and depended upon a strong investment in "Frenchness" in both France and America. Throughout the course of this book, we will see Frenchness deployed by members of the film production community and the industry more broadly conceived; by film critics in their reviews, and by audiences and observers whenever the sources allowed such points of view to be directly expressed. Frenchness both sharpened the distinctions between the national cinemas of France and America as economic and cultural entities, while also sowing the transatlantic cultural field with universalism and internationalism that relied on a new postwar culture of both real and imagined social and cultural mobility.

The French enthusiastically helped package Frenchness for export in the form of mass cultural visual clichés. But even more importantly, Americans did too. In fact, signal images of Frenchness were themselves imports into France from the fertile imaginations of Hollywood's filmmakers. Scholars have already studied the formation of national identity and symbols in an attempt to understand how civic and patriotic ritual connects strangers. But marketing and trading "nation-ness" as a series of visual clichés could and did construct an imagery that transcended the nation as an imagined community.

This study urges us to look beyond national history as the frame for studies of culture in the twentieth century. The term "Atlantic world" has been used to describe the European–North American commerce and culture across the ocean between 1500 and 1800, but is less commonly used for the period after American independence.[18] Yet this Atlantic world has developed in a continuous history, even after the rise of nations and nationalism in the nineteenth century. Important works such as Daniel T. Rodgers's *Atlantic Crossings* suggest the deep connections between American elites, the formation of social politics in America, and developments in Europe during the Progressive Era. Histories of consumer culture, tourism, and youth, especially after World War II, have made clear that transatlantic crossings were central in the marketing of goods and travel for those who came of age after the war.[19]

Recent studies have begun to recast this history through a more Atlanticist framework, showing how France and America formed a particularly important nexus in the Cold War, consumerism, and globalization in the twenty-five years after D-day. In *Cold War Holidays*, Christopher Endy demonstrates that D-day, apart from its well-known military significance, also ushered in a new era of tourism. Americans became the world's great tourists and the French continued to enjoy their role as the world's greatest hosts. Endy argues that the cultural imagery generated by tourism "on the whole offered symbols and narratives that could allow Americans to imagine themselves part of a shared Atlantic Community with France."[20] Mass tourism, he suggests, developed along an axis of exchange that requires us to reconsider simple formulas about "American mass culture" and the "Americanization of France."

Rather than track tourists and their imagery, I follow a culture industry whose currency was moving images. This book emphasizes the way "Frenchness" on screen and as an organizing category of film culture helped foster the emergence of cosmopolitanism in both film images and as a postwar production practice. Investigating cultural transfer between France and America during the 1950s and early 1960s helps to concretize the study of the globalization of film.

There are many types of film history. Because film has become a predominant mode of entertainment during the last century, some scholars have connected it to the history of leisure, pleasure, and amusement.[21] The success of Hollywood's industrial production has engendered an important history of the economic organization of film. The history of the studios and the production, distribution, and exhibition of film in America and throughout the world, the star system, issues of trade and tariffs, and censorship all function as essential elements in understanding the history of film. As the primary medium for the delivery of narrative in the twentieth century, film historians have looked at plots, genres, and subjects to reveal the ideology embedded within them.[22] A broader film culture that includes fan discourse and publications, institutions such as the Oscars, film festivals, film archives, and museums are essential components in the writing of film history as both sources and objects of study.[23]

By integrating important economic and legal components in film history with a more general social and cultural historical approach, this book illustrates that the complexity of film demands a multifaceted approach. Thus, this study also examines institutions such as the Cannes Film Festival, exhibition issues such as independent movie theaters and the coming of widescreen technology, the production and promotion and reception of films, and the connection of those films and institutions to other forms of visual culture such as painting and photography. The French-American exchange I analyze both confirms the importance of Hollywood in the history of film and insists that France, Frenchness, and French film interests shaped that history in ways we have previously overlooked.

This study moves between two nations but does not seek primarily to compare or contrast them. Instead, the object of examination here is a transnational space. Cultural exchange and influence are analyzed in their own terms, rather than as a function of politics or economics. Yet as Pascale Casanova has argued in her recent book about the transnational dimension of modern literary history, cultural influence and political domination do not always coincide.[24] Drawing inspiration from Fernand Braudel's observations about the relative independence of artistic and economic power in the early modern world, Casanova charts what she calls a "world republic of letters" and identifies the central role Paris played as a physical and symbolic center of an international literary space. This book identifies a similar space for film. It looks at how social, economic, and political institutions are shaped by the visual culture they produce and argues that films have agency in shaping and reshaping the nation, the imagination, and the transnational space of film culture.

Cultural exchange does not develop in a simple formula with respect to political contexts. As Margaret Cohen and Carolyn Dever suggest in their collection about literary cultural exchange across the channel between France and England, "political hostilities diminished neither the intensity nor the cultural centrality of Anglo-French intellectual and literary exchange" during the early nineteenth century. Despite political animosity and ongoing warfare between the two nations, a vibrant transnational culture thrived within a "Channel Zone."[25] A history of cultural production must account for and accept these disjunctures between politics and culture. No sphere—political, economic, or cultural—is completely autonomous, nor is the cultural field epiphenomenal, as it has been too often treated. Cultural texts and experiences shape politics and economics as much as they reflect them. In the 1950s and 1960s, long before the end of the Cold War, film culture fostered cosmopolitan production and vision.

Casanova's study also helps illuminate the role Paris played in the international space of the world republic of letters. She emphasizes the remarkable confluence of Paris as standing for both the French Revolution's political freedom and as the cultural beacon of classical letters, arts, and fashion.[26] The world republic of letters operated on the principle that Paris could and did function as a denationalized capital for world cultural production. Although this belief was in part mythological, as Casanova points out, the mythology had social consequences. Paris, as a result, actually became cosmopolitan as it drew the world's writers to it.[27] As Franco Moretti has shown, Paris (along with London) ruled literary production for over a century, and at least half of all European novels in the nineteenth century were published there.[28]

Hollywood became the center of production for film, the twentieth century's quintessential cultural form, in the way Paris had become the center for the nineteenth-century novel. Yet what this study also examines is what happened to and with "Paris" in light of the rise of Hollywood as a capital of cultural production. It argues that because Paris owned culture before Hollywood owned the movies, the Paris-Hollywood story is a particularly important one to tell.

This study also provides cultural explanations for why Paris played such an important role in the postwar struggles between America and the Soviet Union. The persistent importance of French film, despite its own limited commercial value and long after France could wield major political and economic power on an international scale, suggests the complex connection of politics and culture. The postwar American promotion of "freedom" endowed cultural freedom with political significance. Frenchness in film echoed earlier iterations of Frenchness with the cultural freedom of the Enlightenment and its cosmopolitanism. Even if such "international" cultural organizations as the Congress for Cultural Freedom were really Cold War–inspired CIA projects, Paris served as their headquarters because that city denoted an "international" cultural space.[29] This book thus refreshes the narrative of "Cold War culture" by moving it away from an emphasis on the centrality of propaganda about the "American way of life" to establishing its even more complex achievement: the globalization of capitalist culture, the century's greatest weapon against Communism.

No cultural form has been so often and for so long identified with American influence as movies made in Hollywood. Recent research has shown that other spheres of popular culture, especially music, can be marshaled in the name of generational revolt.[30] Because we have come to presume that film helps define or construct nations, it naturally follows that when one country's film culture comes to dominate the markets of another, there is cause for alarm. Bells sound about imperialism, hegemony, "Americanization." Individual national European cinemas have been understood as defenders of the nation against foreign domination, or as united in common European cause against Hollywood.[31] For example, the Film Europe movement of the 1920s combated the initial "Americanization" of film in Europe after World

War I.[32] Victoria de Grazia's *Irresistible Empire* recapitulates the battle between European and American film as one waged until World War II and then lost by Europe. After the war, de Grazia contends, "to create a successful national cinema meant finding a niche within the Hollywood system."[33]

The history of film during the postwar period is about more than the persistence of national cinemas and suggests how they gave way to the establishment of a more cosmopolitan film industry. The French case, has, however, seemed to epitomize the continuation of the ardent European resistance to Hollywood in the form of a government policy of cultural protectionism. If Brigitte Bardot in her own time was France's most famous cinematic icon, the star of the histories of the relations of the French and American film industries are the Blum-Byrnes Accords of 1946, which reinforced notions of the protection of film as a form of nationalism. In fact, histories of French and American disputes over screen-time quotas from the 1930s to the GATT negotiations in the 1990s have so dominated histories of Franco-American film relations that they have reduced the subject to simple cultural diplomacy thus occluding any broader view of Franco-American film culture.

The Blum-Byrnes Accords of 1946 were part of a general negotiation arrived at by U.S. Secretary of State James Byrnes and acting French Prime Minister Léon Blum. The agreements cancelled France's debts to the United States to insure that Léon Blum would maintain power in the postwar era instead of falling victim to a potential Communist coup from within France. The notorious agreement did not limit the number of American films imported into France but it did set a guarantee that French film would get 30 percent of screen time (eventually renegotiated to 38 percent). The Germans were actually the first nation to impose such limits on the import of American films in 1921, and the French followed suit in 1928, subsequently loosening screen-time quotas in the 1930s. After the war and the Blum-Byrnes Accords, however, they became a touchstone for the imbalance of power between France and America.

Not all sectors of the French film industry favored quotas. Film exhibitors did not care about what nation's films were showing in their theaters so long as they drew a crowd.[34] Nevertheless, protests raged in France among certain sectors of the film industry, especially on the Left, which utilized the imbalance of the accords as a political opportunity to bash the United States. Film became a football in international relations. Eventually, numerical quotas on U.S. films were imposed again, but the Americans voluntarily limited their film exports further to 124 films per year; in practice, even fewer were actually viewed, since French films continued to find a healthy domestic audience.[35]

Recently, Jens Ulff-Moeller has tried to modify the singular importance of the Blum-Byrnes Accords while remaining committed to explaining American films' global domination as a function of diplomatic manipulations of political economy. In particular, he has reasserted that the MPEA (Motion Picture Export Association) operated as a "little State Department." With the support of the U.S. Government, the MPEA allowed studios to operate as a cartel, and the Webb-Pomerene Act of 1918 allowed cartels to operate in export markets. The French government, meanwhile, created an unfavorable domestic situation for their own films by taxing theatrical revenues, thereby keeping the French film industry undercapitalized. Ulff-Moeller emphasizes that the battle for screen time between France and America also meant that all the other European cinemas had to compete with the Americans for screen time in France. What he does not acknowledge is how this strategy effectively shored up the postwar French film industry vis-à-vis every nation except the United States. The French film industry thus remained viable, witnessing its greatest expansion in the U.S. market since before World War I. By stressing the points of intersection and cooperation, this book shows that enmity was only one facet of the relationship between France and America in and around their film industries.

World War II marked an important crossroads in the development of a singular global film industry as a response to many of the wartime uses of film. The regimes of Hitler and Mussolini had already seized on the importance of film as a tool of state ideology, although not all the films produced during the fascist era were "propaganda" films.[36] The war also disrupted film trade and instigated a massive reorganization of the film industries in France, Italy, and Germany. In its wake, American films that had not been screened during the war were "dumped" on the European market as part of the victory spoils. According to the American Department of Commerce in January of 1949, 72 percent of all feature films shown in Europe were American. Hollywood producer Walter Wanger noted in 1948: "The motion picture industry has been the nearest thing to Senator Benton's conception of a Marshall Plan for ideas."[37] It is hard to dispute the triumph of American international distribution, especially in the immediate postwar period.

Yet this triumph was short lived as domestic challenges reshaped the film business. First, the 1948 Paramount decrees that busted the studios' monopoly on production, distribution, and exhibition broke up the vertical integration that had made the studios such efficient models of industrial production. Second, the growth of television and the social decentralization of suburbia drained audiences away from movie houses. Finally, the HUAC (House Un-American Activities Committee) hearings and concomitant blacklisting damaged the industry and brought internal turmoil. Cinema seemed to metamorphose from a routine mass distraction into a more segmented element among a growing array of consumer diversions.

But Hollywood did not give up easily, and responded in the 1950s with new strategies to attract viewers. Studios invested in making fewer but "better" movies. New venues such as drive-ins were opened to attract a more mobile and autocentric American public. Finally, theatrically oriented exhibitions (road shows) and new widescreen technologies renewed a sense of novelty for the grand scale of the movies, and further distinguished it from television.[38]

The changes in Hollywood associated with the "decline" resonated in Europe, drawing the transatlantic industries into greater mutual cooperation.[39] This transatlantic practice produced what Peter Lev has called "meta-generic films" of the Euro-American cinema, which combined Hollywood entertainment with the European art film. This study investigates further the way Frenchness worked in two film industries to create the popular cosmopolitan cinema of the decade from the mid-1950s to mid-1960s. Frenchness as a commodity in films and film culture also resonated in economic terms. The Americans correctly believed that the French market was their gateway to Europe; France was the largest European exporter of film to the United States for most of the 1950s and 1960s, following Italy's short-lived dominance in 1947–48.[40] Hollywood's marketing innovations in combination with France's cinematic caché combined to create an environment ripe for cultural collaboration.

This study tracks both the actions of various players associated with the French film industry and the widespread dissemination of images of Frenchness in postwar film. The first chapter, "The Belle Epoque that Never Ended: Frenchness and the Can-Can Film of the 1950s" examines the great era of the "Frenchness film." In 1951, *An American in Paris* won the Academy Award for best picture. In 1958, *Gigi* not only won best picture but also became the most Oscar-winning film in the thirty-year history of the awards. Why was this the "era" of the "Frenchness" film in Hollywood? How was France depicted, and further, what did it signify? By looking at production histories, critical reception, memoirs, and the films themselves, I argue that the Belle Epoque is the most pervasive cliché of Frenchness, but that its signification is complex. The world of the Moulin Rouge coincided with the initial rise of mass culture, and thus became the single most repeated image of France. Impressionist paintings, posters, and early film established the inventory upon which later popular visual culture would draw. While on the surface the films may appear to be simple travelogues supporting the rise of American tourism to Paris, they also signaled France's generative role in the commercial arts while linking French and American mass visual cultures.

The next chapter examines the smashing success of the Cannes Film Festival, which had been founded before the war in reaction to the fascist spectacle of the Venice Film Festival. The Cannes Festival did not open until 1946, but it soon became the world's most important international stage for film exhibition and its most central film distribution market. The Cannes Festival organizers marshaled their own ideas of France's special role as a center of cosmopolitan culture production to simultaneously strengthen the French film industry and become the center of international film culture. One key to the festival's success was that its organizers cooperated extensively with the United States film industry and promoted internationalism as the driving vision of film culture. In other words, Hollywood participated in the French-led establishment of a postwar "world" film headquarters on the shores of the Mediterranean rather than the Pacific. The Cannes Festival embodied an international film culture in which nations, including the United States, coexisted, cooperated, and coproduced. It became a crossroads of the film production community, making possible the international coproductions that came to characterize the cosmopolitan film culture of the mid-1950s to mid-1960s.

The third chapter, "And France Created Bardot" examines the meteoric rise of Brigitte Bardot, the singular phenomenally successful popular French "export" during the postwar period. Frenchness films and the Cannes Film Festival helped prepare the way for Bardot's ascent. Her success rested on her representation as mobile and modern, both connected to and well beyond her status as a sex symbol. Bardot's American popularity catapulted her into the realm of "international" stardom. It would be difficult to explain Bardot's success in the American context without an examination of the history of foreign film in America. Although others have studied the postwar rise of foreign film in the United States, almost all have looked at the weakened state of the American film industry to explain the rise of foreign film in the late 1950s and early 1960s. Instead, this chapter shows that the French themselves played a vital role in the promotion of French film by opening the French Film Office in New York in 1956, encouraged and aided by the American film industry's Foreign Advisory Bureau. Bardot helped cement the viability of the French film industry by assuring it an export market for a brief moment. Yet, the viability of French film did not merely benefit the French film industry. Rather, Bardot's career shows that France and America worked together, marketing Frenchness to the benefit of the transatlantic film business.

The book's last chapter, "The Cosmopolitan Film: From *Around the World in Eighty Days* to Making Movies around the World" shows how cosmopolitan film culture emerged from the ground prepared by Franco-American exchange. The chapter links developments in the business of making films with the content and visual narratives of a group of films I call the cosmopolitan film cycle. The powerful pairing of France and America helped produce the phenomenon that extended well beyond their axis of interaction, inaugurating a key moment in the globalization of film culture. Although the Cannes Festival evokes the small "art film" of the 1960s in our contemporary imagination, it also played a key role in fostering the crass and commercial, massive, multinational all-star coproductions (such as *Around the World in Eighty Days, Exodus, The Fall of the Roman Empire, Doctor Zhivago*) by offering a stage designed for exhibiting "international" production. Critics mostly disdained these films but their very existence and some of their remarkable financial successes (*Around the World* made $68.5 million on a $6 million investment between 1956–58) help us understand the role that cosmopolitanism played in film culture and subsequently the way that this orientation has continued to shape film as a global medium and industry.

In order to understand the development of the increasingly global context of and for film production, I suggest we need to better grasp the roles played by two nations and film industries whose connection after World War II would dramatically shape the course of film's development. This book eschews easy platitudes such as the "Americanization" of culture around the world via film by casting a serious eye to such pleasing sights as Brigitte Bardot and her pride of place next to the failing Eisenhower on the cover of *Look*. Frenchness still mattered in postwar culture, even in mass culture, in a way that suggests cultural influence is neither a mere function of nor reflection of political and economic forces. Finally, this book tells a story of affinity and cooperation between two cultures that have had and continue to have much in common and whose knowledge and appreciation of each other has been beneficial to both. We open this study with one of the most enduring visions of this mutual admiration, MGM's *An American in Paris*.

THE BELLE EPOQUE THAT NEVER ENDED

Frenchness and the Can-Can Film of the 1950s

MGM'S NOW CLASSIC FILM, *An American in Paris*, begins with a credit sequence awash in symbols of France. A tricolor ribbon overlain by a subtle *fleur de lys* sits in the top left hand corner of an embossed invitation doubling as the film's opening credits (fig.1.1). This imagery invokes the long-term history of France through its symbols of kingdom and nation: the *fleur de lys* for the former and the tricolor for the latter. But this film, like so many of the films set in France and made for an international audience, is really a film about Paris. The opening sequence features several panoramic shots of the nineteenth-century monumental city (the Place de la Concorde, the Opéra, the Alexander III bridge). These views are broken up by shots of the gardens of the Louvre at the Arc du Carousel and of the leafy green end of the Ile de la Cité, obscuring what might have been a look at Nôtre Dame. Aside from one shot of the Place Vendôme outside the Ritz Hotel, these are the film's only images shot on location in Paris. The dream factory of MGM's studio in Culver City instead manufactured the city of light.

An American in Paris initiated the "wave" of 1950s Frenchness films, which were, for the most part, Paris films.[1] Bracketed by *An American in Paris* (1951) and *Gigi* (1958), the two most celebrated films of the genre, are *Sabrina* (1953), *Moulin Rouge* (1952), *Lili* (1953), *April in Paris* (1954), *French Can-Can* (1954), *Daddy Long Legs* (1955), *Lust for Life* (1956), *Funny Face* (1957), *Silk Stockings* (1957), and *Les Girls* (1957). Three slightly later films—*Black Tights* (1960), *Can-Can* (1961), and *Irma La Douce* (1963)—complete the cycle, and confirm the familiar postwar themes of the Americanization of Europe and the Cold

1.1 Title image, *An American in Paris*, 1951.

War.[2] One interpretation of these Frenchness films is to read them as vehicles of American ideology and Americanization. Harmless and feminized, France is represented by the dancer-turned-actress, Leslie Caron, who plays "orphan" roles in *An American in Paris, Lili,* and *Daddy Long Legs.* A weak and backward postwar France then encounters dashing America and, eventually seduced, "modernizes" and submits to the confident and forward-looking American way of life. But films are not merely transparent vehicles for ideology, nor are they depictions of measurable "attitudes" of one nation towards another. Although the victory over the Axis Powers in World War II may well have led to a victory for the "American Way of Life," surely these films can and should be understood in a way that does more than reflect what we already know about the political and ideological climate of the period. If not, why study the films at all?

What is most striking about the Frenchness films is that they represent "France" as a particular time and place: Belle Epoque Paris, which straddled two centuries and became the emblematic representation of France for movie audiences in the 1950s. Turn-of-the-century clichés of the Can-Can, Moulin Rouge, Impressionist and post-Impressionist paintings and palette, and commercial art posters came to bear particular meanings of Frenchness when shot through a midcentury context.

Even at the time, critics noted the fascination with the Belle Epoque in the Frenchness films. In 1958, a *Time* magazine film critic described *Gigi* as "the most ornate of the cinema's recurrent funerals for the fin-de-siècle."[3] *An American in Paris,* ostensibly set in the 1950s, was, in fact, a vehicle of fin-de-siècle imagery. By representing Frenchness in an historic setting, one might consider that American filmmakers neatly and conveniently relegated France's potency to the past. Or one could conclude that these nostalgia films use the post–World War I mythology of the fin-de-siècle as an innocent and joyous time in an attempt to side-step the realities of the Vichy regime's collaboration, especially as the Americans positioned themselves as "liberators" in France. These short-term explanations, however, leave cultural expression hanging as an outlet for the political rather than the arena of meaning-making itself.

Thus to really understand such films, it is vital to offer greater contextualization beyond the immediate postwar context and to examine the films' visual narratives and their production histories rather than summarize their settings and plots. Frenchness films were extravagant, expensive, noteworthy, often musical, and often quite memorable. Not only did the studios invest them with great artistic and economic resources, but they also achieved both creative and popular success. They remain among the films most remembered from the 1950s in France and in America. Despite their overt nostalgia, they depict French culture as "modern" at a moment when "modernization" seemed to be an American quality that needed application by the Americans in France. Thus 1950s Frenchness films need to be recontextualized as part of a longer history of visual culture in which Paris served as a beacon. The popular visual culture of the French Belle Epoque came to dominate the new century and shape Franco-American cultural relations after World War II as well. The connection between France and America after the war was marked by affinity and celebration, not the rejection and sense of superiority argued by historians of foreign relations and historians who have described the emergence of an important American art scene in the twentieth century, especially after World War II.[4]

English-language films that featured Paris and the Frenchness it invoked celebrated cinema's heritage in the crucible of fin-de-siècle France. These films link the history of entertainment to a transnational context of development from France to America. As "heritage" films they worked to situate 1950s filmmaking in relation to the generative historical moment of modern visual culture. The films pay homage to France to celebrate film itself as an emblem of modern life and finally, to flaunt cinema's eclipse of earlier static forms of visual representation. At a moment when television introduced grave concern for the future of filmgoing, these films reasserted the magic of the form.[5] The films are impressive, technically rendered aesthetic achievements (some of the best of the period). By self-consciously foregrounding matters of visual artifice, they advocated to filmmakers and audiences alike that entertainment could also be art.

Filmmakers turned to depictions of France as a way to situate the contemporary visual culture they were producing. In what might seem a counterintuitive twist, the Belle Epoque figures were not imbued with nostalgia (as might be said of a film such as *Meet Me in St. Louis*), but rather portrayed the link that helped establish cultural continuity and a historical context for both postwar filmmakers and their cultural product. The films suggest that in the 1950s, American filmmakers and audiences identified France as much with mass entertainment culture and film as with the "high culture" of French painting, literature, and luxury goods. In other words, these films about the French Belle Epoque and its visuality linked America's premier cultural expression, film, to its French origins.

To better understand the way the films connected French and American film culture, it is essential to examine other, perhaps even more obvious, links and contexts forged by the films. The expansion of American tourism to Europe, which had begun after World War I, had been interrupted in 1939.[6] As Harvey Levenstein noted in *Seductive Journey*, in the 1920s, 90 percent of all American tourists who went to Europe went to France: "No matter where an American visitor does not go on his European tour, he almost certainly goes to Paris . . . It's the center of the American tourist's universe."[7] The number of American soldiers stationed in Europe both during and after each world war had already exposed average American men to travel abroad. Jet travel, which opened up significantly in 1958, only increased the numbers of tourists, most of whom still traveled across the Atlantic by boat.[8]

In this context, the films can be understood as travelogues, a subgenre in which one would also have to include other "European" location films such as *Three Coins in a Fountain*, *Roman Holiday*, and *Summertime*. As the director of production of *Funny Face*, writing to get permission to shoot in France, explained to the French government bureaucrat charged with approving the location work, "Our film . . . offers great advertising for Paris and can only help tourism, the hotel and fashion industries."[9] In a review of *An American in Paris*, the *Hollywood Reporter* claimed, "their Parisian interiors make you want to buy a steamship ticket, fly, float . . . to the enchanting city of light."[10] Publicity materials for *Gigi* announced, "Paris co-stars in MGM's *Gigi*." In fact, the French tourist office printed 5,000 special posters promoting the film and the city in 1958.[11] Other films took travel as their main subject. In a note to the French Centre National de la Cinématographie, Walt Disney Studios requested to shoot their film *Bon Voyage* (1961) on location because the film's plot revolved around the return of an American couple to France, where they had originally met. The studio explained that the film played on the American fascination with Europe: "The dream of every middle-class American, as we know, is to salute the old continent."[12] Thus, it should come as no surprise that many American films were shot on location in France as a prelude and accompaniment to American tourist interest. Between 1947 and 1963, 106 American productions (including a handful of television shows and documentary films) requested permission to film in the country.[13]

Italian neorealism's otherwise gritty aesthetic also contributed to the rise of location shooting after the war. Roberto Rossellini made quite a stir when he started shooting out of doors and on location; the success of *Rome*,

Open City, in particular, inspired other filmmakers to follow, even when they were shooting in refined and glorious Technicolor film.[14] In 1949, not long after the excitement about *Open City*, Stanley Donen and Gene Kelly's *On the Town* impressed viewers with its New York locations. Inspired by this success, Kelly suggested that MGM shoot *An American in Paris* on location. The film's production team would thus have set out to do what no MGM film had done to date: shoot a musical on the streets of a foreign country. Aside from the budgetary concerns, the film's art director, Preston Ames, was dead set against it, arguing to Gene Kelly, "Have you ever danced on cobblestones?"[15] In the end, the studio sent a second unit camera crew to Paris to shoot the film's opening location shots and a few shots of the exterior of the Ritz Hotel. Instead, the film's representation of Paris would come in fantasy form, especially in the lavish (but made to dance on) sets for the twenty-minute ballet finale.

Location shooting lent an air of realism and authenticity to Frenchness films. Because Paris had a long history and so much of the nineteenth-century city physically remained well into the twentieth, filmmakers of the 1950s could use the city streets rather than re-create them, as had been the common practice until after the war.[16] John Huston's *Moulin Rouge*, shot in Paris and in studios in London, also frequently used a handheld camera to heighten the realism and avoid tourist clichés. As the film's scrolling narrative explains, "for a brief moment . . . Toulouse-Lautrec, his beloved city and time live again." This sort of authenticity reached its height in 1957 when *Gigi* fulfilled MGM's plans to shoot a major musical on location. Director Vincente Minnelli had already shot in Europe in 1955 while making the Vincent van Gogh biopic *Lust for Life*. In addition, *Funny Face*, released in 1957, had, no doubt, upped the ante for shooting films about Paris, in Paris. Minnelli and his cast and crew filmed in the city for thirty-one days from August 5 to September 4, 1957.[17] The film does not emphasize the tourist's Paris but rather attempts to portray a more authentic "insider's" perspective on the city: its parks, thoroughfares, and open spaces (fig. 1.2). Highly unusual for a major studio film, it even featured many interiors shot on location—including Gaston's residence (the Musée Jacquemart-André) (fig. 1.3); Maxim's restaurant, which they rented for several days; and the old dilapidated ice skating rink, the Palais de Glace, which they refurbished. Alan Jay Lerner and Frederick Loewe wrote the score while ensconced in the Georges V Hotel in order to immerse themselves more completely in French culture. Janet Flanner, the *New Yorker* critic who wrote as "Gênet," visited the *Gigi* set in Paris and

1.2 On location in the Tuileries Gardens, Paris, for the production of *Gigi*, summer 1958. Photo by Joseph Ruttenberg. Courtesy: Academy of Motion Picture Arts and Sciences.

1.3 Gaston's residence, filmed at the Musée Jacquemart-André in Paris for *Gigi*, 1958.

pronounced it the "most authoritative Parisian movie so far filmed."[18] Cecil Beaton, the film's art designer, hated the scenes and the retakes that had been shot in Culver City and claimed "the whole success of the film was the Parisian flavor and that was created by making it in France."[19]

Musicals, in particular, could heighten the experience of viewing a location by creating a "travelogue effect" as Donen and Kelly had shown in their "New York, New York" number in *On the Town*. Such montages created city "slide shows" in coordination with song and dance. Until *The Sound of Music*'s Salzburg "Do, Re, Mi" became the classic musical travelogue sequence in 1965, Donen surpassed his own work in *On the Town* in the Frenchness film *Funny Face* filmed in 1956. A visual tour de force, the film was shot both in Hollywood and extensively in and around Paris. In all, the crew proposed forty-eight location shots for the month and a half they spent working in the French capital.[20] Many of these shots are clustered in the film's most vivid and engaging sequences, "Bonjour Paris" and the Paris photo shoot.[21] Although on the surface, the film is an unlikely love story between its protagonists, played by Fred Astaire and Audrey Hepburn, it is really about Paris and the city in pictures. The film frames the city as a series of tourist postcards as the film's trailer makes clear. The trailer begins with an aerial shot of Paris, centered on the Eiffel Tower, superimposed with white lettering that announces, "You're going to have a marvelous time!" (fig.1.4). It next offers the opening and closing sequences of "Bonjour Paris" and introduces the film's stars. When they arrive jubilantly on the second level of the Eiffel Tower, the white text reappears, "On a Lavish, Love-Happy Paris Holiday" (fig.1.5).

New widescreen technologies enhanced the power and beauty of location shots after the invention of Cinerama in 1952 and CinemaScope in 1953.[22] *Funny Face*'s most ambitious and original production number, "Bonjour Paris" offers a spectacular visit to the city. Kay Thompson, playing

1.4–1.5 From the *Funny Face* trailer, 1957.

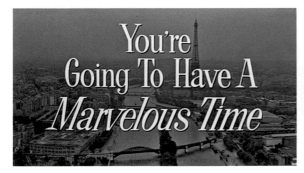

Maggie Prescott, a wily magazine editor, and Fred Astaire as Dick Avery, the suave fashion photographer, lure Audrey Hepburn, playing Jo Stockton, a bookish intellectual, to Paris. In exchange for agreeing to be photographed in Paris for their magazine, she will be able to meet the "empathicalist" philosopher, Flostre. Once the three Americans set foot in Paris at Orly airport, they spurn the cabbies offering tours of the city. With blasé confidence, they protest that they are not tourists but acknowledge that people do not usually consider Paris a place to work. They take their separate cabs, claiming they will rest at their respective hotels but each actually begins to tour the city. Dick Avery begins at the top of the Champs-Elysées, with the Arc de Triomphe behind him.[23] The fashion magazine editor Maggie Prescott tours the rue de la Paix, in front of the Opéra and the young intellectual Jo Stockton heads to a small street in Montmartre with Sacré-Coeur looming in the background. The sequence features an assortment of Parisian monuments—the Vendôme column, the Madeleine, the Louvre, Nôtre Dame, the Place de la Concorde, the Alexander III Bridge, the fountains at Versailles— sometimes with and sometimes without the actors. The three separate journeys around Paris suggest there is a Paris for everyone. This is then visually reinforced in a triptych representing the three characters, each on a separate filmstrip, each having a great time in their Paris (fig. 1.6). Yet the musical number ends with each singing, "There's something missing, something missing I know, there's still one place I have to go . . ." and the film cuts to a long shot of the Eiffel Tower seen from the esplanade of the Palais de Chaillot, replete with fountains dancing with water (fig. 1.7). Maggie, Dick, and Jo then run into each other in the elevator ascending the ultimate Parisian icon—the Eiffel Tower, at once symbol of Paris and the "modernity" of its late nineteenth century moment.[24] Paris is for all tourists, the song projects, as the three emerge from the elevator and gleefully sing in confession, "We're strictly tourists, you can titter and jeer and all we want to say is Lafayette we are here, on a spree, Bonjour, Paris!" (fig. 1.8). They wave happily to the native Parisians seated around them, some wearing French naval costume to indicate their authenticity as Frenchmen. The sequence thus satisfies the touristic urge to see the city, represents it as a series of postcard snapshots made more "cinematic" by virtue of the split-screen triptych that exploited widescreen technology, and ends at the icon of Paris that is at once contemporary tourist symbol and one of the great representations of the city and its Belle Epoque.

Beyond their functional role in promoting Paris, the films also repeated a host of older clichés of Frenchness that guaranteed that Paris would delight

1.6 Triptych from "Bonjour, Paris" sequence, *Funny Face*, 1957.

1.7 Eiffel Tower in "Bonjour, Paris" sequence, *Funny Face*, 1957

1.8 Trio on top of the Eiffel Tower. Publicity still, *Funny Face*, 1957. Courtesy: Academy of Motion Picture Arts and Sciences.

the senses; please the body and comfort the spirit though art. The films combined the titillation of Paris, a place known for sex and frivolity, with its association with artistic quality and cultural innovation as a newspaper ad for *Moulin Rouge* made clear: "Wild, Wicked, Wonderful Paris . . . all her loves, ladies and legends." In this way, Frenchness films could appeal to both the base instincts of the flesh and wrap them in high culture, guaranteeing commercial success while furthering the respectability of film.[25]

Although the Can-Can did not begin as a charged symbol of French sexuality, from its origin in the 1830s and forward, the dance provoked the forces of moral rectitude to object to its performance. It traveled to London and around the United States—the fact that the Moulin Rouge nightclub opened in 1889 during the year of the Exposition gave it a large and international audience, spreading its fame around the world. In those early years, the dancers were really drumming up other business of a sexual nature and the dance's association with solicitation contributed to its eventual integration into the saloon culture of frontier America. By the 1890s, as entertainment venues opened in Montmartre, the dance became the crowning moment of the evening, launching such bright if short-lived careers as that of La Goulue at the Moulin Rouge.[26] The Can-Can dance included the lifting of the leg not only in kicks that revealed the bare upper thigh and the dancer's undergarments, but also the slow lift of one leg in a circular motion that highlighted an exposed and moving buttocks. But it was later in the dance's 1890s revival that introduced greater fetishistic allure as dancers emphasized the actions of the skirt and petticoat that they manipulated with their hands and with their kicks.

The Belle Epoque and its Can-Can eventually codified the old saw of Rabelaisian France in a commercialized and visually provocative and sustainable way through the emergence of the entertainment industry that manufactured "la gaieté française." Histories of fin-de-siècle Paris have traditionally focused on the culture of Montmartre to the point of making it a cliché, although at the time the landscape of urban entertainment cast its net far more widely across the city and, importantly, in its geographic center on the *grands boulevards*.[27] As the French Consul General noted in 1953 about a film about the painter Edgar Degas, "It would come as no surprise if they came up with the title *Montmartre* to capitalize on the success of *Moulin Rouge* (the film)."[28] Such an easy transition between art and entertainment, wherein a film about the painter Degas could be imagined in association with entertainment, underlies many of the Frenchness films.

1.9 Gallery of works by Toulouse-Lautrec (all copies by Vertès) on his apartment wall from *Moulin Rouge*, 1952.

Frenchness films also managed to enhance their reputations through their association with the display of high art. *Lust for Life* featured a range of actual art works by Van Gogh, which the film's director, Vincente Minnelli, had filmed in museums and private collections with still cameras and then photographed in Cinemascope.[29] In *Moulin Rouge*, a suicide attempt by Toulouse-Lautrec is preceded by a long and slow display of his work on his studio walls (the images are copies). As the audience ponders his work (fig. 1.9), so does the character himself, eventually turning off his open gas lines. Inspired by his own work, he chooses to live. In another scene in the film, Toulouse-Lautrec enters a brothel, and the film fades to a montage of some of his actual brothel pastels.

The centrality of French art in the Frenchness films conveyed that they were "quality" productions. Their producers showcased them at the Cannes and Venice Film Festivals in Europe and they garnered Academy Award nominations and prizes, including Best Picture awards for both *An American in Paris* and *Gigi*, a film that received the most nominations of any film musical until that time.[30] Reviewers noted that the films were "so elegant and imaginative in conception that we can compare them only, from this point of view, with Cocteau's *La Belle et la bête*."[31] In other words, these films about France not only merited comparison with French "art" films but also the implication seems to be that because the subject matter was itself elegant, so were the films themselves. A preview report for *Gigi* noted that one viewer found the movie, "the most elegant Hollywood musical."[32] *Gigi* opened in New York in an unprecedented way as a cultural event: MGM rented a Broadway theater, the Royale. For its six month run there, it sold out every performance and then moved to the Sutton movie theater further uptown, where it also broke attendance records.[33]

Given the remarkable range of French art, why choose this particular fin-de-siècle art as the visual inspiration for and sometimes even the subject of the Frenchness films? As the French consul general Raoul Bertrand wrote to Paris in an effort to get permissions to film MGM's Degas film, "The studio's interest in making the film is based on wanting to take advantage of the world-wide taste for the French Impressionists. This taste has also been spread by the global success of films such as *An American in Paris* and *Moulin Rouge*."[34] Thus, while this French diplomat recognized a general taste for Impressionist paintings, in his attempt to get permission from the Degas family, he noted that the films added great public interest and thus value to the artists and the nation where they had worked. Yet his note also makes clear that the popularity of the Frenchness films also offered the French government and its officials a flattering mirror in which they could see their own importance reflected in brilliant Technicolor.

But, of course, filmmakers had to value the Impressionists in the first place. Vincente Minnelli explained in an interview with the *Cahiers du cinéma* published while *Gigi* was still in production: "One can always return to the Impressionists and discover something new: they are eternally striking. It is perhaps the richest school and if I had to satisfy myself with the canvases of only one school, I would choose the Impressionists."[35] Minnelli's comment reminds us of the singular status of Impressionist art in the United States from the 1870s onward.

American interest in Impressionism began in the late nineteenth century, when American art collectors had led the way in cultivating the achievements of contemporary French artworks, especially the Impressionists. Annie Cohen-Solal has noted the rise of American art in the twentieth century and its deep connection with French art: "in the last years of the nineteenth century, most of the innovative paintings, produced by French painters in the preceding four decades crossed the Atlantic to find themselves in another geographic space, in a culture that is different from the one in which they originated."[36] In other words, the cutting-edge of French painting was exported to the United States. As early as 1886, art dealer Paul Durand-Ruel helped the American Art Association organize an exhibition of French Impressionist paintings, capitalizing on the vogue for French art in the United States.[37]

While exhibitions familiarized audiences of art appreciators, the collecting habits of wealthy Americans gave these paintings permanent homes in the United States. Among the most important collectors of the Impressionists were Henry and Louisine Havemeyer. Bolstered by a fortune made in the sugar market and a close friendship between Louisine and Mary Cassat (which eventually ended late in the painter's life), the Havemeyers amassed one of the most significant art collections in the United States, especially of works by contemporary artists and the Impressionists.[38] The Metropolitan Museum of Art received the Havemeyer bequest in 1929, which contributed centrally to the cultivation of the Impressionists in America. Other painters associated with post-Impressionism, such as Cézanne, Gauguin, Seurat, and Van Gogh, also found their way into American museums. In fact, the Museum of Modern Art in New York opened in 1929 with an exposition of the work of these four French "moderns."[39] As historian Neil Harris has duly noted, "America became a storehouse of European art in the twentieth century."[40] The collecting habits of American patrons helped fill American museums with both the old European masters but more so with recent art from France. Impressionists thus became instant classics in the American context in part because they became "museum pieces" not long after the period of their creation.

The Impressionists also appealed to the tastes of filmmakers. This moment in painting coincided with the emergence of the cinema and thus shared both a common visual culture and set of cultural preoccupations about attention, distraction and motion.[41] Robert Herbert has argued that in their depiction of a modern, urban, and leisure-oriented culture, the Impressionists and neo-Impressionists reflected, at least superficially, consumer society's happiest vision of itself.[42] If the Impressionists "inspired" filmmakers and successfully reached their public in addition to collectors and museumgoers, it may well be because they could register as both art and popular culture.

If the French were selling their art with abandon to the Americans since the late nineteenth century, French government officials of the 1950s saw the Frenchness films as vehicles for increasing not only the appreciation of French art but also converting the commercialization of that art into a form of prestige for France. The Frenchness films served as virtual galleries of art. As Raoul Bertrand explained in a memo to the Ministry of Foreign Affairs, "From the perspective of promoting French painting, this project can only be encouraged. It is worth noting, for example, that after the showing of *Moulin Rouge* the reproduction of Toulouse-Lautrec canvasses quintupled in the United States in order to meet the public interest. It is equally worth noting that big color films, of the variety I have just mentioned, have a worldwide audience of 400 million viewers. Put otherwise, we have at our disposal a free and unparalleled means of publicity."[43] The display of French art in the films increased the market value of particular French paintings and turned art into a vehicle for advertising France more generally.

What is more complicated about the films' relation to art is that filmmakers walked a fine line between offering "uplift through art" and the exploitation of familiar visual clichés. The films displayed both paintings and the more familiar and widely reproduced popular art made in Belle Epoque Paris. For example, *Gigi*'s credits unfurl across a set of drawings by the illustrator Sem that were owned by the film's producer, Arthur Freed (fig. 1.10).[44] The films actively promoted a tight connection between painting and more commercial forms of artistic production such as the poster. For example, *Moulin Rouge* opens with tracking shots that detail the crowd at the nightclub and then pans the bar and the mirror behind it in a seemingly obvious reference to Manet's painting, *The Bar at the Folies Bergère*. The camera then settles on the show on the floor—a virtual animation of Toulouse-Lautrec's poster of the *Moulin Rouge*—complete with an actor playing the male dance partner, Valentin, "the boneless" with a prosthetic chin to match the poster's caricatured exaggeration of his features and an actress playing La Goulue posed as in the poster (figs. 1.11 and 1.12).

In fact, no artist seemed to play as central a role as the iconic artist of the period in the Frenchness films as did Henri de Toulouse-Lautrec. His name, his art, Montmartre, the Can-Can all made what became obligatory appear-

1.10 Title image with Sem Illustrations, probably owned by producer Arthur Freed, *Gigi*, 1958.

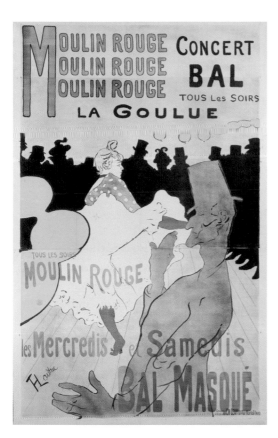

1.11 Henri de Toulouse-Lautrec, *Moulin Rouge, La Goulue*, 1891. Courtesy: Art Institute of Chicago, Mr. and Mrs. Carter H. Harrison Collection.

1.12 Opening sequence of *Moulin Rouge* (1952) based in the poster by Toulouse-Lautrec.

ances in the Frenchness films. In his own time, Toulouse-Lautrec's work tied the Montmartrois leisure depicted in his posters to the aesthetic achievement that Philip Dennis Cate has labeled "the color revolution."[45] His reputation in both Paris and the United States grew after his early death at thirty-seven in 1901. In fact, his untimely death assured that he painted nothing after the Belle Epoque. By the eve of World War II, *The Bulletin of the Art Institute of Chicago* had already dedicated two articles to his work, one in 1929 and the other in 1935. In June 1951, *Newsweek* magazine noted the publication of a book of all thirty-one of his posters in a single volume. Toulouse-Lautrec's popularity and his international fame by the 1950s, beyond the art world, does suggest that his production in oil paintings and pastels as well as in the more commercial forms of the poster and lithograph made his work familiar to a general audience

The late nineteenth century production of French commercial visual culture left an important legacy through the popular imagery, posters, and the paintings that were produced in Paris and that depicted the pleasures of modern life. Long before museum shops reproduced art on coasters, scarves and the like, reproductions of Parisian fin-de-siècle imagery probably circulated in America, as the earlier observation by the French consul general suggests. Many viewers of the Frenchness films knew the Toulouse-Lautrec posters, and the films thus transmitted familiar visual clichés dressed up as art. In addition, the films' production teams had access to visual materials to inspire the look of their films. When Cecil Beaton needed inspiration for the costumes for *Gigi*, he turned to the readily available images from the fin-de-siècle periodicals *Les Modes*, *Le Théâtre*, and *Femina* available in most American city libraries.[46] The sheer volume of the images produced as posters, lithographs, and periodical illustrations no doubt contributed to their continued circulation after the late nineteenth century. Ad agency creative teams used copies of Toulouse-Lautrec posters to put in the background, as in this advertisement for Van Heusen's *Moulin Rouge* shirt (fig. 1.13), a tie-in with the film. Since the shirt's cut and style had nothing to do with the Moulin Rouge, the film's star José Ferrer modeled it in front of Toulouse-Lautrec posters.

A materialist explanation for the way that Toulouse-Lautrec and Montmartre became the touchstone for representing Paris 1900 emerges. Many of his images began their lives as illustrations, lithographs, and posters—not paintings. Yet because he also painted, his commercial work was more easily understood as art than the work of Chéret and Sem. And who better than Hollywood directors to seize on the notion that commercial art was art nevertheless? Familiarity with the French visual imagery shored up the status of the most "artistic" of directors and the most "quality-oriented" of producers in the studios. The fact that so many of the images depicted an environment of leisure and entertainment only reinforced their suitable presence in films whose own creators imagined themselves as the paragon of both art and entertainment.

The films, however, do more than simply display art or underline the compatibility of art and commerce. Fin-de-siècle visual culture, with its illustrated press, wax museums, and posters, was cinematic before the fact.[47] These films make explicit both the importance of visual culture in late nineteenth-century Paris and its connection to contemporary film culture of the 1950s. Paris and Hollywood formed an axis of cultural circulation

1.13 Van Heusen's "Moulin Rouge" shirt ad campaign, c. 1953. Collection of the author.

in which the former served as the cultural crucible for the latter. Although there were important "extra-cinematic" forces at work (such as increased tourism to France after the war that stimulated the production of travelogues, and economic reasons to shoot on location), the Frenchness films also suggest that American film was connected to French culture beyond the mere exploitation of clichés of Parisian gaiety and the association of France with "art."[48]

By literally animating the static visual culture of the bygone French 1890s, Frenchness films both connected to and updated the classic fin-de-siècle cultural form of the poster. Aside from the opening of *Moulin Rouge* described above, the film includes a tracking shot of a Morris column, the characteristic Parisian street furniture that served as billboards, with Toulouse-Lautrec's Jane Avril poster dissolving into Zsa Zsa Gabor as Jane Avril, turning and moving toward the camera as she performs on stage (figs. 1.14 and 1.15). As one reviewer noted, *Moulin Rouge* offered a "moving poster of the splendid '90's . . ."[49] In *Gigi*, Eva Gabor skates in the Palais de Glace

1.14 Image of Jane Avril poster, *Moulin Rouge*, 1952.

1.15 The Jane Avril poster animated in *Moulin Rouge*, 1952.

in a dress that makes her seem as if she just stepped out of the Jules Chéret poster (figs.1.16 and 1.17). Although French painting inspired the entire ballet finale of *An American in Paris*, the Toulouse-Lautrec sequence explicitly demonstrates the way that film works to animate still images. It begins with a poster of the Afro-Cuban acrobatic dancer and clown "Chocolat" and then dissolves into Gene Kelly as Chocolat in a still pose that comes alive (fig. 1.18). This vivification of the drawn image is further emphasized in a sort of exaggerated and vivacious choreography that includes the by-now notorious and seemingly unmanly wiggle of Gene Kelly's behind.

Plot and character took a backseat to the goal of creating stunning visual effects in the Frenchness films, which is one reason why studying them as mere ideological constructs for the postwar era can be a problem. *An American in Paris* developed around Gershwin's score of the same title, which Gene Kelly decided he wanted to transform into a ballet. The success of the British-made ballet film, *The Red Shoes* by Emeric Pressburger and Michael Powell in 1948, had, no doubt, been a revelation to both the MGM producer Arthur Freed and Gene Kelly. It had been nominated for the Academy Award for Best Picture, shot on location in Monte Carlo and along the Côte d'Azur, and featured a twenty-minute ballet.[50] According to Michael Powell's memoirs, Kelly told him he screened *The Red Shoes* at MGM fifteen to twenty times for the executives before they green-lighted the project. Kelly told Powell the film was full of "quotes from *The Red Shoes*." Powell claims never to have seen the American film.[51]

The ballet in *An American in Paris* is the crowning achievement of an already aesthetically ambitious film that linked its Parisian setting to its artistry and to the visual spectacle of the dance. As studio head Dore Schary

1.16 Jules Chéret, *Palais de Glace* poster from *Le Courrier français*, 1894.

1.17 The Chéret poster reproduced in *Gigi*, including the dress, 1958.

1.18 The start of the "complete Toulouse-Lautrec environment." *An American in Paris*, 1951.

1.18a Gene Kelly as "Chocolat." *An American in Paris*, 1951.

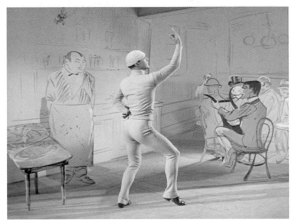

recounted, "I told Schenck (Nicholas in the New York Office) this picture is going to be great because of the ballet—or it'll be nothing. Without the ballet it is just a cute and nice musical."[52] The goal of the ballet, according to its script summary, was "to accomplish choreographically, dramatically and scenically what the great impressionist painters accomplished in their medium through the use of color and light and forms."[53] In his memoir, Minnelli explains that they approached the ballet as a painter would, "with bold splashes of color." The art department ran a contest to see which designs "would most closely approximate scenes of Paris as they might have been painted by Rousseau and Lautrec."[54]

The film's reviews must have delighted its creators; critics celebrated the ballet as a major achievement, despite its borrowings from *The Red Shoes* and the Kelly-Donen ballet in *On the Town*. Nevertheless, *Variety* called it "a masterpiece of design, lighting, costumes and color."[55] *Time* called it a "grand show" and tellingly noted its "brilliant combination of Hollywood's opulence and technical wizardry with the kind of taste and creativeness that most high-budgeted musicals notoriously lack."[56] French reviewers were equally enamored of the ballet. *Libération* called it a "total success" and noted that, although it was filmed in Hollywood, the film was not the usual "gay Paris seen by the cowboys" but rather it had sets that were "inspired by the famous canvases of Renoir, Cézanne, Rousseau, Dufy, Toulouse-Lautrec and Utrillo."[57]

Although each of the ballet's sequences evokes an artist's work, the one featuring the work of Toulouse-Lautrec does more than evoke the painter's style and canvas. The script called it "a complete Lautrec environment." The scene is replete with image after image from his paintings and posters—some as cartoon cutouts such as La Goulue and Valentin, others as waxlike figures: Aristide Bruant with his red scarf, the singers Paulus and Yvette Guilbert as they were portrayed in Lautrec's imagery (figs. 1.19 and 1.20). These figures are lifeless and frozen against the prancing Chocolat who is soon joined by Can-Can girls, one of whom is Leslie Caron as Jane Avril. These cinematic sprites jump, twist, and dance as if to announce that the filmmaker can achieve what the artists of the Belle Epoque could only aspire to: to capture and represent the sensuality of entertainment by filming it.

The Frenchness films insistently link filmmaking to the world of late nineteenth-century Paris as a sort of tribute and self-conscious portrayal of their own origins. Announcing their genealogical debt, the films also display their advancements over the work of the Belle Epoque artists. In *Moulin Rouge* John Huston films a number of Toulouse-Lautrec's still images and

1.19 The Toulouse-Lautrec environment. *An American in Paris*, 1951.

1.20 Henri de Toulouse-Lautrec, *At the Moulin Rouge*, 1892/95. Courtesy: Art Institute of Chicago, Helen Birch Bartlett Memorial Collection.

goes back and forth by cross-cutting between the legs of a dancer and a gaping spectator, creating a "flip-book" effect and injecting a sense of animation, but one slow enough for the film viewer to remember that persistence of vision allows us to see moving images (figs. 1.21, 1.22, 1.23, 1.24, 1.25). This technique contrasts still and moving images and emphasizes motion, reminding viewers that film as a form both emerged from the world of spectacle, consumption, and commercialized sexuality that we associate with the Belle Epoque but film represented the next stage in the development of that culture.

The films visually link film as a medium to what was a new visual culture in the French 1890s, emphasizing their own superiority not only through the craft and technique of motion, but also to the aesthetic of artifice, especially one that depended on the creative manipulation of color photography. While Italian neorealism seemed to associate European filmmaking with the small-scale, black and white documentary, Frenchness films worked in an opposite register. They brought the viewer France in Technicolor, which became the 1950s equivalent of the Impressionist palette. The films reinterpret the interest in "Europe" that the immediate postwar curiosity about neorealism appeared to suggest but drew on a visual idiom both more familiar and more popular on both sides of the Atlantic. In this way, the films associate France and popular visual culture. For example, in a key scene in *Moulin Rouge* that involves the transformation of Toulouse-Lautrec's painting for the nightclub into a poster, the craft involved in mass cultural image making becomes an allegory for filmmaking. When he arrives at the lithographer's shop, the printmaker explains to the artists that his color palette cannot be reproduced lithographically. Toulouse-Lautrec replies, "I mixed the paints, I shall blend the inks." Thus begins the collaboration between the artist and technician in which both perform aesthetic and technical tasks—the artist improves the mixing technique by using a toothbrush; the lithog-

1.21–1.25 Toulouse-Lautrec pastels from *Moulin Rouge*, 1952. Images are photographed as still and then edited to make them appear as though they were in a flip book and thus animated.

rapher explains how the image requires the right amount of acid to be properly printed. We then see the mechanical reproduction of the poster and its distribution around Paris as well as the critical attention and excitement it receives. The scene is extraneous to the film's plot but underscores its deeper message about the development of art in the context of its intersection with craft and technology in the modern world. That a film about a French artist's life would pause on this meditation about art and technology echoes what filmmakers in the 1950s, who surely practiced a technologically mediated and reproducible art, might have thought about their own identity as "modern" artists.

An *American in Paris* also links Paris, art, and the movies. As Jerry Mulligan, a GI turned painter, Gene Kelly introduces his position in a voiceover that features establishing shots of Paris. "For a painter the mecca of the world for study, for inspiration and for living . . . is Paris . . . Brother, if you can't paint in Paris you might as well give up and marry the boss's daughter." Yet the plot turns on Jerry's poverty, the impossibility of being a painter in a world where you need to make a living, and the tension between the affections of a rich older American and the innocent French girl with whom he falls in love. Jerry insists on the purity of art: he won't paint for money and he can't paint on a deadline. The film's thin plot is a mere device for a film that sings and dances its visuality and in which color is one of the film's greatest subjects. Aside from linking France and art as the movie's theme, the director Vincente Minnelli and art director Preston Ames also managed to emphasize their own art by linking it to the film's theme of painting. For example, Lise, the French love interest played by ingénue Leslie Caron, is introduced in a sequence of dance scenes that start with her fiancé looking in a mirror embedded in a picture frame that then transforms into a "painting" of her; the background set is monochromatic and she is dressed in a starkly contrasting color to the set behind her (fig. 1.26). Minnelli explained

1.26 Framed in a mirror that doubles as the frame of a painting with monochrome but colorful set. *An American in Paris*, 1951.

that "the colors were poster colors, absolutely like from a child's paint box." He also asked Irene Sharaff to design the costumes and the color combinations.[58] Each tableau represents Lise's different moods and personal qualities, which are inflected by the different dance she performs and the starkness of the colors in the sets. In another sequence, the film's music hall number, "I'll Build a Stairway to Paradise," color is emphasized through illumination as the stairs light up a pinkish-white with the singer's every step. The scene's very theatricality also recalls the fact that Minnelli's original métier was that of theatrical set designer.

The flimsy plot resolves in the film's last half hour in an abrupt summary: the American painter gets the French girl. This is wrapped up in a wordless thirty-second scene in which Jerry runs and embraces Lise who leaves her music hall Frenchman behind. This moment follows what became the film's greatest achievement: the twenty minute ballet of "An American in Paris" that narrates Jerry's love for Lise but is also a danced celebration of Paris through its turn-of-the-century paintings.

Although the Belle Epoque had already been visually evoked in the music hall number and on the studio set of Jerry's quaintly lost in time Left Bank street, complete with old-fashioned café, the final half hour explodes in the evocation of a painter's Paris: the beaux-arts ball followed by the ballet both form the film's visual tribute to Paris and its painters. *An American in Paris* distinguished its ballet technologically as well as aesthetically. Although Kelly's screen ballet cites the main dance number in *The Red Shoes*, its editing, dissolves, and transposition create actions and moves that could not happen in an actual stage performance; furthermore it does not share the look of a classical ballet like the Ballets Russes' *Red Shoes*. While the Powell and Pressburger film may have "staged" their film's ballet to take advantage of the cinematic medium, its costumes and style are that of a classic fairy tale ballet. By contrast, *An American in Paris* takes the filmed ballet and combines it with the staging and style of a movie musical to create a hybrid dance that, like Paris and the painters featured in the ballet, combined art and popular culture, the turn-of-the century moment in France and mid-century Hollywood.

As an artistic device intended to make the colors of the ballet more stunning, the beaux arts ball scene that immediately precedes it featured costumes and sets in black and white only. As Minnelli explained, "There will be no color in it except the flesh tones. Even the serpentine confetti will be black and white. I thought this would give the eye a rest, so that when the black and white turned into color, it would be so much more dramatic."[59] The ballet fantasy (an important device regularly employed in dance-based stage musicals since *Oklahoma* in 1943) is introduced by way of a singular red rose set against a life-sized version of a ripped sketch Jerry has made of Paris. As Jerry picks up the rose, Gershwin's musical symphony really begins and the charcoal sketch is washed with the colors of France (and America)—red and blue—that begin to fill the otherwise white canvas (fig. 1.27). Jerry, dressed in a modern dancer's black with a white collar, picks up the rose as a remembrance of the woman he is in the process of losing and the scene comes alive. The ballet's script describes the change, "Suddenly, the metamorphosis takes place. Colors sweep into the set."[60] A group of furies in white lead to the explosion of color onto the set—red furies, costumed marching bands, policemen, youngsters in stripes appear in fast order in a Paris inspired by Raoul Dufy. Jerry sees Lise dressed in white, but she disappears on the rim of the fountain in the Place de la Concorde as the set

1.27 Charcoal sketch becomes blue, white, and red as the ballet begins. *An American in Paris*, 1951.

becomes green and then fades in a fog. The color and motion build throughout the ballet to the Lautrec sequence discussed earlier. The ballet itself crescendos in a return to the Place de la Concorde (in which it began) mobbed with schoolgirls, military men, policemen and other picture-book Parisian characters only to have the music diminish and the crowds and the girl disappear. The color also departs from the scene.

Against the wishes of the film's art director Preston Ames, Minnelli brought in cinematographer John Alton to light the ballet. In Alton, Minnelli and Kelly saw a flexible, risk-taker who would embrace the spirit of lighting the ballet in experimental ways. Alton liked to use colored filters but Ames enlisted Irene Sharaff and they complained about the yellow and purple distortions of their sets and costumes. According to Ames, the filters were removed. Kelly and Minnelli, however, have credited Alton for the important contribution to the look of the sequence and he shared an Oscar for best cinematographer with Alfred Gilks for their work on the film.[61]

Reviewers at the time celebrated the film for its visual achievement. *Variety* argued that the ballet was "a masterpiece of design, lighting, costumes and color photography." It further noted that the film distinguished itself because it could be compared to the "art house" film *The Red Shoes* but was remarkably geared to a mass audience.[62] *Time* called it a "brilliant combination of Hollywood's opulence and technical wizardry with the kind of taste and creativeness that most high-budgeted musicals notoriously lacked."[63] This Hollywood gloss on the City of Light resulted in what *Commonweal*'s William Pfaff called the Paris of "prettiness." His review highlights not only what he noted as the artificiality of *An American in Paris* but also the Hollywood-Paris connection: "This is Paris, the cultural center of a beautiful land which has Oz as its capital . . . where the trees are always green."[64]

For the most part, however, the visually opulent and artistic "Frenchness" films dodged charges of superficiality. *Gigi*, according to *Time* was a "full course feast for the eyes and ears."[65] Perhaps no comment summarized the visual power of these films as concisely as Stanley Kauffman did in the *New Republic* when he quipped "a deaf man could enjoy *Gigi*."[66]

The Frenchness films' visual originality in part resided in their use of color in much the same way that the Impressionist use of color had drawn attention in the last third of the nineteenth century and has continued to help define the terms of painting ever since. *Catholic World* noted that "the extent to which the movies have learned to use Technicolor as an artist does his palette has never been better demonstrated."[67] *Newsweek* claimed that John Huston's *Moulin Rouge* was a "ravishing Technicolor portrait of Paris."[68] Bosley Crowther, critic for the *New York Times*, declared that "color, of course, is the big thing in this film . . . color that flows in a creation that quite overshadows the famous painter's poster art."[69] Of *Funny Face* reviewer Philip Hartung declared, "the real stars . . . are the photography and color which are used magnificently."[70]

The use of color not only drew attention to the art of filmmaking itself but also helped make the films look like the photographic imagery of glossy magazines, thus connecting visual culture of the late nineteenth century to 1950s photojournalism and contemporary filmmaking. If this aesthetic were tied directly to the budding consumerism of the nineteenth century, by the mid-twentieth it became as ubiquitous as consumer culture itself. In short, color was everywhere.[71] The movies did not just look like magazines. They even employed magazine personnel. For example, Eliot Elisofon, a photographer for *Life*, served as a special color consultant for *Moulin Rouge*. Fashion photographer Richard Avedon consulted on *Funny Face* and provided the inspiration for the character Dick Avery.

If the films drew a line of aesthetic development between France and America, their production histories played an important role in defining a transatlantic cinema in the 1950s. Huston used a French source—Pierre La Mure's biography of Toulouse-Lautrec called *Moulin Rouge*—as the basis of his film. *Gigi*, a quintessentially French novella by one of the country's most popular authors, made an international transition from print to stage to screen. Colette wrote *Gigi* during the occupation of France. It was published first in serial and then book form in Switzerland in 1944. At the Liberation, it was published in Paris and then translated and published in *Harper's Bazaar* in the United States in 1946. In 1948, Colette coauthored the script for a French film, which starred Danièle Delorme. Anita Loos then adapted it for the stage in New York and London, where Audrey Hepburn and Leslie Caron played the title role respectively. Colette then translated and adapted the Loos production for the Parisian stage, where it premiered in February of 1954, seven months before the French author's death. Arthur Freed bought the rights for an American film adaptation. He had one of his assistants translate the French film, and began deliberations between the studio and members of the Production Code Board until a censorship-proof plot had been approved. Celebrating women who made their livings as courtesans was not within the moral parameters of Hollywood's self-censorship organization. Despite efforts to adapt the film, Freed worried it was too

French. Lela Simone, a key member of the unit, explained Freed's concerns: "The French play, French characters, were very strange to Americans. . . . The whole frame of the story is very un-American."[72] When the MGM film opened in Paris, it was promoted as starring, "the triumph of French talent." In fact, the French actors involved in the film, Leslie Caron, Louis Jourdan, and Maurice Chevalier each had more significant careers making films in the United States than in France.

French personnel also labored behind the cameras on the production whose long location shoot in Paris in August 1957 involved a team of French cameramen as well as set decorators, carpenters and the like working for the MGM production. Even more interesting, French film lab technicians made an important and original contribution to the finished film. Vincente Minnelli wanted to review the daily work they were shooting and thus needed the film developed nearby. He used a lab on the outskirts of Paris in Saint Cloud. As Minnelli explained in a French interview about the film's production: "There, the technicians were not following the Eastman development protocols, and were themselves experimenting and the results proved themselves to be marvelous. Ruttenberg (the film's director of photography) was so thrilled that at the end of this experiment, our labs in California decided to copy French methods."[73] Minnelli, himself, was quick to discuss the influence of French filmmakers on his own work. As he explained in an earlier interview with *Les Cahiers du cinéma*, "I think I was more influenced by European directors . . . Cocteau, Jean Renoir . . ."[74] Perhaps the influence of these French directors even made Minnelli more open to recognizing the techniques in the French color lab. In any event, the French experimentation with color helped create the look of MGM's *Gigi*. Although Hollywood production had, since its inception, drawn talent from around the world to the studios (as much as the rising tide of war had pushed a substantial group out of Central Europe, often via France to Hollywood), the postwar productions of English-language films in European locations and in France, in particular, not only produced enough critical and popular achievement to warrant a fairly steady flow of Frenchness films, but even the most characteristically "American" of studio productions, the MGM musicals created by the Freed unit, became differently transcultural. Hollywood did not just serve as a magnet for the world's talent. Especially after the war, when studio units like Freed's went off the lot, they brought more than the location shots back with them.

Frenchness films carved out an early production niche outside the studios. John Huston was an American-born director, the son of a respected

Hollywood actor, and had worked at Warner Brothers and MGM, but he directed United Artists' *Moulin Rouge* in London and Paris.[75] Film historian Tino Balio's definitive history of United Artists suggests its financing of such independent productions for much of the 1950s and 1960s made the development of international production possible. That business model worked by differentiating the studios and their films, but also by building on cultural interests and tastes such as "Frenchness" early in the 1950s and later cosmopolitanism in the 1960s. Consider, for example, other UA projects such as the James Bond films. Frenchness films also opened the door on the critical bemusement about transatlantic film production. As a French reviewer noted of the success of *Moulin Rouge* at the Venice Film Festival, "the film is English, the director American and the subject French."[76] As suggested earlier, "Frenchness" could be marshaled in complex ways as a theme, a topic, and as a set of representations. English-language "Frenchness" films of the 1950s were instances of cultural exchange between France and America. The very act of making such films, however, resulted in the greater "internationalization" of film culture. Making films about France became as much about making films *in* France.

During the seven-year period from *An American in Paris* to *Gigi* the French audience for these films also grew. The strength of the French reception was celebrated by Robert Vogel in a report to Arthur Freed describing its August 1952 opening at the Colisée Theater: "The final ballet was watched in complete silence and followed by a thunder of applause." He noted that the number of admissions were 40 percent higher than *King Solomon's Mines* and twice that of *Caruso*, and he foresaw both a long run and receipts that would break the theater's record.[77]

Not only did *Gigi* garner more attention than the other films (if the number of reviews is any evidence) but it also benefited from an unprecedented, successful publicity campaign. *Le Film Français* noted that French magazines plastered their covers with promotions for the film and that Le Printemps, a major department store, devoted their display windows to the film, featuring dresses worn by Leslie Caron in the movie, which had now been copied for the French consumer (figs. 1.28 and 1.29).[78] Even back in Los Angeles, the Freed unit marveled at the French frenzy over the film. As Edith Lapinière, MGM's Paris liaison, reported to Peggy O'Day in Culver City, "This is no longer a publicity campaign; it is becoming fun to prove to the greatest French producers and distributors that we can double (and I repeat double!) the amount of publicity received in the French press by their greatest pictures since the war."[79]

1.28 Display windows at Au Printemps department store, Paris, late fall, 1958. Courtesy: Arthur Freed Collection, USC Special Collections, Cinema-TV Library.

1.29 Interior display, mannequin in Gigi dress with publicity still. Au Printemps department store, Paris, late fall, 1958. Courtesy: Arthur Freed Collection, USC Special Collections, Cinema-TV Library.

The films were popular with audiences and the critical reception in France offered a blend of antagonism and appreciation. For some critics, the films were simply too clichéd, especially in their depictions of Paris. *An American in Paris,* one reviewer noted, depicted only "certain picturesque elements that mix it up with a crazy salad of frenzied American gaiety . . . In short, a charming Paris but one only looking backwards . . . This is the image fixed for generations to come of an old-fashioned and delightful toy that the American tourist can play with for a while longer, as long as it doesn't break."[80] If reviews such as this objected to the hackneyed and nostalgic views of Paris, others identified that Hollywood was doing a better job with French cultural patrimony than the French cinema itself. As one of the most vituperative critics of *Moulin Rouge* noted, "Let's continue to let Hollywood spoil our cultural patrimony by bringing together, in the studios of London, a Puerto Rican actor, an Hungarian émigré and an American director to create 'Parisian' atmosphere. French cinema should have the right to make prestige films."[81] Although this critic urged the French onwards in making films about their own culture, the Hollywood he depicted was less American than it was a motley global intersection of cultures in which France and French art served as the greatest common denominator for such international productions.

On balance, French reviewers focused instead on the use of French sources and personnel, identifying the films as sites of cultural exchange and even conceding that clichés of Paris always bear a modicum of truth. In that way, the critics admitted that the films went beyond any simple notion that they were American "Frenchness" films. They praised *An American in Paris* for its tribute to French painters in the ballet sequence.[82] Others applauded the use of the contemporary French artist Vertès in *Moulin Rouge* who painted the half-finished canvases and whose hand could be seen sketching Toulouse-Lautrec's drawings. French critics relished in the French actors who starred in *Gigi,* especially in Maurice Chevalier, who was called "the real miracle," "our national Maurice," "a valuable export item."[83]

If Maurice Chevalier became the perfect Frenchman for export, reviewers recognized the positive elements in the postcard clichés that permeated the films. As Eric Rohmer wrote of *Funny Face* in *Arts* (when he was a young critic before becoming a filmmaker himself), the film depicted a "postcard Paris but one that was, after all, neither terribly false nor ugly since what is most beautiful and rightly well-known about Paris has been represented on postcards."[84] While Rohmer identifies the film's visual idiom as "unoriginal," he also underscores the authenticity of the cliché in a way that suggests this was a Paris equally recognizable to the French as it was to a foreign audience. There were some critics, needless to say, who could not help but invoke clichés of American provincialism as facilitating the enjoyment of the films. As one put it, "all this should enchant the Wisconsin farmers and will not miss making the shop girls of Iowa swoon."[85]

Most striking perhaps, one finds that both French and American reviews singled the films out for their visual and technical virtuosity and for the intertextual visual culture they established with fin-de-siècle art and the related media of photography. As one critic put it, "*Gigi* is a film made solely for the pleasure of the eyes, a purely retinal film."[86] Of *Moulin Rouge* one critic argued that "for the first time Technicolor has given birth to a style, a sort of essay on the relation between the pictorial and the cinematographic."[87] Another review stressed that the film foregrounded "the beauty of cinematographic language."[88] Eric Rohmer mused extensively about *Funny Face*'s engagement with photography: "The effects . . . are related to the technique of pure photography, without pictorial reference and with irrefutable evidence that color, far from bullying the art of the image actually opens new and intoxicating horizons."[89] French critics joined their American counterparts in celebrating these films as breakthroughs in their use of color and visual refinement.

But the influence of these films can be detected beyond box office figures, reviews, and publicity. Their popularity in America and in France may well have resulted in the French themselves producing "Frenchness" films to capitalize on the recognition of these clichés. If the American productions seemed to represent a transatlantic exchange of talent, technique, setting and source material, so did the French-made Frenchness movies. Trying to capitalize on the popularity of the Belle Epoque films, French filmmakers themselves participated in the celebration of the Belle Epoque and thus paid Hollywood a backhanded compliment.

The film that best exemplifies the French production of Frenchness comes from the director most valued as a national treasure at the time: Jean Renoir. There are other films (*Folies Bergère* and *Le Ballon rouge* among them) that share the palette of the Technicolor films and the association of Frenchness with Montmartre or the music halls, but it is Jean Renoir's film *French Can-Can* (1954) (whose English language title is *Only the French Can*) that exemplifies the extent of the traffic between France and America as well as the centrality of the cliché of the Belle Epoque in 1950s filmmaking. Renoir's *French Can-Can* is another example of the mutual American and French influence in creating Frenchness in film after the war. It also underscores the exchange not only in images but also in personnel between France and America that the war had further extended. In addition to Renoir's famous exile, stars such as Michèle Morgan, Jean-Pierre Aumont, and Jean Gabin each came to Hollywood during the war, despite the burdens of working in a foreign language.

Jean Renoir, son of the celebrated Impressionist painter Pierre-Auguste Renoir, was the best-known wartime filmmaking émigré from France to America. He arrived in New York for the first time in February 1941 at age forty-seven. Renoir left France to protest the collaboration of the Vichy government and the complete domination of the French film industry by its German occupiers. Once in the United States, he moved to Los Angeles.[90] His time in Hollywood is often described as a constant frustration as he made few films (five in seven years). After the war, Renoir never fully returned to France—he died in Beverly Hills in 1979, a naturalized American citizen—but it was not until long after the war's 1945 end that he returned to make movies in Europe. In 1953 he made a Franco-Italian coproduction, *Carosse d'or,* which was filmed in Rome; released in French, Italian, and English-language versions; and set in eighteenth-century colonial Peru. He returned to France the next year to make *French Can-Can,* a film that recounts a fictionalized version of the opening of the Moulin Rouge. The film, released in 1955, was the first he made in France after twelve years spent in Hollywood.

French Can-Can is a tenuously plotted and colorful movie musical. When Renoir returned to France, despite his nationality and lineage, he seemed to be imitating the Hollywood-style films he complained about while living there. Of *French Can-Can,* Renoir claimed that he "desired to make a film in a very French spirit."[91] But when the film opened in New York in 1956, the *New York Times* noted that it presented "a tale (that) might have been cribbed directly from some of the pictures made . . . in Hollywood.[92] Like the English-language Frenchness films, *French Can-Can* takes place in and around the Moulin Rouge. But beyond treating the same subject matter as the Hollywood productions, Renoir also visually evokes the other films by using their pictorial vocabulary and techniques.[93] Impressionist works, including his father's *Moulin de la Galette,* come to life in the film. The film is also littered with Belle Epoque posters. At the start of the finale set in the Moulin Rouge, a poster of a dancing girl on the interior wall of the Moulin Rouge splits open and a line of girls comes leaping through it as if stepping out of the

1.30 Woman bashing though poster in *French Can-Can*, 1954.

poster (fig. 1.30). Like *An American in Paris*, Renoir's film ends with a long final dance number: a twenty-minute Can-Can finale held in the Moulin Rouge. While it differs from the American film to the extent that the dance is more of a classic backstage musical number, its structural placement is entirely imitative of the MGM film.

Despite the similarity to Hollywood's Frenchness, French reviewers invoked the director's heritage as a measure of the film's authenticity. "The color is exceptional. Renoir used his father's palette,"[94] the critics wrote, invoking the filmmaker's artistic heritage. "Penetrated by his father's Impressionist colors, M. Renoir has made a beautiful and dreamy color film."[95] Renoir himself suggested that his own goals in the film were to underscore visual virtuosity and the powers of the cinema, as did the American Frenchness films. In his memoirs he noted that "*French Can-Can*'s subject is resolutely childish . . . I was more and more drawn by these sorts of stories, weak stories that would free me to enjoy myself with cinematography."[96] For Renoir, as for Minnelli, the Belle Epoque seemed the perfect setting to allow the director to indulge a desire to underscore film's aesthetic and visual aspects instead of its capacity for great storytelling.

"Frenchness" as the Belle Epoque—whether in American or even French film—and its association with spectacle, color, movement, song, dance, girls bashing through posters, and the Can-Can itself, highlights the power of film as much as its depictions of France. Certain clichés that stood in for "France" had a particularly long shelf-life. The Belle Epoque "stuck" in film for a number of reasons, including the history of the American collecting of French Impressionists as well as the prolific reproduction of these French visual entertainment clichés in poster art. Long before Hollywood, art and commercial art shared the same palette in France. This may help explain why, aside his lurid biography, Toulouse-Lautrec and his world appear as a leitmotif of the 1950s Frenchness films.

Frenchness films reinforced "nationness" and simultaneously helped to build stronger transatlantic and transnational ties among the film production community as well as among film spectators. When attention is paid to the visual work of the films themselves, when their production and reception are studied in detail and when these elements are connected to the broader context of the history of visual culture, we are able to offer a picture of Franco-American cultural exchange that differs from both rivalry and "Americanization" that has characterized other descriptions of the postwar era. In particular, production histories suggest the increasingly international context of production after the war: directors, actors, story materials traveled the Atlantic in what might be thought of as "circular" patterns, chasing after a set of half-century old clichés of Parisian life. In the moment considered to be the height of postwar American cultural imperialism, some of the most commercially successful, critically acclaimed, and eventually cherished films were tributes to France rather than transparent ciphers for promoting the "American way of life." That France and Frenchness played a special role in film must be placed into the longer history of French-American affinity and left at that. For the Americans, French Republicanism served as a political inspiration. French art and literature were paragons of "high" culture; their fashion and champagne stood at the apex of luxury production. France offered a pretext for films dealing with romance and sex.[97] But films are visual expressions that need to be both contextualized and read as such. By foregrounding the films' production and reception and by taking a more careful look at the films as visual expressions, we can see that the use of Frenchness had a more precise significance going back a half century to the medium's origins. The 1950s Frenchness films served as vehicles through which filmmakers, in both America and France, could locate themselves as part of a shared and significant popular cultural tradition that began in France at the century's dawn. The success of the "Frenchness" films would make the Franco-American film connection the kernel of an increasingly global film culture after the war. The Franco-American film partnership was to extend far beyond a successful film cycle and the increasing transatlantic film commerce it generated. The partnership also produced the most significant film institution of the postwar era, the Cannes Film Festival, to whose history we now turn.

THE CANNES FILM FESTIVAL AND THE MARKETING OF COSMOPOLITANISM

LE FESTIVAL INTERNATIONAL du film de Cannes first opened on the unfortunate date of September 1, 1939, as Hitler invaded Poland. Reborn in April 1946 as the first major postwar international cultural event, the Festival promised the "finest films in the world presented in the finest setting in the world."[1] With its glamorous sheen, it would help project an image of the recovery of France and would serve, more concretely, as an ideal vehicle for renewing tourism to the Côte d'Azur. But it did more than that.

In the context of film history, "Le Festival de Cannes" as it was later known, or the Cannes Film Festival, became the shooting star in an ever-expanding cosmos of film festivals after the war.[2] It played a key role in the development of the postwar "art film," helping to launch the French New Wave when it awarded François Truffaut best director for his *Les 400 Coups* in 1959. The Festival also provided an international venue for the exhibition of films made in countries that would emerge after the war as having national cinemas of international value: Mexico, Japan, Egypt, and India.

But the Festival is also central to the cultural history of the postwar era. It showcased the importance of film to the project of the postwar globalization of culture. At a pivotal moment in American domination of the international film market, the French-run Festival developed an international platform for the world's films and film personalities. In Cannes, films and their stars had access to an unprecedented scope of publicity, disseminated by the increasingly photo-oriented mass international press. While studies of cultural diplomacy have underscored national chauvinism, rivalry, and the frigid battles of the Cold War, the history of the Festival describes the forging of a collaborative international film culture.[3] At Cannes, nations, including the United States, coexisted, cooperated, and coproduced. A confluence of certain vital elements allowed the Festival to succeed: the association of France and the Riviera with cultural cosmopolitanism, the Festival's creation of a press juggernaut, and the transformation of this spot on the Riviera into a literal crossroads for the world filmmaking community all conspired to make the Festival the world's largest film market. Though the Festival fell short of achieving the true cosmopolitanism to which it aspired, it successfully shaped the filmmaking community's practices more than we have understood.

Cosmopolitanism was the Festival's driving cultural value, photographic stills its primary mode of international publicity, and film commerce its underlying practice; these elements enabled the Festival to attract the world's film producing community to participate. France established its centrality in international film culture by playing host to the world's most important Festival and market. If French national products did not dominate the box office in most parts of the globe, Cannes promoted internationalism and eventually auteurism instead. The Festival contributed to the internationalization of the film industry in symbolic and actual terms. The Festival activities organized at the behest of French cultural diplomats and film professionals show that the French moved beyond the notion of "national cinema" as both an ideal and as a mode of film production. In the process, they had an important influence on Hollywood and in developing a global film community. The Cannes Film Festival, from its inception in 1939 through the end of 1968, marking its first phase, shows how important the French were in shaping the direction of world film culture in the postwar era. The Festival cultivated the idea that such an international film culture existed in the first place and that France could serve as the perfect staging grounds because of the long-term French investment in cultural cosmopolitanism.

The Festival managed to become world famous because of this universalizing vision as well as the actual films shown there. But the historically specific configuration of other factors—its location, the management's canny organization of the press, their ability to draw the stars the press favored, and the development of the film market—worked together to establish its success. Although there can be no doubt that the Festival served French national and economic ends, more significantly, it helped give renewed validation to the notion of film as an international business and cultural form in a period of apparent American dominance.

The Festival organizers sought the cooperation of countries around the world, but it forged its strongest partnership with the American film-producing community, for whom the benefits of participation seemed less obvious than for smaller countries. Though few would dispute the rise of American film hegemony in the first half of the twentieth century in the wake of World War I, only the French had the confidence, know-how, and sheer nerve to challenge American rule after World War II. Most studies have characterized this confrontation as cultural protectionism and focused on the postwar impositions of film quotas by the French government to reserve screen time for French films; scholars also stress the French governmental subsidy of the film industry that made loans for the production of high-quality French films.[4] The Cannes Film Festival, however, created an international stage for films and film culture, and also promoted international film business. Its direction forged an alliance with Hollywood that would define such concepts as "global Hollywood."[5]

The Cannes Film Festival may be the most celebrated film festival, but it was not the first. That distinction goes to the *Mostra Internazionale d'Arte Cinematografica*, better known as the Venice Film Festival, which began in August of 1932 as an extension of the *Biennale d'Arte*. By 1938 when the Venice festival awarded Leni Riefenstahl's *Olympia* (*The Olympiad*) the grand prize, observers and participants rightly saw the gathering as a platform for fascists rather than as an international competition. The British, American, and French delegations responded by claiming they would no longer participate at Venice. Philippe Erlanger, director of the Association Française d'Action Artistique, the agency responsible for the travel of French art and culture abroad, in his capacity as the French representative to the Venice festival, teamed with the French government's minister of foreign affairs and the minister of national education to establish that France would host a genuinely international film festival the following year.

Though it vied with other attractive locations such as Biarritz, Vichy, and even Paris to host the Festival, boosters from the city of Cannes were strategic in securing the selection of their town. The organizers of the first Cannes Film Festival set out to democratically promote film on an international scale in pointed distinction to the propagandist mission in Venice. Regulations from 1939 stated that Cannes would "encourage the development of the cinematographic arts in all its forms and to create among all film producing countries a spirit of collaboration."[6] The Festival proclaimed it would be free of "all ideology and nationalism," and competition rules underscored that intention.[7] To ensure fair competition, Axis powers Italy, Germany, and Japan were excluded. The jury was to consist of members from each of the nine participant nations: Belgium, the United States, France, Great Britain, the Netherlands, Luxembourg, Sweden, Czechoslovakia, and the Soviet Union. France would simply compete as one among the nations. Each country would propose its films, and the jury would select the best of each nation's offerings in addition to awarding an overall international prize.[8]

A radio ad in July of 1939 announced, "the international capital of film" was set to debut its festival at the start of September 1939.[9] Louis Lumière, the French father of film, was to preside over the three-week event. MGM sent a special boatload of stars including Tyrone Power, Douglas Fairbanks, and Norma Shearer. A giant papier-mâché Nôtre Dame decorated the Palm Beach sands to promote William Dieterle's film *The Hunchback of Notre Dame*. Journalist Maurice Bessy, who many years later became the Festival's director, noted in *Cinémonde* on the eve of the event that it would be a "peaceful victory" and that the nations gathered "no less in art than in politics are not prepared to bend before tyranny."[10] But events intervened. Hitler invaded Poland at the same moment and attendees scrambled to return home. As Erlanger noted, "the name of the festival was up in lights in the front of the Casino Municipal when human folly turned out the lights."[11]

Although there would be no film festival in Cannes until 1946, it was not for lack of trying. Traces of various wartime plans offer glimpses into French cultural bureaucrats and their wartime experience and remind us of just how central film had become not only to government propaganda but also to everyday life during wartime. The "phony war," as it has been called by historians, began in October 1939, but Georges Huisman, the director of Beaux-Arts wrote in November 1939 to Jean Zay, the minister of national education, hoping to keep the festival idea alive despite the impending doom. In particular, he worried that this new war would repeat the devastation that the war of 1914–18 had wrought on the French film industry and argued that a festival might keep their national industry alive.[12] Philippe Erlanger maintained plans to reopen the Festival in March 1940, but urged the mayor of Cannes to keep the local press quiet to avoid enflaming the Italians while he worked the proper diplomatic channels.[13] Although he considered the idea of a winter festival a terrible one, mostly because the war had distracted the press from reports concerning any other topic, the mayor cooperated but warned Erlanger that nothing could be worse than "news of a festival taking place in front of empty seats."[14] The city of Cannes, he reminded Erlanger, had a high standard of event planning, which the conditions of war might spoil. Better to hold no festival than a mediocre one.

Discussions continued into the next year. Georges Prade, a Cannes booster in Paris, wrote to the mayor urging him to consider supporting a wartime event so that the city would maintain its hold on the Festival and not lose it to competing sites if the Cannes municipal authorities lost interest.[15] No one seemed to worry about the dangers of the actual war intervening, echoing Marc Bloch's famous indictment of France's lack of preparedness for the war when it eventually came.[16]

The invasion of France in May and the defeat in June had important implications for all French industries, film among them. In the reorganization of many of its agencies, the Vichy government created the Comité d'Organisation des Industries Cinématographiques (COIC), whose connections to the German occupiers were strong. The COIC would lay the groundwork for the postwar structure of French cinema, developing after the war into the postwar Centre National de la Cinématographie. After a pause starting in June, film production began again at the end of 1940 in studios in the southern unoccupied zone while the Germans set-up Continental Films in Paris. The French moviegoing public was unaware of any of the distinctions since Continental's French-language films were not meant as propaganda vehicles but rather to keep up the veneer of normality and morale in occupied France.[17]

The COIC extended the hope that a wartime festival might happen. In October of 1941, a note from the Action Artistique to the secretary of state of national education and youth informed the secretary that Count d'Herbemont of the COIC had approached them, having made certain advances with his connections in German film. His ambitions ran high. The note says the count planned to accomplish what even Venice never had: "a gathering where, despite the current state of affairs, the peoples of Europe, America and Asia would meet."[18] How they planned to accomplish this is left unarticulated.[19] Two months later the escalation of the war with the bombing of Pearl Harbor and the American entry into the war made the gathering of the peoples of Europe, Asia, and America impossible.

The archival paper trail relating to the Festival runs cold for the rest of the war until October 1944, only months after the liberation of Paris and only a month after the Germans were driven from France. At that time, Philippe Erlanger and Henri Gendre, a Cannes hotelier (and father of actor Louis Jourdan), suggested to the new general director of cinema that a festival be planned for December 1945. Erlanger himself had not even been officially reintegrated into his civil service post in the Action Artistique service. (That came in December 1944. Because he was a Jew, Erlanger had been decommissioned on December 19, 1940.)[20] Such determination on his part was prescient but also suggests the central place that film would occupy in the cultural and economic agenda of the nation after the war. The Ministry of Foreign Affairs certainly understood this. Its cultural affairs officer commented, "It is clear that French cinematic production will be called upon, after the war, to become one of the most effective means of French propaganda abroad."[21]

Planning for the Festival officially began in the spring 1945, but the postwar conditions presented many challenges. In April of that year, the organizing committee of the Festival wrote to the Ministry of Foreign Affairs explaining that all the major hotels in Cannes had been requisitioned and occupied by French and American forces. In fact, Cannes served as the officers' site in the United States Riviera Recreational Area. (Enlisted men went to Nice.) A note from Henri Gendre informed the Quai d'Orsay that the American colonel Gum had promised that when hostilities actually ceased they would take up Monaco's offer and move their offices and troops there to make way for the Festival.[22] For a variety of reasons, many budgetary, the Festival was pushed back again to September 1946. The organizers excluded Germany, Spain, and Japan but invited Italy, mostly to fend off the potential revival of the Venice festival.[23] The Soviet Union was counted among the twenty-one participant nations in what its organizers heralded as the first postwar international cultural event.[24]

Fireworks, flower parades, receptions, and an impromptu movie house in the municipal casino made the first Festival a stunning few weeks in an era of otherwise profound deprivation. The opening evening party also featured Grace Moore, the American star of the Metropolitan Opera, singing such popular French favorites as selections from Jules Massenet's *Louise* and performing a rousing rendition of the French national anthem, the "La Marseillaise." Married at the time to a Frenchman, Moore's presence signaled the vital importance of American participation in the Festival. As a press release announcing the Festival in 1945 boasted, it would be "a big show of friendship between nations, and particularly between France and the United States who began the project."[25] This comment came on the heels of particularly tense moments after the war when the flooding of France with American films led to the plagued negotiations of the Blum-Byrnes Accords.[26] Despite the bitter anti-Americanism that the quota battles produced in the filmmaking community, the Festival organizers clearly believed that cooperation between France and America was possible and mutually beneficial.

Although the first Festival would be remembered in the long term as a significant event in the history of film aesthetics because it introduced Italian neorealism with Rossellini's *Rome, Open City*, its inaugural program also confirmed the overall health of France after the war and the role film and other forms of culture might play in promoting international understanding. The poster for the Festival in 1946 featured a film camera operator with a globe for a head, posed to evoke the transformation of a machine-gun into a movie camera. Through his camera runs films composed of different national flags (fig. 2.1).[27] French observers echoed the Festival's graphic message of internationalism, stressing film's capacity to promote universal understanding in the era of newly achieved peace. As Léon Moussinac, correspondent for the Communist film publication *L'Écran français*, remarked in his opening commentary describing the Festival, "There are thousands of ways to serve peace. But cinema's power of rapprochement and influence goes beyond that of other modes of expression in that it directly and simultaneously touches the worldwide crowds."[28] People associated with the Fes-

2.1 Cannes Film Festival poster, 1946, Paul Colin, reprinted in *France Illustration*, September 21, 1946. Courtesy: BIFI.

tival such as poet, writer, artist, and filmmaker Jean Cocteau, a regular on the Riviera social scene and president of the jury several times, perpetuated the notion of film as the universal language. He applauded the Festival as "an apolitical no man's land, a microcosm of what the world would look like if people could speak to each other directly and speak the same language."[29] War-torn Europe looked to the popularity of film and to the seeming universalism of both entertainment and the language of images to repair its fissures. This rhetoric recalls prior discussions of early American cinema's role in integrating immigrants, but in postwar Europe it took on new meaning and urgency as the need for international understanding emerged.[30]

The first Festival may have been a success but the event's future was hardly assured. Competition from Venice presented the new Festival with its foremost problem. At the time, it seemed to both the Festival organizers and the press that there would be room for only one festival.[31] In fact, when the French learned in late spring of 1946 that plans were afoot for a Venice renewal, shuttle diplomacy by Erlanger resulted in an accord between the two festivals in which each would host a major international event every other year and in the off-year the other would offer a "film week" that involved no international competition.[32] This competition from Venice and the unsure budgetary contributions of the French government compromised the Festival's stability between 1946 and 1950. In fact, the French government's support of the event declined in the initial years. In 1946 government money accounted for 89 percent of the event budget. By 1953, the government's contribution shrunk to 55 percent.[33] After the 1947 event, the Festival also took on the hybrid administrative status of an "Association de 1901," which meant that it became an independently run organization in the public interest, the equivalent of a nonprofit organization, but one that, because of its general public interest, would and could receive government money. This established its independent status while guaranteeing a long life of dependence on the government for financial support.

A diverse cast of characters ended up leading this hybrid organization from its headquarters in Paris. While Philippe Erlanger remained an active member of the Cannes team, Robert Favre Le Bret became the Festival's administrative director in 1947. Favre Le Bret combined the finesse of a cultural diplomat with commercial experience garnered from some years spent working as a journalist. During the years he ran the Festival, he also headed the Paris Opéra, where he organized foreign tours. He set the tone for the *mondain* quality of the Cannes Festival (he was often photographed looking at ease in a white tuxedo and sunglasses) and was accused over the years as director of not caring or even knowing enough about film. Thus, although the Festival reported to the government, its personnel had experience in the private sector. Also joining Favre Le Bret were film professionals such as Marcel l'Herbier, who represented the producers and writers organization the Syndicat des Producteurs Français et de l'Association des Auteurs de Films. French film producers always had representation in the Festival's decision-making bodies. Although France is reputed for its "statism," the Festival's administrative operation suggests that the commercial and public sector worked in tandem as it organized this international cultural event.

In the wake of Cannes Film Festival's success, film festivals popped up from Carlsbad to Punta del Este, from Berlin to Beirut. The Cannes's files list about eighteen festivals in 1963 alone. On the surface, festivals promoted tourism, which helps explain why many localities yearned to get into the festival game. As one Cannes city official reasoned, given the usual cost of advertising, the seventeen Festival days and "the hundreds of magazines, weeklies and dailies that publish articles, photos and colorful reports of Cannes, . . . it is easy to see that the festival gives Cannes immeasurable publicity."[34] Film professionals, however, did not always meet the multiplication of festivals with great enthusiasm. As early as 1947, *Variety* noted, "the plethora of film festivals in Europe is becoming a permanent headache for the bona fide picture people. . . . Everyone is hoping that some regulation will provide for one festival a year in all of Europe similar to the ones governing the Olympic Games and international fairs."[35] A 1951 dispatch from the U.S. Embassy in Paris discusses a movement to create a single "Nobel" prize film festival, a proposal that had gained the approval of the International Federation of Motion Picture Producers.[36] In 1952, André Lang, representing the French Critics Association, explained to the Cannes Film Festival organizers, "there aren't enough good movies to divide them between festivals in a single year."[37]

Each festival sought to distinguish itself from the next but a clear hierarchy emerged in which the Cannes Film Festival became the first among them. As early as 1953, the organizers noted that it had become "the universal meeting ground for film. . . . We can say that the Cannes Festival has become, little by little, a sort of Olympic games of film."[38] In 1956, the Paris correspondent for *Variety*, Gene Moskowitz, declared, "it is possible to say that Cannes' prestige is far greater than its chief rival, the Venice Film Festival."[39] The next year, *Variety* called Cannes "unquestionably the major film event on the Continent."[40] The *Saturday Evening Post* proclaimed it "the most important (festival) from every point of view—in attendance, publicity, number of films shown and amount of business transacted."[41] Darryl Zanuck, head of Twentieth Century Fox, wrote to Favre Le Bret that "there is need for only one festival in the world and I would say it is Cannes."[42]

The Festival's scale and genuinely international quality helped Cannes achieve recognition. While it may have promoted French economic interests by stimulating tourism, it did not serve as a mere pretext for showcasing French films. French aspirations were grander. The Festival organizers sought to establish and direct world cinema from the beaches of the Mediterranean and readily envisioned France as the perfect place because of its association with both internationalism and a commitment to excellence in culture. As a press release boasted, "No nation other than France could better preside over such a gathering with a spirit of artistic independence and absolute impartiality."[43] In a later moment of self-congratulation, the Festival administration noted, "we must never forget that our liberal and open policies, especially towards countries without a distinguished film industry (the festival must also offer encouragement and a model), contributed enormously to our world-wide fame and to the success of the festival."[44] The Festival offered small but significant film-producing countries such as Sweden an incomparable audience for products made in Northern Europe. It also invited people interested in film from countries with little or no national film production to participate as observers, hoping to help stimulate filmmaking around the globe.

When officials boasted (and boast they did) about the success of their event, they often defined their achievement in creating the crossroads of the world's film culture. As a Festival official noted in 1959 in a report destined for the newly created Cabinet of the Ministry of Culture, headed by André Malraux, "all the big stars of world film have come to Cannes in the course of the last few years."[45] The Festival measured its success by its ability to host the world's cinema community, calling it in 1949 "a sort of International Conference on the cinematic arts . . . the biggest film gathering."[46] In Cannes, argued the Festival's promoters to the government, France would host the world, reinforcing both the nation and its leadership in the greater international community.

Others touted the event in similar terms. The executive secretary of the Motion Picture Academy of Arts and Sciences applauded the Festival's internationalism: "it did bring most of the current films of the world into the focus of a single show place. . . . small countries and large ones were accorded the same courtesies and privileges."[47] Cannes' mayor also noted "the presence of a cosmopolitan crowd speaking all the world's languages gives the festival its incomparable ambiance."[48]

How broad was the Festival competition? Over the years diplomatic issues came into play at specific moments, but an overall ethos of inclusion and participation prevailed to embrace as many of the film-producing nations as possible. The Eastern bloc nations, for example, came in and out of the list of participant nations. In attendance at the Festival in 1946, the USSR abstained in 1947 and 1949 and returned in 1951. Absent again until 1954, the Soviets participated from then on suggesting that actually being a part of the event was more important than posturing or using the event as a political football. The Chinese in Taiwan sent a film in 1959; in 1960 the People's Republic of China began to visit Cannes. The former Axis powers (except Italy) were absent from the participant nations in 1946; by 1949 Germany participated and in 1951, Japan and Spain joined the participant nations. Latin American countries participated and presented films, and Mexican cinema, in particular, received a great deal of positive critical attention. Most of the European nations (such as Sweden, the Netherlands, and Finland) participated frequently, but only when they felt they had a sufficiently good film to exhibit. The Festival cast its net wide: the new state of Israel sent a film in 1949; India, Egypt, and Morocco regularly sent films. The original seventeen participant nations eventually numbered, on average, about twenty-eight. Although some nations would come and go, the Festival exhibited the broadest range of the world's films in one place at one time. What this ever-shuffling list of nations suggests is that the worst of political enemies could come together to participate in an international cultural event.[49]

Visitors and the press brought a host of associations and expectations with them to the South of France and this played an important role in the construction and reception of the event. Like the rest of the Riviera, Cannes had been an international playground since the early nineteenth century. Yet unlike Nice, tinged with faded nineteenth-century Russian and British aristocracy, Cannes was perhaps best known for sumptuous villas and its swank beach clubs, and for its new American money. Frank Jay Gould built his first Riviera palace in Cannes; its 1929 beach and casino club was called Le Palm Beach and movie stars such as Charlie Chaplin, Rudolph Valentino, Gloria Swanson, and Douglas Fairbanks helped found the summer season in the late 1920s and '30s (figs. 2.2 and 2.3).

Cannes' success in drawing film people from around the world was due in no small measure to its billing as "Hollywood on the Riviera."[50] By connecting the Riviera and Hollywood in the public imagination, the Festival also underscored filmmaking's link to a "Mediterranean" climate. Atmospheric comparisons were constantly made; it is not clear whether the movies were associated with the sun and beach because of Hollywood or because the sun and beach embodied the glitz and glamour with which film culture had early become associated. Recalling the rhetoric of California boosters who imagined their state as an American Mediterranean, Cannes boosters invoked California.[51] Georges Prade, municipal deputy of Paris, explained in arguing for the Festival in its planning stages,

CANNES.   Le Palm Beach (Roger Scassal, arch.; Nice

2.2 Postcard of the Palm Beach Club in Cannes, c. early 1930s. Courtesy: Cannes Municipal Archives.

63 CANNES
La Piscine du Palm Beach

2.3 Postcard of the pool at the Palm Beach, Cannes, c. early 1930s. Courtesy: Cannes Municipal Archives.

As one American producer recently told me: Noon on the Croisette, the boat for the islands, the water at Juan-les-pins, at Cap d'Antibes, the yachts, the planes that cross with their white trails . . . is this not "la joie de vivre," and the same climate as that of the cinema itself? This is something that will transform the Côte d'Azur into a center of one of the most important industries in modern times. With its climate, with the astonishing range of its cultures, by the proximity to snow, the Côte d'Azur, a night away from Paris and a few hours from London by plane, will become the Florida and California of Europe.[52]

Americans saw in the Riviera an environment that evoked California, but the French also appeared bent on promoting this association as well. Philippe Erlanger applauded the Festival's ambiance and its parties and receptions by remarking that "they give the festival the actual atmosphere of California."[53] The French associated sun and filmmaking with California, but the allusion had its own local reference as well. As the news bulletin from Uni-France Film suggested, "the Côte d'Azur may well be called a French California. And foreigners from all over the world, even California itself, do not deny it."[54]

Just as movies became associated with the sunny climate of Los Angeles during the same period in the United States, so they did in France, where many people in the film industry hoped that the studios in nearby Nice, where films had been shot as early as 1911, would take root. The studio La Victorine was officially opened in 1919 by Serge Sandberg, an early film exhibition pioneer in France who believed that the South of France was a potential paradise for filmmakers as it had been for painters.[55] French filmmakers from then on attempted to establish the Riviera as a center for filmmaking. A truly remarkable wartime attempt by Jean Renoir to create a studio in nearby Valbonne (Renoir has otherwise been represented as having never had any intention of staying in Vichy France), underscores the interest by French filmmakers in transforming the south of France into another Hollywood.[56] In addition, like California, the South of France immediately became associated with the new culture of the automobile and stood out in France, much as Los Angeles did in the United States, as a motorist's paradise (fig.2.4).[57] Finally, to many observers, Cannes seemed so picture-perfect as to resemble a film set. Critic and filmmaker Alexandre Astruc noted in 1946 that the city was a "ville cinéma" which seemed to emerge "like a prefabricated set from a Technicolor film. One might say that a set designer had plopped down a sumptuous construction at the edge of the Mediterranean"

2.4 *Robert, Hugette, Arlette, Florette, Antibes 1953*. Photograph by Jacques Henri Lartigue. © Ministère de la Culture—France / AAJHL.

(figs. 2.5 and 2.6).[58] Cannes was an excellent backdrop for any festival, but it was the perfect site for a festival dedicated to film. When contrasted to the charming but decrepit lagoon-city of Venice with its Lido beach, one cannot help but draw the Hollywood-Cannes comparison.

In Cannes' resort culture, festivity and pleasure became a fundamental part of the Festival's image. One critic asked whether Cannes was a "film festival or a festival of festivities?" He complained about the frantic pace of events: "screenings, screenings outside the competition, press conferences, cocktail parties, receptions, luncheons . . . Too many banal society

2.5 View of the Festival Palace, photographed from the beach, c. early 1950s. Courtesy: BIFI, FIF.

2.6 View of the beach from the roof of the Palace, c. early 1950s. Courtesy: BIFI, FIF.

receptions where cinema has nothing to do with it."[59] Another critic had it both ways: "across this enormous Carnival, this fair of film and *mondanités*, film (which is after all an art!) still manages to find its place."[60] The *mondain* ambiance seemed to matter so much that the organizers insisted that evening screenings were to be attended in formal attire by guests and reporters alike.[61] The Festival organizers invited journalists to the main beachside boulevard, the Croisette, in black tie. Other events included the flower parades along the avenue, press conferences, and appearances by movie stars. The press, decked out in their finest, covered the Festival as one big party.

The social events and their accompanying spontaneous and planned rituals that prominently featured in the popular press presaged the "pseudo-events" of mass media culture.[62] By 1951, most Festival events and press coverage were in place, except for the creation of an overall first place prize, the Palme d'Or, first awarded in 1955. Until then, the prizes were a hodge-podge designed to honor as many films as possible. Continuity in administrative leadership also assured a coherent development of these rituals and their publicity. Erlanger continued to participate actively in the event's organization and Robert Favre Le Bret served as the primary organizer and director of the Festival until 1968 when the winds of social and cultural upheaval affected even the film world. Henri Langlois and his partisans used the broad events of Paris in May 1968 to shut down the Festival and it was subsequently reorganized.[63]

Though some critics faulted the Festival for its frivolity, the parties gave reporters something to talk about. In fact, the Festival was so associated with paracinematic events that Favre Le Bret, writing to *L'Express* editor Françoise Giroud, complained about journalist Pierre Billard's coverage of the Festival, lamenting that he was most upset about the magazine's notion that the Festival preferred parties to film: "I will limit myself to reminding you that from Italian neo-realism to the New Wave, the entire evolution of film for the last twenty years has been formed at Cannes."[64] Favre Le Bret needed to remind the press that the Festival was about film because he had helped the Festival succeed by staging an unrelenting series of extracinematic parties. The press, relying on clichéd notions of the *gaieté française*, enthusiastically covered the fun in Cannes.

Movies alone could not establish the Festival as a worldwide stage for international film culture but press coverage of "events" could. For the exclusive ears of the Festival's organizers, however, Favre Le Bret admitted that extracinematic events were essential as he looked back over more than fifteen years of festivals in 1966: "If the Festival is recognized worldwide, it is much less due to film reviews . . . than to all the extra-cinematic events.

Whether we like it or not, this is what gives the Cannes meeting its appealing shape and provides an alluring atmosphere that pleases all the foreign guests and provides their memories with lively and brilliant images."[65]

The key vehicle for the representation of the international gathering became the worldwide press corps. The press assured the greatest international buzz. Print journalists, especially related to film trade and fan publications, attended from many countries. The photojournalists covering Cannes tended to be either French (the Mirkine family became the key Cannes photographers and were given excellent access), but by the mid-1950s photographers arrived from all over the world; they often worked for one of the big photo agencies such as Magnum and Rapho. Once television coverage increased in the mid-1960s, the audiovisual press corps included journalists mostly from Europe and America. Cannes events and the photo opportunities they generated played a central role not only via print, but also by the international dissemination of photos as a primary vehicle of publicity. As Favre Le Bret noted, "this extraordinary publicity, that reaches millions of people around the world, is due in large part, it must not be forgotten, to the hundreds of photographers and reporters of French and foreign TV."[66]

The Festival had a fairly straightforward approach to the international press: more is better. In fact, much of the Festival's budget went toward paying for journalists, both French and foreign, to attend. From the start, more than half the Festival's invited guests were journalists. Over time, and as the Festival had hoped, the number of journalists who attended at their own expense far outnumbered those who were invited. In 1951, 300 journalists attended, of whom 150 were invited. In 1954, of the 400 journalists in attendance, 177 were the Festival's guests. Only a year later, 614 arrived to cover the Festival, of whom only 201 were invited. The Festival steadied its invitations at about 200 but by 1963, 808 journalists attended. In 1972, there were 1,000.[67] A team of seasonal employees, led initially by a young woman who would become the well-known novelist Christiane de Rochefort and her assistant Louisette Fargette, who eventually assumed the director's position, were charged with the onerous task of handing out press certification, which also guaranteed admission to the films and press conferences. In a tribute to Fargette on the occasion of her fortieth year working at the Festival, noted television interviewer François Chalais remarked, "I saw her office under siege as if an impenetrable fortress. . . . I'd often ask myself, 'How does she do it? Your job put you in front of the worst of the starved savage beasts of the jungle . . . journalists.'"[68]

The press did not simply "cover" the Festival. Its presence also helped create the Festival's ceremonies. Photographers' needs created the Festival's

2.7 The staircase in the Festival Palace at what Cocteau called, "a Festival about the staircase," 1952. Courtesy: BIFI, FIF.

great ritual—*la montée des marches* (the staircase climb). In the old Palace, the staircase stood at the center of the interior hall, not unlike the stairs at the Opéra in Paris. Journalists fought each other to get a photo of the stars as they entered the theater. This led Jean Cocteau to utter his famous regret: "c'est un festival d'escalier" (a staircase festival).[69] In the Palace, the live crowd outside missed the ascent of the staircase entirely and its design made it difficult for photographers to shoot entries and even more difficult for television cameras to film. In fact, most of the images of the evening arrivals were taken not on the steps but as stars entered. As the Festival grew in size, pressure for better photographic access to the stairs increased. The new Palace, which opened in 1983, allowed the show, complete with a huge red-carpeted outdoor staircase, to take place on the sidewalk—better for onlookers and still and television cameras (figs. 2.7–2.9).[70]

2.8 Entrance to the Palace with frenzy of photographers, early 1950s. Courtesy: BIFI, FIF.

2.9 The new Palace, built in 1983, with the staircase on the outside. Courtesy: Corbis.

Once filmmakers and cultural diplomats from around the world understood the extent of the media presence, they wanted to send their films and stars, and even attend themselves to take advantage of the well-organized, free publicity. As the Festival organizers noted, "outside the attribution of the prizes, the Festival is an extraordinary publicity launch for a good movie."[71] Nathaniel Golden of the Department of Commerce, the American delegate to the Festival in 1959, urged even greater American participation in the Festival for its "goldmine of world-wide free publicity."[72] In particular, he observed the large numbers of still and newsreel photographers who acquainted audiences around the world with an actor or actress's image before their film performance was even known.

But the "news" from the Festival came in a variety of forms. Newspapers, glossy magazines, and the burgeoning field of telejournalism made a global audience spectators at the Festival. In particular, the rise of such publications as *Time, Life, Vu,* and *Match* in the late thirties had spawned new players in the profession—the photojournalist and the photo agency such as Magnum and Rapho.[73] The confluence of the Festival with the rise of the photojournalists—or "paparazzi" (as they became known after Fellini's shutterbugging hound "Paparazzo" in the 1960 film and Palme d'Or winner *La Dolce vita*)—and of television journalism favored coverage of the Festival as a series of photo opportunities. If, as noted earlier, Cannes appeared as the perfect studio lot set, film stars, film professionals, starlets and onlookers stood out against this backdrop as the beautiful subjects photographed in the foreground. As an American journalist observed, "Since photographers are the elite of the Festival and are welcomed everywhere, a good ploy is to borrow a camera and, looking hassled and irritable, push through."[74] Being photographed was the name of the game. As the same reporter for the *Saturday Evening Post* remarked, "the Festival's host is M. François Mitterrand, the Minister of Justice—chosen for the honor not because justice has anything to do with the film industry, but because he is the most photogenic of French ministers."[75]

The history of the press coverage of the Festival also dovetailed with the rise of the new medium of television and its reporting. Festival organizers sought to use television in a variety of ways. As early as the 1951, they considered featuring a simple demonstration of television. After all, the medium was still in its infancy. Another year they contemplated that, in light of the Palace's limited number of spectators, they could retransmit the Festival films on a giant television screen. But they worried that the potentially poor quality would only magnify public aggravation with the exclusivity of

Festival events.[76] In general, this group charged with the promotion of film did not imagine the new medium as a threat to the seventh art. As one organizer noted, "television has enriched film."[77]

The press—print, filmic and televisual—represented the Cannes Festival as an elite international gathering to which millions around the world were invited through the voyeuristic powers of the mass media. If staged events drew the press, the movie stars drew audiences. As Favre Le Bret noted,

The seductive nature of the site of this international meeting of film is decidedly favorable to the development of such an ambiance but it is not the essential element. That element can be found more so in the animation that goes on during the entire event; this animation is crystallized around the presence of certain artistic personalities which confirm its spectacular physiognomy . . . it is those personalities that also allow the journalists from all over the world to write stories that will interest a broad public.[78]

Stars were a key lure. They paraded in convertibles on the Croisette, gave press conferences, and most ritualistically, appeared in formal attire for the evening screening, the apogee of the day's events. As one Canadian newspaper explained, "compared to all the distractions that Cannes offers during this international event, the highlight of the day is the arrival of the stars for the evening performance."[79] The evening screening showed stars "going to the movies" as well as stars accompanying their own films. At these screenings, formal and ritualistic star appearances were on offer. Unlike traditional star iconography, which relied on the single star or the fan magazine coverage of events such as film premieres that related to a single film, the Festival offered a collective portrait of the film world comparable in scale only to the Academy Awards, which it could even claim to exceed because of its international reach. In fact, the Academy Awards, which only became a "theatrical event" in 1944, was not telecast until 1953. By then, Cannes had already garnered a great deal of international press coverage.

The connection between stars, photography, and film was integral to how the star system functioned in general.[80] But the Festival also contributed to the development of the star system as a symbolic order (as opposed to an economic structure). Edgar Morin, one of the first sociologists of film and celebrity, commented on the Festival even before he published his landmark books, *Le Cinéma ou l'homme imaginaire* (1956) and *Les Stars* (1957).[81] As other observers had also noted, it was not the films, but "the film world on parade" that made the Festival exciting.[82] At the center of this world, Morin argued, were stars whose actual presence seemed to prompt great curiosity about their status as "real" people as opposed to their cinematic image. What one could observe at the Festival, much like on a safari, were the interactions of stars with each other as well as their individual and collective display for the public. Yet Morin observed that the lived reality of the star was simply one extended photo shoot. The Festival itself was like a soundstage: "If the star's real-life is like a movie, it is also that the Festival life is essentially cinematic [c'est que la vie du festival est essentiellement du cinéma.]"[83] For Morin, at the heart of cinematic culture was photography itself: "All that is filmed is photographed a hundred times. All that is photographed resembles that which is filmed. All that is photogenic aspires to be photographed."[84]

Morin interpreted the Festival's iconography in an essay written in 1955 in which he developed many of his important observations of the star system as embedded in long-term cultural habits and rituals. He identified several types of image: the star's entry to the Palace; the "staircase climb," which he compared to the Roman triumph or the ascent of the Virgin; the classic poses that suggested the lives of stars are filled with joy, happiness, and love; the Madonna and child sequences in which a female star is paired with a child. In addition, he noted that the images served over time to humanize the deific stars. Finally, he commented on the image of the starlet, whose structural necessity inhered in the fact that she shone light on the grandeur of the more important star. In other words, Cannes, it turns out, provided Morin with the material for what became some of the earliest and most influential ideas about film stardom as a system.[85]

Yet in trying to render the Festival within a longer visual cultural tradition, Morin missed the particularity of the Cannes mix of star imagery. Cannes' novelty included juxtaposition of the classic "star" photography of the staged Hollywood premiere and other official "photo shoots" alongside the seeming spontaneity that the beach seemed perfect to exploit. For example, for every traditional star photo of celebrities in formal attire (figs. 2.10 and 2.11) there is an image of a Kirk Douglas or even Sartre on the beach (fig. 2.12). This informality reinforces the gay life that Morin identified but also goes beyond it to emphasize what the paparazzi became famous for—the unauthorized image.

If glamour functioned to present a sophisticated star, the Cannes images offset that with a certain natural and spontaneous style. In the early years, stars and filmmakers did stroll on the promenade, and photographers were as likely to catch them off-guard (see figure 2.13 of Bardot and older theater and film star Edwige Feuillère at a café) as they were to ritualistically photograph them at the staged photo shoots. In fact, the spontaneity of the Festival photography led to heightened concerns among stars that had something to hide. In a note from publicist Rupert Allan to Robert Favre Le Bret, Allan suggests that Gene Kelly be hidden away at a less central hotel than the Carlton where photographers lurked day and night. As he explained to the Festival director, "Gene has a hair problem, which means that he must wear a cap or a headpiece for photos. This, in a way, presents a problem for him in Cannes with all the photographers around."[86] But careful management of a studio-perfect image did not work here as it did in Hollywood. The stars whose careers were made by Cannes were stars such as Brigitte Bardot, who basked in the spontaneity of the Festival events and its convivial atmosphere. A nineteen year-old starlet in 1953, Bardot's natural charm before the cameras at Cannes would make her the most famous woman of the decade.

Cannes played a crucial role in the career of Brigitte Bardot, who in turn played a crucial role in promoting the Festival. At her first Festival she was described as a "charming . . . young starlet" who was "so adorable."[87] She had, in fact, just completed her first starring role that year in Willy Rozier's film *Manina*, whose English title is sometimes *The Girl in the Bikini*. The film's publicity materials underscored that the character lived a "free and almost wild life." This quality would become a key element of Bardot's style— happily repeated in the beach photos at the Festival.[88] The crossover to the real beach in Cannes was thus not a big leap from the theme of Bardot's first film. In that debut year at Cannes in 1953, she also had the good fortune to be photographed with one of the most famous stars in attendance, Leslie Caron, whom she knew from their days at dance school in Paris. Caron was by then on her own rise in Hollywood, having already starred in *An American in Paris*, and was present in Cannes with *Lili*, a film that received much positive response at the Festival.

IT IS NEVER easy to explain why some are elevated from the ranks of starlets to become stars, let alone definitively explain the sort of phenomenal fame of someone like Brigitte Bardot. Yet, to consider her celebrity without attaching it to the photojournalism of the Cannes Film Festival misses a major element in both her meteoric rise and in the influence of the Festival on international film culture more generally. Bardot and her husband Roger Vadim mastered the Cannes-style photo by making even arranged photo sessions seem spontaneous. This sort of spontaneity became synonymous with the "acting" career of Bardot, but its quality and cultivation may well have

2.10 Warren Beatty and Natalie Wood in Cannes, 1962. Courtesy: Dalmas.

2.11 Alain Delon and Estella Blaine at the Festival. Note photographers on stairs. 1958. Courtesy: Mirkine / Sygma / Corbis.

2.12 Jean-Paul Sartre on the beach during the Festival, 1947. Courtesy: Getty Images.

2.13 Edwidge Feuillère and Brigitte Bardot at a café in Cannes, 1956. Courtesy: Lido/Sipa.

2.14 Kirk Douglas and Brigitte Bardot in the beach, 1953. Courtesy: Kobal Collection / Hawkins, Bob.

been first developed for the still images of the shutterbugs on the beach at Cannes. Her early champions such as François Truffaut, writing when he was a film critic, noted, "she is founding a new movement in cinema."[89] Yet rather than see this new style as emerging merely as a response to the staginess of the traditional French cinema, Vadim and Bardot first cultivated their "cinematic" style in relation to the photojournalism of Cannes. Outside of considerations of style, as Favre Le Bret wrote to Raoul Lévy, the producer of *Et Dieu créa la femme* (*And God Created Woman*), as if it were self-evident, "the Festival served as Mlle. Bardot's launching pad from the start of her career."[90] The Festival and its cosmopolitan culture advanced her career in a way that allowed her to emerge as an international superstar who was clearly thought of as "French" at the same time.

The canny management of photojournalists at Cannes helped Bardot go from starlet to star. Photographers hung out on the beach and stars and starlets appeared in suitable lack of attire to take advantage of the photo opportunities. While images such as figure 2.14 of Bardot with Kirk Douglas were staged (in this case to promote his film *Act of Love* in which Bardot had a bit part), Bardot also had a knack for just showing up on the beach when the photographers were loitering waiting for people to shoot (fig.2.15).

If the Festival took its "discovery" of certain films as a point of pride, starlet iconography served as the more popular visual equivalent of the hunt for artistic talent. As Maurice Bessy, longtime film journalist who directed the Festival immediately after Favre Le Bret, observed in retrospect: "It was the era when young women, rather than recording an album wanted to get into films. They went to Cannes."[91] The Festival, in short, became an international "Schwab's"—the drugstore on Hollywood Boulevard said to have launched a thousand careers. The fact that Bardot could rise from starlet status to superstardom encouraged photographers to lurk in search of other pretty young hopefuls. And careers were made. American Tina Louise, not long after her appearance at Cannes in 1962, became Ginger on *Gilligan's Island*, a show on which she played, of all things, a starlet. But most of the young hopefuls photographed remained nameless for posterity.

2.15 Brigitte Bardot on the beach in Cannes, 1954. Courtesy: Corbis.

The starlet photos were part of the growing genre of the pin-up.[92] The commodification of female sexuality may, in fact, have been as universal a language as film. The beach setting offered a seemingly legitimate reason for their state of relative undress. Fairly lax censorship laws and a long tradition of nudes and erotica in France encouraged risqué photos. *Variety* noted about the Festival, "What's 'news' to a photographer? Girls, Girls, Girls."[93] As the *Saturday Evening Post* reported of one starlet, "she is usually clad in the absolute minimum of clothing allowed by law, and that, in France, is two tiny wisps of fabric known as a bikini. . . . She will also do almost anything to get herself photographed."[94] Since the launch of the bikini in 1946 by Cannes designers Jacques Heim and Louis Réard, the French reinforced their reputation as a sexually open society, and the photographers at the Festival used the occasion to sell these sexy photos around the world under the veneer of legitimate reporting, even of the racy monokini (figs. 2.16).

But starlet photos also provided an interesting critical commentary on motion pictures themselves. As a *Life* magazine headlined punned, "Lady, do you want to get in Pictures? You CAN at Cannes."[95] If you couldn't get into "pictures" as in motion pictures, there was always the world of paparazzi photos. This starlet hunt reinforced still photography's importance to film, while highlighting the social and cultural hierarchy between the two photographic forms. The introduction of television at the same time as the Festival took hold as an important yearly image-fest added a third mode of photographic representation to the relation between still photography and moving photographic images.

The first postwar festivals were covered in fairly simple one-minute newsreels, which filmed the openings and closings or panned the Croisette and beach but did not offer visually distinctive coverage. These films were made by Gaumont and distributed worldwide through newsreel outlets. The filmed iconography of the Festival would find its great director under the tutelage of journalist François Chalais (fig. 2.17), who attended the Festival as a newspaper journalist from the start (and was then married to equally important journalist France Roche). His *Reflets de Cannes*, beginning in 1951, and then *Cinépanorama* (1956), a weekly film show broadcast by the French national station RTF, were essential elements in the spread of the Festival's public image.[96] Like newsreels, Chalais' *Reflets* captured the palm trees, the Palace, and the general ambiance of the Festival on film. Always set to jazzy music with an up beat and swinging tempo, his broadcasts emphasized the event's festive element. Like the still imagery, it featured many images of the

beach and women in bathing suits. In fact, some members of the Festival direction complained that Chalais emphasized the *mondain* and frivolous qualities so much that he was giving the event negative press. As one organizer noted, "This broadcast gives a false impression of the Festival, and can only do it a disservice in the eyes of, among others, the public servants who already think that it is consists of nothing but trifles and parties."[97] Chalais' coverage particularly irked Festival organizers since they were supported in part by public monies and the government was also responsible for television. But Chalais refused to be controlled by the subjects he covered. He responded to these complaints by reminding the organizers "I'm not here to be a Festival apologist."[98] Chalais seemed far less the dupe of the Festival than most of the press corps, or at least he understood that the journalist had the right to represent the Festival as he or she wanted and not as the Festival did.

2.16 Starlet in monokini, 1965. Courtesy: FIF.

2.17 François Chalais and friend at the Festival, 1963. Courtesy: FIF.

Despite the complaints and defenses, the *Reflets* established its difference from the paparazzi and the newsreels in two ways. First, Chalais' team filmed not only the event being covered, but also the press coverage of an event. There are countless images of the photographers taking pictures in the television broadcasts; thus the television cameras filmed the subject of the photos and the subject being photographed at the same time. The television programs emphasized what could already be found in the still photographs, which often had trouble getting their subjects without photographing photographers as well. (See fig. 2.9, a shot of Warren Beatty and Natalie Wood, as well as fig. 2.18 of Alfred Hitchcock and Tippi Hedren on the staircase with photographers lurking behind and in the center of the composition). The television camera's "eye" reveals the fabrication of the event as an event by showing the photographers at work. Television transmitted a sort of metacritical perspective—coverage and the coverage of coverage.[99]

2.18 Alfred Hitchcock and Tippi Hedren at the Festival, 1963. Courtesy: FIF.

Perhaps this is what bothered the Festival organizers, since it was their job to produce the event as smoothly and seamlessly as possible.

Chalais' shows also carved out the terrain of the celebrity interview in France. Like the imagery that seemed to underscore image making, Chalais' interviews often focused on celebrities. He interviewed most of the major figures that visited the Festival—although French-speaking stars were clearly at an advantage. Americans such as Jayne Mansfield, Mitzi Gaynor, and Dorothy Dandridge did not attempt to speak in French and were thus filmed in motion—on boats or dancing—to mitigate their mute status. For those who could speak, he prompted them to complain about the difficulties of celebrity and in so doing reveal their "private" selves. Sophia Loren explained that she had no more privacy because "you have to pay the price of celebrity."[100] Brigitte Bardot pouted that "my life is a big prison," and Martine Carole explained that one's celebrity status "destroys your private life."[101] Some had more clever replies to his asking about the power of celebrity. Simone Signoret reminded him that if she had been truly powerful they would be doing the interview at a time she selected and not the reverse. Jane Fonda, with a fairly good facility with the language, underscored the fact that when the camera is on, an actor always acts—undercutting the charade that the Chalais interview would really bring audiences closer to those interviewed.[102] In sum, television coverage combined the spontaneity of the paparazzi photos with an attempt to achieve greater intimacy. Yet, television differed from paparazzi photos in its more self-reflexive stance. It offered a discourse on image making rather than acting as just another medium for seamless representation.

Photo and television journalists cultivated the spontaneous image at Cannes and thus helped underscore the special cosmopolitan space of the Festival. Only here would such international groupings of stars be possible (figs. 2.19 and 2.20). Riding in the convertible in figure 2.19 are the Italian Sophia Loren, the Frenchman Alain Delon and his girlfriend, the Austrian star Romy Schneider who had become a superstar in Europe in the wildly popular Sissi films. Figure 2.20 features French and American "twins"— Bardot and Kim Novak. This iconography embedded American stars into a broader cosmos of stars from all over the world.

The Cannes images represent one of the Festival's signal qualities: the constitution of a film culture broader than Hollywood's. Yet, both Hollywood and the growing community of English-language independent filmmakers also attended in force, which the Festival organizers achieved through steady cultural diplomacy with film professionals rather than any government. The Cannes organizers recognized the international importance of American product and people and sought to exploit its status. They trotted out the American presence like a prized pony; American participation in and endorsement of the Festival not only contributed to its success, but also suggested that the Americans felt they had something to gain by coming to France.

Before the war, it had been the rejection of fascist propaganda that the Americans shared with the French and British, which resulted in their support of the Festival's creation in the first place. Despite the short life of the 1939 Festival, Philippe Erlanger wrote to the minister of education that "American film people, notably, have made it their business to assure the success of the event."[103] Their attendance at Cannes helped re-establish the importance of France in the international film world. The story of the American participation offers a different sense of "film relations" between the two

2.19 Sophia Loren (Italy), Alain Delon (France), and Romy Schneider (Austria) at the Festival, 1962. Courtesy: Dalmas.

2.20 "Twins." Brigitte Bardot (France) and Kim Novak (USA) at the Cannes Festival, 1956. Courtesy: Kobal Collection / Hawkins, Bob.

communities than scholarship about quota battles narrates.[104] Rather than taking any stance against Hollywood, the Festival organizers saw their role as promoting film in general and accepted that Hollywood's participation would enrich and enliven their event. In fact, when negotiations in Washington in 1954 threatened to prevent American participation in the Festival, *Variety* editor Abel Green reassured Favre Le Bret that this would not affect American stars from coming to the Festival. Although his position was probably incorrect, his reasoning is of interest: "the Franco-American breakdown on the film treaty . . . doesn't have any effect on Hollywood stars. After all, the American motion picture industry is an international industry and French-American relations are always of the highest."[105]

Explicit cooperation emerged from the first postwar Festival. In a message to the Festival organizers from Eric Johnston, president of the Motion Picture Association of American (MPAA), he granted that "we Americans have much to learn from our talented colleagues around the world. . . . No people ever had a monopoly of talent."[106] Perhaps such a disposition facilitated observations such as this from the executive secretary of the American Motion Picture Academy of Arts and Sciences who attended the 1952 Festival: "I never encountered the supercilious dislike of Americans and American films which I had been warned I might meet at every turn. My experience was one of good-will and eagerness to narrow the inevitable breach caused by our quotas and business agreements."

Between 1946 and 1952, American participation appeared insufficient to some observers. The publisher and editor of the expatriate newsletter *Ilma's Paris Grapevine*, American Viola Ilma, wrote to Dwight D. Eisenhower after the 1951 Festival and called the paltry American presence "an outright insult and disgrace to ourselves and to our hosts."[107] The problem persisted the following year as evidenced by a report from the executive secretary of the American Motion Pictures Academy of Arts and Sciences: "the impression at Cannes was that the U.S. film industry had snubbed the Festival and had sent prints of whatever films were easily available; that we had not tried to present either our best pictures or a varied impression of life in the United States."[108] This comment suggests some lack of mutual comprehension since *An American in Paris*, the winner for best picture of 1951, represented the United States, among other films that year.

The problem of perceived lack of interest on the part of the Americans seemed to disappear over time. Hollywood's most important film professionals, from its producers to directors, from its distributors to independent theater owners, started to make an annual pilgrimage to the Riviera. New

York art-house theater owner and distributor Walter Reade wrote to Favre Le Bret noting, "many of the theater owners of our country have been interested in [the Festival's] activity and its great international significance."[109] Reade attended in order to buy the rights to show films from around the world in the United States. That the Festival facilitated the rise of foreign film exploitation in America is another variation on the two-way street of film relations. Even studio heads such as Spyros Skouras, president of Twentieth Century Fox, lauded the Festival in non-nationalistic terms:

My faith in the universally important good the Festival of Cannes performs to the benefit of the world industry is as steadfast as ever. . . . Providing as it does a mirror reflecting the best creative achievements of artists and craftsmen of so many countries, the Festival has assumed a public and world industry significance. . . . You have my own and my company's complete co-operation in the perpetuation of the purpose and objective of the Festival International du Film.[110]

Although much has been made of the jingoism associated with the "patriotic" efforts of the studios during the war and Hollywood's subsequent flooding of Europe with American films, their level of interest and cooperation in Cannes indicates a recognition of the key role played by the French-led Festival in its cultivation of film as a "world industry."

The Festival helped the American industry develop this broader outlook. Hollywood's participation was of the highest priority for the Festival's organizers who systematically cultivated their presence. As much as they wanted American films, they also wanted American personalities to attend in order to feed, in particular, the photographic corps that the Festival worked hard to gather. In a letter to Madame Georges Bidault (née Suzy Borel), wife of the president and an attaché at the Ministry of Foreign Affairs (herself an organizer of the Festival in 1939), Favre Le Bret confided that "it is without doubt the participation of American stars and personalities who already have an international reputation has created an atmosphere that has furthered the Festival's success."[111] The Festival organizers identified the Americans as key: "It must be admitted that it is thanks to the American participation that we have not only the best film selection but also the presence of big stars."[112]

Procuring the participation of American studios and stars was in part achieved by the yearly trip made by Favre Le Bret to the United States. He visited New York, Washington, and Los Angeles, meeting with the likes of Eric Johnston, Howard Hughes of RKO, Arthur Lowe of MGM, Luigi Luraschi of Paramount, and "Elby" Mayer at his home in Bel Air.[113] He saw French journalists such as Léo Sauvage, *Le Figaro*'s New York correspondent, and French ex-pat director and writer, Robert Florey in Los Angeles.[114] These trips also depended on two great Cannes friends in America: Rupert Allan, a publicist who had been with the MPEA (Motion Picture Export Association, originally known as the MPA) in Paris before moving to the West Coast in 1950 as the editor for *Look*; and Anne Buydens, a German-born, Belgian-raised, and Swiss educated "diplomatic hostess" who served as a protocol officer for the Festival after the war before marrying Kirk Douglas and relocating to Hollywood. During the 1950s and '60s, Allan and Anne Douglas voluntarily served as the central liaisons between the Festival and the American industry.

The Festival archives are filled with correspondence in which Allan and Douglas identify films and the stars that might accompany their films to Cannes. They seemed to pay careful attention to French-themed films in particular. After seeing *Funny Face*, Allan noted in a letter to Favre Le Bret, "I don't think any other film has ever paid such a tribute to Paris as it does," and suggested they procure it for the Festival.[115] Douglas reported to Favre Le Bret that she had seen *Can-Can*, which was charming but not as good as *Gigi*, which they had screened two years earlier.[116] Allan favored young starts, his logic evident as he explained to Favre Le Bret the selection of Mitzi Gaynor: "Mitzi is sure to get a great deal of publicity because of her cuteness, her animation, and enthusiasm, her amiability, and above all, she looks terrific in bathing suits!"[117] The careers of Americans such as Kim Novak were launched at Cannes. Jayne Mansfield took advantage of the beach setting to show off her assets. Francophiles such as Edward G. Robinson, Kirk Douglas, and Gene Kelly, hairpiece or no, attended on several occasions. Rupert Allan's publicity stunt of introducing Grace Kelly to Prince Rainier of Monaco in 1955 at Cannes became the event around which the next year's festival was organized—the royal wedding in Monaco.

The presence of stars was easier to negotiate than that of the films. The subject of the exhibition of American films is a complicated one, which first needs to be embedded in a more general understanding of the Festival's film screenings. Both structural and aesthetic factors led to the selection of films destined for exhibition at Cannes. Most countries used national panels, usually composed of governmental film authorities, to select the films to be sent to Cannes. In the United States, the Motion Picture Association, working most closely with its Paris office, selected the American films to be sent. Over time, however, Favre Le Bret became involved in the selection of American films on his yearly visits. This set the precedent for what would, in 1971, become one of the Festival's major policy changes: the Festival selected the films and those films no longer represented a nation. There are several reasons why this shift happened. First, by the late 1960s, as Favre Le Bret noted, "It has become harder and harder to determine the nationality of films."[118] The increase in coproductions in Europe (and Franco-Italian ones in particular), the decline of the Hollywood studios and its star system, and the rise of "auteurism" also started to brand films by director as opposed to nation. This development of cosmopolitanism within film culture was not just reflected in the Cannes program, it was a product of the internationalism of Cannes itself.

The Festival awarded prizes for the best film from each nation and with one overall international prize. Although categories of awards have come and gone over the years, the Palme d'Or was first awarded in 1955. But to study that award over time to establish some sort of pattern would be futile, since the small group of around ten jurors changed from year to year and was always eclectic, not only in its composition but also in its tastes. Journalist France Roche cynically commented on the jury awards in 1957: "The jury did not judge quality. Its awards are a titration of politics, commerce and tourism. They give a small award to one, another small award to another and a big prize to the Americans to make sure in exchange they will get Hollywood stars the next year."[119] Contrary to Roche's claim, America did not win a disproportionate number of awards and only won its first award for best film with *Marty* in 1955.

The initial jury was composed of a member from each exhibiting nation. The following year the jury was all-French, though its makeup shifted again until eventually returning to including as many non-French as French members. There were all-French film professional juries, international panels of cultural celebrities (académiciens) such as Jean Cocteau and Jules Romains. Eventually panels included an increasing number of film stars and directors. From the mid-1950s onwards, internationalism, glamour, and two and a half week availability guided the selection of members to the Cannes jury.

More salient to a discussion of "Cannes films" might be the kinds of films exhibited, especially once the Festival itself made those selections (which is beyond the scope of this study chronologically). Even then, it is critical to remember that production schedules and distribution deals contributed to what could be shown in Cannes, since Festival rules specified that films shown had to have their European premiere in Cannes. (Exceptions, however, were made to this rule. For example, in 1964, *Les Parapluies de Cherbourg* screened at Cannes and actually won the Palme d'Or, despite having already been released in Paris. Protests abounded from interested parties in Italy, the Soviet Union, and Japan.)

Both the Festival leadership and the press valued films for their status as discoveries and revelations. Just as "discovery" marked the Cannes events discussed earlier—the spontaneous photo, the new star, the starlet who becomes a star—this quality marked film exhibition as well. Discovery could mean many things. Films could "discover" stars (Kim Novak); uncover new film aesthetics (neorealism and the New Wave); or reveal the work of filmmakers whose films had not previously been exhibited outside their own country. The Festival would "discover" such directors as the Indian Satyajit Ray, the Egyptian Youssef Chahine, and the Greek Michel Cacoyannis, major directors within their national and regional contexts, but largely unknown in the major film-producing nations such as France, Italy, England, and the United States. For American films, Cannes would discover modest budget character-driven films such as *Marty*, which went on to win the best picture of 1955, awarded in March 1956 after having won the Palme d'Or at Cannes in May 1955.

Although films were not awarded prizes based on their likely success at the box office, potential commercial value certainly drove film selection in the first place. Films such as the Italo-French coproduction *Black Orpheus*— set in contemporary Brazil during Carnival—exemplified the sorts of films favored by Favre Le Bret. Exotic, shot in a rich color palette, with a lively samba beat and untrained actors of color, it packaged the popular taste for spectacular color and music in the pretension of the classical tradition, since the story is that of Orpheus. *Black Orpheus* did, in fact, win the Palme d'Or and went on to great box office success (selling 573,496 tickets), making it the fifth most successful film at the box office in France between 1950 and 1963.[120]

If small nations might have benefited from the publicity machine at Cannes, what did the Americans gain by being there? There were obvious drawbacks: the Americans never believed they had enough films exhibited at Cannes because their level of world film production was so much greater than other countries. American producers feared that failure in competition might hurt a film's box office abroad, a segment of profits that was on the rise during this period. Yet the benefits outweighed these concerns: enormous press coverage; a cold-war inspired need to be present where and when the Soviets were in international cultural settings; and to present proof of their international cooperation to counteract accusations that Hollywood wanted to purge the world of foreign production.[121]

There were economic incentives as well for every nation, but they were particularly appealing to American studios that struggled with French-imposed postwar quotas. In a brilliant move that helped guarantee the Festival high-quality films from all nations, any films entered in the Festival would not count against quota limits and $250,000 in profits from each film could be repatriated directly back to the producer domestically instead of being frozen in European accounts. Ordinarily, the American studio profits in France stayed in French accounts in order to stem the flow of dollars out of Europe. Five American films shown at the Festival could mean as much as $1.25 million dollars back to the States. At times, the Americans screened films such as *Gigi* and *Around the World in Eighty Days*, but refused to enter them in the competition to avoid risking the reputations of these big investments.

For these occasions, the Festival created the *hors compétition* category devoted mostly to blockbusters because their scale would allow, "especially for opening night, an opportunity for extra-cinematic events that would likely add to the Festival's glitter."[122] This privileged forum of the film screened outside the competition became an essential part of the Festival and included such blockbusters as *Ben Hur* (1959), *Exodus* (1960), and *Doctor Zhivago* (1965). In this way, the Festival fostered what might be called the "international" film of the late fifties and to the mid-sixties—massive, international all-star co-productions such as *Around the World in Eighty Days*, *The Leopard*, *Exodus*, *The Fall of the Roman Empire*, *The Fabulous Adventures of Marco Polo*, and *Doctor Zhivago*, which played at the Festival, and such popular series as *The Pink Panther* and James Bond films which constituted a popular, cosmopolitan international film.

Hollywood acknowledged the Festival's importance, and the Festival knew that without American film there could be no "international" Festival. This cooperation emerged because of a shared affinity between the Festival organizers and the Americans: the French film community grasped and promoted the commercial quality of films as much as they valued artistry. Time and again, Favre Le Bret and his team underscored their commitment to film as reflecting popular taste and felt they should never abandon that stance. The notion that the Cannes film is an "art" film is a function of two things: the prizes ended up being eclectically awarded to many noncommercial films while Cannes' blockbusters played outside the competition. Increasingly, non-American film was associated with noncommercial film. Because Cannes showcased international film, it has been seen as promoting art film. Quite the reverse is the case: the Festival organizers cared deeply about promoting commercially viable films not only from the United States, but also from all over the world.

The Festival proclaimed itself at once concerned with art and commerce. In a summary written by the Festival directors describing its significance to the new minister of culture André Malraux, they noted, "It is undeniable that the Festival serves both the cinematic arts and industry."[123] From its conception, the Festival favored the logic of production: the number of films exhibited per nation was proportional to the number of films produced in each country yearly. Thus, film production trumped both quality and diplomacy. The organizers did not see quality and popularity as necessarily in conflict. As the Festival organizers noted in 1958, "One of the reasons for the Festival's success is that the direction has always been as liberal and eclectic as possible, not limiting its choice to a few esoteric films whose qualities could not be appreciated by a large audience."[124]

The quality/commerce debate emerged early in discussions of the Festival's films. In 1951, journalist Simone Dubreuilh mockingly defended film festivals as gatherings where qualities other than commercial potential mattered. As she put it, "without festivals, the Temple merchants would not have their yearly moment of disinterest," as if to say that the competition at least encouraged the consideration of artistic merit.[125] Marxist film critic and scholar Georges Sadoul as early as 1949 pronounced that it was "once a glorious festival which has become a publicity fair used exclusively to promote commercial products and casinos."[126] André Bazin, more interested in the development of "film art," complained as early as 1949 that the Festival had lost its soul to commercial interests.[127] Yet defenders of the Festival responded with vigor. Roger Vadim argued that the importance of festivals inhered in the very juxtaposition of art and commerce at the heart of film: "festivals orchestrate a commercial and artistic movement that benefit cinema, it seems to me that they offer a practical interest for the seventh art."[128]

Some critics may have been interested in the discourse of cinematic quality (on which their existence depended), but those who produced the Festival and the thousands who attended and who reported on it (film critics aside) did not separate quality from the development of the industry. Favre Le Bret articulated this philosophy in a letter to John McCarthy, vice president of the Motion Picture Association: "The strict goal of the Festival . . . is to facilitate, by virtue of the comparison of the best films from all over the world, a focus on world-wide production that invigorates the film industry while helping to advance the artistic evolution of film."[129] In the late 1960s when the Venice festival had fallen on hard times, Favre Le Bret commented that the problem was the Venice festival's "intellectualism." Although he noted that this approach was, without doubt, commendable, he also insisted it was "more appropriate for a conference, of the ciné-club variety than for a festival which, after all, contains the term 'fête' within it."[130] Venice, to the Cannes organizers, became known as the "ciné-club de luxe," which amounted to calling it a high-end film appreciation circle.[131] By contrast, commerce and popular film remained the guiding principles of the Cannes Festival's organizers.

This open door policy toward commercial film made the spontaneous development of the world's largest film market possible. Cannes was no mere highbrow film exhibition; it was centrally engaged in promoting the industry. The Festival not only promoted films from all nations but also became an international marketplace for film. As the Festival organizers noted as early as 1948, "virtually side by side with the Festival is a real and true film market."[132] This market took many forms. Some producers rented out theaters in town to screen movies that had not been entered in the competition because the number of film professionals in attendance at the Festival offered unprecedented exposure to distributors and other film professionals from around the world. Movies were bought and sold at cafés, on the beach, and at parties. The market business increased to the extent that the organizers wondered whether they should integrate the unofficial market activity into their official domain as part of the Festival's sanctioned events. As the American participant reporting to the Academy in 1952 noted, "the Festival is an excellent showcase for the best wares currently available in the world film market," and he urged Americans to participate even more.[133] The "market" developed in and along the movie theaters on the rue d'Antibes where films were screened. Deals were struck in bars, cafés, on napkins and with handshakes before being written up. In 1953, the market did twice as much business as the prior year. In 1955, one source estimated it did about one and a half million francs of business; by 1957, the market was thought to generate two million francs in film trade.[134] Eventually, the market came under the Festival's official sponsorship in 1959 and is an important indicator of the Festival's central role in the economics of the world film market. By 1965, *Newsweek* noted rather matter-of-factly that the Festival was "the movie world's biggest commercial event with 35% of the year's films dealt at Cannes."[135] Long before Miramax struck gold in 1989 at Cannes with *Sex, Lies and Videotape*, producers such as Carlo Ponti and Raoul Lévy made fortunes buying and selling films there.[136] As the Festival organizers noted in the late fifties, "the Festival owes its success to its commercial value. . . . it is a real stock exchange of film."[137] The French weekly *L'Express* reported that business was so big that "the number of deals struck at Cannes would suffice to keep the movie business afloat for ten years."[138]

The film market developed in part, as Festival organizers grasped, because the particular geography of Cannes turned the resort into *une cité du cinéma:* the dense cluster of hotels, the Promenade de la Croisette and the beach made for excellent and easy encounters among film professionals who sought to conduct the business of buying and selling films already made or developing projects and deals.[139] As the American delegate remarked in 1959, "the primary purpose of the Cannes Film Festival is as much to get film people together from all parts of the world as it is to show the top films."[140] Of the thousands of people who descended on Cannes for the Festival's two weeks, the overwhelming majority were members of the film community. Professionals and journalists so dominated the event from the start that the local authorities in Cannes complained that all the seats to the films were already given away: "To attract tourists, you can't only promise them the possibility but also the reality of actually attending the films."[141] Edgar Morin summarized it best: "The purpose of a festival is to commercialize that which is aesthetic and aestheticize the commercial."[142]

By the mid-1960s, the Festival in Cannes had firmly established itself as the major yearly crossroads of the world film community. While the Festival may have helped French film and certainly played a key role in the emergence of the French New Wave, the event itself also facilitated the internationalization of film culture. The Festival combined the market exchange with rhetoric about the international advance of film culture and the press glitz of a galaxy of movie stars in bathing suits by day and turned out in formalwear by night.

But because of film's peculiar and privileged status in relation to the real world as represented in films, the Festival also created more than a global filmmaking community. As a Brazilian newspaper celebrated in 1951, "we have spent these weeks in a splendid spectacle of universal humanity from the four corners of the world with these sixty films; its spirit, its customs, ways of life, of thought."[143] The Festival appeared to re-present the world itself through the films shown and talked about. Although the very success of the Festival in Cannes spawned other film festivals, thus creating the festival circuit of today as its direct legacy, it was a vital force in developing the postwar internationalization of film. Rather than hardening national identity through international contests, the Festival eventually broke down its own rules of competition between nations in order to achieve its self-professed goals of presenting a cosmopolitan smorgasbord of films. In so doing, I hope to have shown that "it was so French" to claim that France could, would, and should be the logical host to such an international event.

Yet, the cooperation between Festival organizers and Hollywood and the press delivery of the cosmopolitan spectacle they orchestrated forces us to reconsider postwar Franco-American film relations. By privileging stories of competition and conflict, we have missed the Franco-American film partnership that formed a cornerstone in the emergent "international" film culture of the postwar era. If institutions such as the Festival in Cannes embodied this new film culture, it fostered two significant elements of the emergent global film culture of the late 1950s and 1960s. The first was the seismic eruption of Brigitte Bardot to international celebrity that reveals a great deal about the France-America connection. The second was the development of the international system of coproduction that generated the cosmopolitan film cycle, which took off after the record-breaking success of the film based on a late nineteenth-century novel by the Frenchman Jules Verne and made by an American "showman" Mike Todd, *Around the World in Eighty Days*. It is to these "bastard" children of the Cannes Film Festival we now turn.

AND FRANCE
CREATED BARDOT

IN 1965 WHEN an American family comedy starring James Stewart called *Dear Brigitte* opened across the country, the film's title needed no explanation. Brigitte Bardot had become the most famous French export of the postwar period. In fact, the film's plot turns on the ubiquity of her fame. So well known was this Frenchwoman that the film narrates the tale of an eight-year-old American boy and mathematical prodigy whose talents are minimized by his father, a professor-poet infuriated by the domination of science on the campus where he teaches. Father and son come together over the boy's "healthy" obsession with Bardot to whom he writes nightly. Happily for the boy, he visits Bardot in Paris in the film's final ten minutes. She turns out to be kind, friendly and, of course, beautiful. Her association with both sex and animals is underscored: she gives the boy a kiss and a puppy to take home to the States.

The sensational career of the woman who became known by her meaningful initials (BB means "baby" when pronounced in French)—stands at a crossroads for any study of the fortunes of France after the war, especially as one considers its "baby boom."[1] Although the demographics of the post-war baby boom put adolescence on the social agenda, the mass media were more instrumental in framing and defining youth than any official state organization of youth policy after the war. As Susan Weiner suggested in *EnfantsTerribles*, the "problems of youth" and "bad girls," in particular, became the locus of anxiety over the future of France.[2] But the media's emphasis on young girls also created a sense that France belonged in the contemporary world. As all European countries that fretted over Americanization after the war realized, producing successful commercial culture defined cultural leadership on the international stage. Although France had a long-established reputation as a beacon of traditional culture, exporting Brigitte Bardot gave France a fighting chance to continue to lead into the future.

The great luxury exporter had managed to find in Bardot a commodity for the mass-market. In fact, she may have been the last great vehicle of popular Frenchness that did not rely on the sort of snob appeal that cultural critic James Twitchell has called "populuxe."[3] Although Bardot was known throughout the world during the height of her celebrity from 1956 to 1965, her triumph in the United States marked a key moment in U.S.-French cinematic relations. Bardot conquered the world because her success with American film producers and audiences held globally significant symbolic capital by virtue of Hollywood's singular role in making films. That culture of cooperation between France and America, as demonstrated in the countries' intertwined interests in Cannes, characterized Bardot's success as well.

Bardot was hardly the first international celebrity from France. Sarah Bernhardt became the most famous actress in the world at the turn of the twentieth century. In the interwar years, one of Hollywood's most important and best-paid stars of the early sound era, Maurice Chevalier, was a "transatlantic" Frenchman who traveled back and forth between France and America making movies on both sides of the Atlantic. Like Chevalier, Bardot's success with the American media and audiences is a central part of the story of her fame and fortune. For both figures, in fact, their celebrity in America catapulted them into international stardom. Yet the differences between them are significant. Chevalier actually worked in Hollywood, but Bardot did not set foot in the United States until 1965, at the end of her career. She never made a film in Hollywood—her small part in *Dear Brigitte* was filmed in France. Thus Bardot was, in her day, a French "export" rather than an "ambassador of the French."[4] Simone de Beauvoir, one of the first intellectuals to analyze the Bardot phenomenon noted, "The receipts [for *And God Created Woman*] are the equivalent of the sale of 2500 Dauphines [Renault car]. Brigitte Bardot now deserves to be considered an export product as important as Renault automobiles."[5] But Bardot was more than a successful export. She emerged within the historical context of the postwar film business in which Hollywood's connections with Europe and France were creating international films and international markets.[6] Bardot's career must be read against and through the many developments of the film industry as well as in the context of the dissemination of her image as an icon of Frenchness. Finally, Bardot's success is another powerful instance in which we can observe postwar American and French film industries bound in mutual dependence rather than antagonism.

THE POSTWAR PERIOD ushered in the heyday of both the foreign film and art film among American audiences. Although there had been a wave of immigrant audiences that enjoyed films from their countries of origin before the war, the market for non-English language film declined over time in the United States.[7] Despite the "nationalization" of film that developed after the advent of sound, New York managed to play foreign films as a niche market in the 1930s. As Barbara Wilinsky documents in *Sure Seaters*, before World War II, New York functioned almost exclusively as the single outlet of foreign film exhibition in the United States.[8]

Foreign films began a new chapter in their exhibition history in America after the war. As GIs returned from service in Europe and Asia and higher education expanded, ordinary Americans were now more sophisticated and receptive to foreign films. One of the main boosters for foreign film was Lillian Gerard, who helped manage the Paris Theater and also wrote ad copy for the Rugoff and Becker circuit of prestigious "little theaters" in Manhattan. Gerard noted that the excitement about foreign film rested on its status as "art" and because it helped renew contact with European culture, which had been cut off to Americans who were not serving there:

We were working as much for love, because foreign films, while not really profitable, were intellectually seductive. . . . during the war years, there was a total blackout of foreign films. . . . it was a relief when, not long after VE day, the French sent us the epic *Children of Paradise*, made during the Occupation to prove the undying artistry of the French and their belief in the dignity of true love, with Arletty symbolizing La Belle France and her lover, Jean-Louis Barrault, groping for her in a surging, insensitive crowd.[9]

Before the war, French film had developed a niche in the American market in what has been seen as one of the great eras of French filmmaking, although the same could be said of Hollywood in the 1930s.[10] After the war, first *Les Enfants du paradis* from France in May 1945 and then the Italian film, *Rome, Open City* gave a hungry market something to talk about.

Among the postwar centers for foreign film, the 570-seat French Pathé Company's Paris Theater on 58th Street, just West of 5th Avenue, stood out. Opened on September 13, 1948 with the French film *Pastoral Symphony*, the Paris openly targeted a "fine film niche." "In this sumptuous Gotham locale," announced the theater's inaugural program, "Pathé Cinema, the original French Company, has built a new motion picture theatre to present films from its own studios and from other Gallic producers. The Paris will bring to the screen the most noteworthy films made abroad, combining the artistry and talent of leading continental directors and artists."[11] The Paris received good press in the trade papers as they began to report on the increasing interest in foreign films. As the *Motion Picture Herald* remarked, "French pictures have a big vogue in New York because they always accent romance." The article also went on to credit Lillian Gerard's choice of films and the ad copy she wrote for the newspapers: "She has been remarkably successful, and has given the smart little French film house a national following."[12]

The highbrow appeal of foreign film was also linked with a seductive commercial element: distributors of foreign films often avoided getting a Production Code seal. Audiences considered their films "racier" than American studio productions because they had not been through the Hollywood precensorship machine. Jacques Chabrier, the Paris Theater's manager, strove to reassert the upstanding dignity of French film, however: "We would show French pictures here in the same way that American pictures are shown. We would have a comfortable modern theater, and we would have a dignified exploitation. We have kept to that."[13]

But foreign pictures were not, in fact, the same as American films. Not long after Chabrier's remark, the Paris Theater, Lillian Gerard, and *New York Times* film critic Bosley Crowther became involved in a epochal censorship case concerning the forty-five minute Roberto Rossellini film, *The Miracle*, which came under attack by the Catholic Legion of Decency as sacrilege for depicting a delusional peasant woman who believes she is the wife of Joseph and gives birth to an illegitimate child, "away in a manger," where she has been marginalized by the people of her village. Galvanized by the cause, Crowther championed freer expression and served as a vocal advocate for European film in the process: "Most of the bold innovations in cinema expression have been made by the creators of films abroad. . . . Artistic quality and commerce are two obviously different things. Foreign movies—those seen in this country—have represented an artistic cream . . . foreign film makers have been free to explore dramatic themes with an attitude of candor and inquiry that has simply not prevailed in Hollywood."[14]

The Miracle case eventually went to the United States Supreme Court, which ruled, for the first time in 1952, that the First Amendment's protection of free speech applied to film and all other forms of cultural production.[15] Foreign films already simply avoided the Production Code in the United States, and the Supreme Court ruling raised the bar against the power of censors in general. The victory promoted both free expression and foreign film on the American market. American distributors of French films delighted in the results of the case. In 1954, distributor Arthur Davis boasted to Georges Cravenne, director of UniFrance (the French film export association), that the latest Martine Carol film *Caroline, Chérie* was then screening with no cuts from the censors in the wake of the case.[16]

The growing commercial success of foreign films in the United States interested independent distributors who eagerly sought out this new niche within the exhibition sector. Noel Meadow, director of publicity for the independent distributor Siritzky International Pictures noted in the *Independent Film Journal Year Book and Buyers' Guide* as early as 1947 that "The most sudden and dramatic development in many years in the field of motion picture exhibition has been the growth of popular interest in foreign films, especially French, and the sharp upward leap in the number of houses devoted to them—exclusively, or even partially. [The] dissatisfaction with Hollywood's epics of gingerbread castles in the air . . . [is] a reflection of a correspondingly growing belief in One World. . . . it is natural that French, one of the world's two universal tongues, should lead the way." While seemingly universal, France also had a strongly identifiable culture of the particular. As *Holiday* magazine put it, "The best French films of the past have been successful here because they did not compromise their nationality. And, in giving a true picture of French life and a true feeling for French characters, they achieved a universal appeal."[17] But this lofty rhetoric could not disguise the fact that France's "particularity" seemed to be sex. Films such as *Olivia* (also titled *The Pit of Loneliness*) were marketed for their edgy and taboo sexuality. In its distribution package, Arthur Davis sold it as "the picture everyone has been speaking of in whispers."[18] The film depicted the boarding school romance between the school's headmistress and one of the girls. Jacqueline Audry, who had scored a success with the French language *Gigi* in 1948, directed the screenplay adapted from an English pulp novel. The ad copy emphasized the film's "frank" and "sensitive" treatment of the subject, while the images exploited the explicit lesbian content by picturing two women embracing.

Foreign film exhibitors often worried about the sexploitation quality of French (and other foreign) films. As foreign film distributor Walter Reade said, "Because many imported pictures are made primarily for adult audiences, they are often more candid in their treatment of sex than are conventional American films. . . . There have been some fringe operations which seized on this product solely for its sex exploitation possibilities and advertised in a near-blatant manner—certainly in questionable taste."[19] Thus, when the ad campaign for Bardot's breakthrough film, *And God Created Woman* used the tag line "But the Devil Created Bardot," it fit into a pattern of audience expectation of what a French film would offer.[20]

Whatever the draw among increasing numbers of Americans, some filmmakers saw in the rise of foreign film the chance to renovate the idea of film as a universal form that had been much talked about in the silent era after the World War I.[21] The notion that film was a "universal language" also implied it was a universal business. Just before the Paramount decrees broke up the studios' control of filmmaking and distribution, Barney Balaban, head of Paramount, explained in an address to the Theater Owners of America that the phrase "One World" "gave expression to the concept that this modern world has made all of us interdependent. We might very well apply the same principle to our own industry. This is 'One Industry'—not separate and isolated entities of production, distribution and exhibition. What happens in London and in Paris does have an effect upon your business in Walla Walla and Oshkosh."[22]

Although it seems at first glance that Balaban, a studio head, was trying to reassure worried exhibitors that they still shared a mutual interest despite the decoupling of production and distribution from exhibition (which would in ten years time have the exhibitors far more tied to London and Paris than they ever thought they would be) the American studio chief articulated that the film business, like film itself, in all its "modern" qualities extended beyond national borders and boundaries.

THE REDUCED NUMBERS of films produced in Hollywood as a result of the Paramount decisions have stood as one major explanation for the growing popularity of foreign film in America. The decoupling of distribution and exhibition ordered by the United States Supreme Court responded to claims of monopoly practices among the studios by independent exhibitors. In short, the court case resulted in separating the studios from theatrical exhibition. Because they now had to sell films on a film-by-film basis and abandon the practice of "block booking" in which exhibitors had to buy "blocks"—that is—large numbers of a studios' films as a package, the studios responded by taking the approach of making fewer "high-quality" films that would be guaranteed longer runs to minimize risk and labor costs to sell the films to exhibitors. Whereas Hollywood produced about 350 films a year in the late 1940s, the number decreased to about 200 a year ten years later.[23] The net outcome of this decision did not ultimately benefit the small theater owners who originally brought the suit because they now lacked films to show. Of course, other changes in American life—such as suburbanization, automobility, and new kinds of leisure such as bowling alleys and television—altered the pattern of weekly moviegoing and changed the nature of the movie business as well as the Paramount decisions.[24]

Film exhibitors turned to films made outside the United States in their search for new product. Independent distributors often ran theaters and thus championed foreign films because they needed more films in the wake of the product shortage. Their trade group, known since 1966 as the National Association of Theater Owners (NATO) but then known as the Theater Owners of America (TOA), began to pin its hopes on foreign films by the mid-1950s. As a result, specialized theaters increased in number from about 100 in 1952 to 448 by 1957, despite the overall decline in the number of movie theaters in the United States.[25] The TOA invited foreign producers and governmental film representatives to its annual convention to meet with theater owners. The largest delegation came from France but there were also representatives from Great Britain, Italy, Germany, New Zealand, Canada, and Mexico. This practice became known as the "foreign film fair," which was designed "to stimulate interest in foreign productions as a supplement to the shrinking American product." Thus for TOA membership, generating interest in foreign films made good business sense, and would bolster receipts at the box office.

There are no definite promises that the existing domestic sources of supply will increase the number of pictures that they will produce and release. It is, therefore, recommended that officers of TOA undertake to do everything available to them to encourage the wide acceptance of films made abroad. . . . Convention ACTION: It is the feeling of the Board and the Executive Committee that release of American-made pictures are at a record low and that interest in British and other foreign product is at a record high; consequently the screens of members of TOA are more open than ever before in industry history for suitable and playable British and other foreign films.[26]

In March 1957, the TOA began publishing a Foreign Film Directory, a list of foreign films currently available for exhibition in the United States, foregrounding the current first-run offerings in New York. In addition to that group, the directory listed films by distributor, including information such as: the film's stars, running time, genre, language, whether they were subtitled, dubbed or both, whether it was in black and white or color, year of release, Legion rating, and Code Seal. A small number of the best-known films were Legion rated; only a few of the United Artists import releases had a Code Seal.[27]

Although the attention to foreign film emerged as a do-or-die business strategy, it did not prevent the theater owners from trying to legitimate foreign film distribution as contributing to the promotion of international understanding. As Walter Reade explained to the TOA,

It must be noted that the playing time accorded foreign films is enabling the American theater industry to make a definite contribution towards better international understanding. Just as Hollywood films are recognized as good will ambassadors for the American way of life when shown abroad, so too the showing of imported films in America's theatres contribute positively to the cultural interchange so necessary to achieve better understanding and sympathy for our Allies and the people overseas."[28]

But as distributors promoted foreign film, exhibitors began demanding a different kind of product. Whereas foreign film had been associated with "artsy film," the more foreign films American distributors and exhibitors saw, the more they realized Europeans could make "commercial" films. At a meeting in Italy, TOA president Myron Blank implored foreign producers to think strategically about tailoring films for commercial export and, in particular, for import into the United States. "What one country might consider successful entertainment will not be true in another country," he fretted.[29] Blank applauded the quality of European and Japanese films, while imploring their producers to better understand the American market. He explained that Americans liked action and suspense over costume and period dramas; sex within the parameters of the Production Code; and high-level production achievements in sound and photography. He also advised,

You must properly exploit your talent in the American market. Perhaps casting American stars with your stars can hasten this. . . . And keep in mind that making pictures for the American market should also make them saleable world-wide since American pictures are definitely very acceptable in the world-wide market. . . . my sincere plea is for you better to understand our country so that you will be able to make pictures that will be commercially successful and bring an understanding of your country to the people of the U.S.[30]

Blank's message was clear: American films are internationally successful. If your films can better resemble ours, they will find a market not only here but also around the world. Although independent theater owners did contribute to the increased screening of non-American films in the United States out of pure need, they also urged Europeans to adopt the Hollywood-style of filmmaking, which, they astutely argued, served as a universal gold standard. These pleas did not fall on deaf ears. In "French Film in America," a report prepared for the Centre National de la Cinématographie, the author noted the importance of the American film market " because it constitutes

a key market: a strong French position in North America will open new outlets around the world."[31] The independent exhibitors, however, were not
the first group to actively promote the development of a market for foreign
film in America or to offer advice on how to strengthen their appeal abroad;
Hollywood had already beaten them to it.

HOLLYWOOD OBJECTED vociferously to the European quotas placed on
American films. Yet historians have characterized Hollywood's lobbying in
the name of "free trade" as a ruse to expand Hollywood's share of the European market to further the "Americanization" of Europe. Yet, like most stories of transatlantic film culture, this one has two sides. Hollywood's attitude toward European films in the American market reveals a surprising
consistency in the American attitude toward free trade. In an annual report,
Eric Johnston, director of the Motion Picture Export Association, supported
the work of the Advisory Unit by arguing "the broader distribution of good
foreign pictures in this country heightens our appreciation and understanding of foreign nations and cultures; that it results in a greater flow of sorely
needed dollars abroad; and that the competition spurs our own studios to
even greater efforts and achievements."[32] A few years later, Johnston continued this promotion of free trade on Hollywood's home turf: "The industry
readily recognizes the logical corollary (of huge American export), namely
that channels from the importation of foreign films to the U.S .must be kept
open."[33]

In 1950, the Motion Picture Association of America (MPAA) put its
money where its mouth was by creating the Advisory Unit on Foreign Film
(AUFF). The short-lived unit surely helped in the expansion of foreign films
on the United States market while perpetuating Hollywood's commitment
to free trade. The unit conceived of itself as "the crystallization of a plan for
friendly and constructive development of motion picture relations between
film producing countries and their industries and this important industry
in the U.S. . . . Its purpose is to offer help and guidance in every way possible
—short of business dealings—to foreign film producers and distributors.
In accordance with recommendations from Marshall plan . . . (it will) stimulate the flow of dollars to foreign producers."[34] Operating in concert with
the Marshall Plan, the board would cite the unit's objectives when Europeans complained that Hollywood wanted open markets in Europe but did not
provide them in return. As the MPAA's 1950 annual report explained, "the

project was launched to overcome an impression then widely held by film industry people overseas that the American market was virtually closed to foreign films . . . the unit encourages and equips foreign producers to gain wider audiences for their pictures in the American market."[35] The fact that the MPAA cultivated an "official" stance of promoting the spread of foreign film in America as a sort of defense against criticism by Europeans does not mean that it did not genuinely help foreign film.

Bernard Kreisler, an economist who had produced a study for the Ford Foundation on the status of postwar cinema around the world, directed the unit. In its first year, 113 foreign producers from twenty-two countries visited the United States under the program's auspices. The unit provided lists of potential outlets for screening foreign-language films in the United States. It also offered a screening service for the trade-showing of the films, arranged for their importation through customs, provided services to negotiate taxation regulations, and acquainted foreign producers with the Production Code. Kreisler designed a questionnaire sent to 563 colleges to determine the commercial potential of foreign language films on campuses and designed a separate survey of every specialized movie house. The MPAA was proud of its services, noting in a press release that "the American film industry, through AUFF, is the only industry in this country known to extend a helping hand to foreign competitors. The objective of the program is to spur the importation and exhibition of more select foreign motion pictures in America and thus help stimulate a greater flow of dollars to film-producing nations abroad."[36]

The unit, at least from the French point of view, was designed in large measure to help them especially. As the newly established French para-governmental unit, UniFrance Film explained, "The committee is taken with the MPAA's project, whose goal is to create in the United States a permanent organization that through its information services and legal and technical advising will facilitate the spread of non-English language film and French films especially. . . . The MPAA hopes to get a representative of the French cinema to go to New York to study the best methods through which to achieve these objectives. The MPAA will be happy to pay for the costs of the trip."[37] UniFrance Film decided to go on a mission at the unit's invitation, but paid its own way so as to not seem too dependent on the generosity of the United States. The delegation visited New York, Washington, and Los Angeles and met with studio heads, circuit theater operators, independent distributors of foreign films, and owners of a number of important movie theaters. They also met with Eric Johnston, head of the MPAA; John McCarthy, international vice president of the MPAA; Joseph Breen, head of the Production Code; and Bernard Kreisler. The trip resulted in a very positive view of the American industry's support for French film. According to one report, "the MPAA has indicated that it is ready to support all activities of the French motion picture industry to find a broader outlet for their films in the American market. As regards commercial showing, the Advisory Unit program calls for aggressive encouragement of the exhibition of French films, as well as the initiation and facilitation of contacts with the directors of large theatre circuits."[38] At the same time, the French government agency in charge of export also sought the advice of its supporters already working in the United States such as Jacques Chabrier of the Paris Theater. Chabrier, writing to UniFrance chief, Robert Cravenne, wondered whether the AUFF was a mere ploy to soften resistance to upcoming renegotiations over the quotas on American films: "It is interesting to note that at the time the agency in question was founded, the trade papers also reported that the MPAA affiliates were set to renegotiate the accords that actually govern the import and dubbing of American films because of a renegotiation clause in the agreements."[39] Chabrier also doubted the viability of the service in general: he believed that foreign films would never play in wide release in America nor would subtitled American films succeed outside of Paris.

Even after the increasing success of French film in the United States later in the decade, some observers still wondered why anyone would bother to compete in the American market. At the height of the French expansion in 1958, an observer writing for a French periodical puzzled at the French film community's interest in the American market when there were countries around the world: "with little or no production of their own rather than in the United States where national production occupies an unchallengeable position. It would never dawn on a French automobile maker to compete with the American car industry in America itself."[40] Of course, the French industry never thought it would rival the American market for its own product, merely that it would find an audience and expand its own profitability there. French filmmakers also cared about how they were seen in America. They thought it would enhance their profitability throughout the rest of the world and also sought validation of their culture and its product in the expansion into the American market.

The French diplomatic corps resisted the move to greater commercial success. They feared the French film industry's focus on greater profitability would result in an Americanization of French film and a dilution of what was particularly French in their films. In their minds, both strategies left little hope for commercial triumph. "If we give them Hollywood products, we could never succeed with this fairly specialized menu; then there would be no particular reason for them to choose, among this mass production, films they don't understand."[41] The French diplomats instead promoted the fact that Paris had an extraordinary resource in its film school, the Institut des Hautes Études Cinématographique (IDHEC), which would allow Paris to become for young filmmakers "the spiritual capital of film, since it will never be its industrial capital."[42] It is not surprising that the diplomatic corps would promote educational institutions run by the government, but French film professionals tended to see things somewhat differently.

IF THE AUFF were a mere public relations stunt, it certainly coincided with serious exploration of the American market by French film interests. Not all of those who assessed the situation were as negative as Jacques Chabrier. The rise of French film in America resulted from the efforts of the French themselves, coupled with the changes in the conditions in the American market.[43] In particular, the founding of UniFrance Film (UFF) and eventually the French Film Office (FFO) in New York facilitated the export of French film to potentially profitable markets. The French initially concentrated on Italy (where, in fact, they had an office before the establishment of UFF); Francophone markets such as Switzerland, Egypt, and the Congo; Spanish-speaking countries Spain, Mexico, Argentina, and Uruguay; and finally Sweden and Finland in Northern Europe.[44] The organization, like the Cannes Film Festival, was an "association of 1901," which is to say a private organization in the public interest, paid for with money from the government-run Centre National de la Cinématographie (CNC) and various French industry production syndicates. Its first president, Georges Lourau, had been the French head of the German Universum Film AG (UFA) before the war and the head of the CNC after the war. The organization's operations were actually run by its director general, Robert Cravenne. Cravenne held a law degree, but before the war worked in the film industry, dubbing and subtitling French films for export. During the war, Cravenne had participated in the French Resistance and was rewarded by being immediately integrated into the film services after the Liberation, serving as the under-secretary for foreign relations of the newly formed CNC in 1946 until UFF was formed in 1949. In many ways, UFF was the French equivalent of the Motion Picture Export Association of America.

The formation of UFF offices abroad involved a haphazard process by which delegations emerged from already existing networks of diplomats and public relations circuits. For example, despite the centrality of the German market in the consumption of French film, the UFF only established a German office in 1953.[45] The interest in expanding further into the American market emerged because of the MPAA's AUFF's encouragement. The French visit in 1950 sponsored by the unit resulted in UFF's hiring Meyer Beck, an American public relations man, to assess the possible expansion of French film into the U.S. market. In a summary report, Beck reported that the French officials were convinced "in the American market only exceptional films will make it and that most French pictures do not have the general appeal necessary for mass audiences in the U.S." But Beck believed there were multiple "selective audiences" who would embrace French film. Further, he urged the French to establish a "permanent representational unit working with the MPAA on all phases of the motion picture industry to achieve the cooperation necessary to bring the fullest success to our mission."[46] The suggestion would bear fruit a few years later when UFF founded the French Film Office in New York in October 1955, after several years of planning.

With offices in New York, UFF and FFO leadership could assess and strategize how best to market French film in the United States. UFF director Cravenne frequently met with American film professionals to assess the perceived difficulties of the American market. He believed this market required a large and permanent operation and argued that the press served as the vital component in the exploitation of foreign films in the United States. The UFF's goal in the United States, he argued, would be to "keep journalists up-to-date on our cinematic productions."[47] UFF's only obstacle to maintaining this level of publicity for French films was the FFO's relatively modest budget.

To clarify the UFF and FFO's mission and to persuade the larger CNC organization to pay to undertake such an expensive venture, UFF hired another American, Henry Kaufman, to produce another report on how to manage such a propaganda effort on behalf of French film in the United States. Kaufman recommended a carefully organized public relations program that would issue press releases, a weekly newsletter, and a monthly information folder and bulletin. They would organize special events to familiarize the public with French product. He also suggested that they organize contests involving French film stars, create tie-ins with other French organizations in the United States, and work with film clubs.[48]

In addition to such reports, Cravenne insisted to the higher-ups at the CNC that the Americans were eager to open their doors to the French. In a memo about a conversation he had at the film festival in São Paolo in March 1954 with Eric Johnston, Cravenne explained that Johnston wanted French film to succeed in America despite his discomfort with French protectionism. Cravenne also reported that Johnston advised him to start making films that would be more suitable for export; they could then be backed up with an effective public relations presence. Again the French were being advised to adopt American practices to compete by better tailoring their product to the market. Cravenne wrote that Johnston reminded them that to play in the large theater circuits, their films would need to be Code-approved, which meant no erotic or antireligious material. Last, he suggested that French films be more diligent in their practice of the star system. As Cravenne translated Johnston's suggestions, "If you want to sell a French car in the U.S., you can't just show a picture of it. You have to see the car itself. The same is true with stars, and you can sell a film more with the names of its stars than with its content."[49] Cravenne believed Johnston was sincere about his support for the French cinema, and that he believed that "France is the country among the world's whose cinema has the greatest artistic qualities."[50]

As French film interests began to commit to serious expansion into the United States, they were deeply aware that their growth had to be based on commercially broad appeal, rather than on an exotic kind of differentiation. UFF knew what they needed to do: "It is no mere publicity campaign, with external activities, through which we could hope to interest the Americans in our product. It is rather with as big and wide a penetration of their markets as is possible, in order to accustom the general film public to our formulas, our character, our civilization. It is also, above all, by familiarizing the public with our usual actors: the star factor actually plays a considerable role in pleasing the public."[51] They sought to increase exhibition in as many venues as possible, thus giving American audiences opportunities to become familiar with France and its film style. By making French film accessible and familiar, Americans would become comfortable with French foreignness and the French film style. Neither claims to art nor the promotion of a cultural high ground would produce the kind of results that filmmakers, producers, and even the French government sought: a large audience for their films that would be economically beneficial and culturally indispensable. If the Americans could use film to promote "the American way of life," a view that many people held at the time (despite its more complex reality as has been discussed in earlier chapters), why couldn't the French do the same?

The FFO had opened under the direction of Joseph Maternati, a diplomat from the ministry of industry and commerce who had been in charge of its film division and, in that capacity, knew many film professionals in France. He was, however, unknown in the United States. *Variety* miswrote his name as "Martinatti" in a skeptical article doubting the mission of the FFO. Rather than creating a liaison between French producers and American distributors, the article wondered whether the French might be more successful if they would just send French stars on U.S. tours.[52] Maternati himself worried that the problems of promotion were at their core commercial ones, and that film producers were in a better position to handle them than he was. Among the other problems he faced were the concerns of American distributors, who worried that the FFO would act as a representative of French producers and become a controlling middleman that would interfere with their access to producers and their films.[53] He nevertheless reassured Cravenne that the office was poised to achieve results, in both prestige and commercial success.[54]

Into the expanding apparatus for promotion also came several relatively commercial films made in France, notably *Du Rififi chez les hommes* and *Diaboliques*. Jules Dassin, an American blacklisted by Hollywood, made the former. The film's style was as familiar as its genre: a noir tale of a jewel heist. Of further interest, the film uses sounds (as opposed to language) in a variety of suspenseful ways; the robbery itself is entirely a pantomime except for those sounds. With its dialogue-free twenty-five minute major sequence, *Rififi* was a perfect film for export. *Diaboliques* was a murder-filled thriller whose suspenseful narrative set the terms for the psycho-thrillers for which Hitchcock had already become well known.

This flurry of French releases in America coincided with the opening of the FFO. *Diaboliques* premiered in the United States in November of 1955 and played for twenty-one weeks in New York. It shared the New York Critics' best foreign film award and was listed in the National Board of Review's list of top five foreign films of the year, as well as being the first foreign-language film to play drive-ins. *Rififi* opened in June of 1956 and played for twenty weeks on the RKO circuit in a dubbed version. Aside from these high-quality thrillers, the Jacques Cousteau–Louis Malle underwater film *Le Monde du silence* (given a lift by the Palme d'Or at Cannes) also played to great acclaim during the same period. It played to solid box office in the United States between the end of September 1956 and the start of January 1957.[55]

The successful distribution of these films resulted in an overall increase in the play of French films in America. This achievement seemed to prompt critics to give French films greater critical attention. Critic Bosley Crowther named *Le Monde du silence* one of the top films of 1956. He also named three French films—*Les Orgeuilleux* (*The Proud and the Beautiful*), *Rififi*, and *Les Grandes manoeuvres*—among the top five foreign films of the year. In an FFO report Maternati explained that more French films opened and were in wider distribution in the United States in 1956 than ever before: "The year 1956 has been the best year that the French film industry has known in the United States. Results from the sales of these films have reached about 1 million dollars as opposed to $200,000 in 1955. . . . This financial success and the growing interest among the critics, the public and American exhibitors is due, first and foremost, to the quality of our product and also to sustained effort in distribution as much as that of the circulation of general information."[56] Although Maternati naturally confirmed the importance of his own mission and its potential to be effective, he concluded with the uncertainty of predicting commercial success in film exhibition. Despite what he perceived to be improved knowledge of French film and producers' efforts to get a better sense of public taste, he nevertheless fretted, "there is no sure way to predict whether a film will succeed or not in the United States."[57] But that didn't stop them from trying.

The FFO's publicity included a monthly information folder (whose distribution in the course of a year went from 1800 to 3500 copies) and the distribution of 65,000 photos of French stars and film stills in its first year of operation.[58] The staff also helped coordinate visits to the United States by French stars. In June of 1956, director Christian Jacque and actress Martine Carol spent two weeks in San Francisco and New York doing interviews and making public appearances on television and at receptions and film screenings. The following year Gérard Philippe, Françoise Arnoul, Micheline Presle, and Jean Marais made a similar tour of the United States. The FFO also helped organize a retrospective of French film held at the Museum of Modern Art, which opened in late May 1957, coinciding with the star tour. During this tour, the FFO public relations specialist Donald La Badie boasted to Cravenne that he had managed to secure a spot for the French actors on *The Ed Sullivan Show:* "The stars who will be in the program at the time of the Museum opening will, in one hour, be playing to an audience far greater than the cumulative gathering for one of their films." Aside from the Sullivan show, they also appeared on *Person-to-Person, What's My Line, I've Got a Secret,* and *This Is Your Life.*[59]

The Paris CNC also sought to use the FFO as a lobbying force within the United States. For example, Jacques Flaud, the head of the CNC, wrote to Maternati asking him to go out to Los Angeles and lobby on behalf of the Jacques Tati film, *Mon Oncle,* to help it win the Oscar for best foreign film in 1958 (a category that had only officially been established two years earlier and been won by Italian films, both directed by Fellini—*La Strada* and *Nights of Cabiria*).[60] The creation of the Academy Award for best foreign film in 1956 at the suggestion of independent producer Walter Wanger is another example of Hollywood's interest in promoting foreign films. As MGM executive Robert Vogel explained, "Walter Wanger came up with foreign film award. The day must come, and soon, when these pictures come to be recognized around the world and the Academy will be in the terrible position of appearing provincial if it ignores pictures that are produced outside Hollywood."[61]

The American trade press took notice of the French efforts. As *Variety* remarked after it doubted the FFO's mission, "Distribs of French pics are aided by Joseph Maternati's French Film Office," and a few years later, "the French Film Office is a more enterprising action than the Italians have ever managed."[62] Crowther also noted the "extraordinary number of French films [that have] opened in New York this year." On November 13, 1957, *Variety* also noted it had been "far and away the best year for their [France's] films yet," and concluded that French films paced the field of foreign films by a wide margin.[63] In the end, *Variety* finally granted that the French were making progress "due in part to their own exertions."[64]

The number of French films distributed went from twenty-three in 1956, to thirty-two in 1957. Maternati boasted of three "mores" in 1957: "more theaters, in more cities, showing more French films." *Variety* commented on the rise of foreign film, singling out the French releases, which lagged behind only England's thirty-six releases while far surpassing Italy's nine films. The same article noted that that very week, four Italian films were playing in four theaters in New York, in contrast to twenty-one French films showing in nineteen theaters.[65] At the MOMA opening, the French ambassador Hervé Alphand celebrated the rise of interest in French film in the United States, noting that in 1956 the United States was the second ranking market for the export of French films, whereas it had only the year before it had been tenth.[66]

Although events such as the retrospective at MOMA tied French film explicitly to "art" (the show's catalog copy went so far as to claim that "no country's intellectuals have been more irresistibly attracted to the exploration of the new medium. . . . French films have won an enduring audience, wherever the spirit of inquiry and experiment is valued"), the successes of films from France in the 1950s seemed to be emerging as part of a "popular" rather than "artistic" cinema.[67] The marketing and publicity efforts of the FFO were critical influences in the changing tide. The FFO was an effective liaison with distributors and theater owners; it assured that the TOA directory had proper information about French films; it helped arrange for Jacques Tati to attend the TOA convention in 1958. But the FFO by October of 1958 had one thing that no one else could offer, which created a sea change not only in the commercial potential of foreign film in America but also in the fortunes, expectations, and singularity of French film. And that was Brigitte Bardot.

THE TOA'S ANNUAL report proclaimed the singular film story of 1957 was the "world's most spectacular personality: Brigitte Bardot. Without question, this young French girl's got more of the total newspaper and magazine coverage of movies than any other actor, actress or picture." The TOA was particularly excited about the fact that the moment's major star emerged from their "specialized films" theater world, thus anticipating this would enhance the standing of the TOA's contribution to the film industry. The TOA noted that Hollywood, "with its reduced studio staffs and lesser number of pictures," might no longer be able to develop itself.[68] Surely the postwar period had seen other European stars come and go, but none seemed to have as powerful an impact as Brigitte Bardot. Her meteoric rise did wonders for the export of French film and, in fact, inspired many producers to believe that the New Wave that followed in her wake might be commercially successful. That was a pipe dream. While the commercial success of the French cinema in America lasted as long as Bardot's career, the New Wave, whose films were inspired in large measure by Hollywood, managed to weave their films into cultural capital gold, giving French film a lasting place in the minds of young American intellectuals rather than in the minds of boys like the star of Disney's *Dear Brigitte*.

Bardot's emergence was a broader sign of the times. For some critics, she represents changing notions of female sexuality as a protoicon of the sexual revolution.[69] Ginette Vincendeau, in particular, amends the usual perspective on Bardot's "break-out" sexuality by arguing that it also depended on "old" values: traditional myths of femininity and the display of her body. She concludes that "Bardot's stardom rested on the combination and reconciliation of these opposed set of values."[70] For others, her sexuality was part of a broader change in youth culture. As Antoine de Baecque has argued in *La Nouvelle Vague: Portrait d'une jeunesse*, her performance and Vadim's films secured the notion that film would represent contemporary youth culture in France. In that way, Bardot paralleled the persona of James Dean: young, brooding, beautiful, and rebellious. De Baecque is correct to focus on the connection between film and youth culture, but in so doing he overlooks the way Bardot fueled the exportation of French film culture. Not only was this Frenchness designed for export, but also nothing could have pleased French modernizers more than the notion that France could be seen as producing a popular form of contemporary culture on a global scale.

Though French film in the 1950s has been characterized by its protectionism, Bardot's career is proof that the story is more complex than that. Her film career is evidence of the successful, if short-lived, "program" of filmmaking in France for a global commercial market. Bardot was the result of a concerted French effort to develop a commercial film presence in the United States, aided by the American market and exhibition interests enumerated above. Bardot was France's most visible export. Her success rested on her identity as a French product made for international export, especially to the target American market. One cannot sufficiently explain her career without embedding it in the context of the industrial history of film. Her sexually frank roles and the public persona she cultivated underscored the international but especially Anglo-Saxon association of the French with sex and a laxity of moral standards. Bardot was another iteration of the Frenchness cliché associated with *la gaieté française*, the Belle Epoque Can-Can girl, and the decadent world of the Moulin Rouge.

Bardot's exportability also depended on her hip and modern qualities. She did not represent France as class-bound, elitist, or Old World. Bardot's spontaneity, youth, mobility, and hedonism enhanced her broad appeal to American audiences of the 1950s. Bardot hit the American market as "commercial" cinema made in France just as Americans could begin to imagine that not all foreign films were "art films." Her emergence coincided with the rise of the paparazzi and their photography of spontaneity made possible by the worldwide explosion of glossy magazines, new telephoto lenses, and the international glamour of the Cannes Film Festival. These shifts in popular culture jolted stardom, as a system, out of its studio-generated timeless mythologizing, making Bardot an iconic figure of this new, more "caught-off-guard" notion of modern celebrity.

Bardot is "cinematic" in two related ways: her roles in film and her representation in the press emphasize her mobility and its association with contemporary culture. While stardom may have always been fleeting, the star system also promoted the timelessness of stars. As Norma Desmond says in *Sunset Boulevard*, "stars are ageless." In fact, François Nourissier, who wrote an early full-length description of the Bardot phenomenon, compared her stardom to Swanson's portrayal. Bardot, he wrote, is the opposite of Norma Desmond. "She's someone you'd meet. Instead of the glorious old car, a Simca sports car like that of your Aunt Henriette, the oh-so-modern and hip woman."[71] Bardot pulled France out of the Belle Epoque and into the flashy red sport cars of the leisure culture of the midcentury. This made her a particularly valuable commodity to French entrepreneurs, especially those in film and journalism, and even the diplomatic corps that were desperately trying to perpetuate their country's reputation for cultural innovation. They already knew that having a vibrant and successful film culture had economic benefits and, in a more general way, maintained a presence in an international industry with enormous cultural influence. Bardot gave the French modernizers the future they needed.

ALTHOUGH THE FAME of Brigitte Bardot seemed to explode in the United States in one fell swoop with the release of *Et Dieu créa la femme* (*And God Created Woman*), she was already an established model (having appeared on the cover of *Elle* several times) as well as a movie actress in France. She had been cast in sixteen films, including small parts in the Franco-American *Act of Love*, starring Kirk Douglas and Dany Robin, and the epic *Helen of Troy*, directed by Robert Wise. In reviews of these movies in the United States, however, she went unnoticed. She appeared in supporting roles—including such historical films as *Si Versailles m'était conté* and *Les Grandes manoeuvres* —that played in the United States with little or no fanfare and certainly with no recognition of Bardot.

And yet, French film exporters envisioned her as a future star from the start. Her first appearance in UniFrance Film's news bulletins was a still from the 1953 film *Manina* in which she was photographed in a bikini and the newsletter promoted her as "France's youngest actress." She was regularly featured in the columns of the UniFrance publication, usually replete with photos and predictions of her eventual stardom. In another early promotion piece in the newsletter penned by her husband Roger Vadim for the August-September 1955 issue, he described her as the "young girl of today, I know her well. . . . When she acts, she invents nothing. . . . She drives her own car in Paris with more confidence than a cab driver."[72] These qualities were to become the great clichés of Bardot's persona: her youth (it is no wonder she ended her acting career before she turned forty), contemporaneity, mobility, confidence, and freedom. She was a woman in the modern world. Bardot "moved"; she was not simply a pin-up who played in the movies, but rather a "movie" star who could be photographed. This peripatetic quality contributed greatly to her exportability.

As a teenager growing up in swank Neuilly in the Western part of greater Paris, Bardot studied ballet in the same school as Leslie Caron and began her career as a cover girl and fashion model for junior clothing lines before she turned eighteen. She aspired to be a dancer, but her father's amateur moviemaking habit captured her dancing before the cameras at a very early age.[73] The success of Caron was often mentioned in the early press coverage of Bardot in both the United States and France, as if she would be the next star from France to have a career in Hollywood. One of the first American articles dedicated to Bardot, published in the *Los Angeles Times Magazine*, essentially duplicates an article and its images published earlier the same year in *Paris-Match*. It announces that "the French movie industry, which lost Leslie Caron to Hollywood, thinks it has the perfect replacement in 17-year-old Brigitte Bardot, who, like Caron, is both a ballet dancer and a movie star."[74] Rather than "lose" Bardot to Hollywood, the French industry (looking for viable export), American exhibitors (looking for foreign product), and American companies (beginning to invest in foreign product), were more than happy to have her stay and make films in France.

The early years of her career from 1952 to 1956 were punctuated by her relationship with Roger Vadim, Marc Allégret's young assistant. Vadim proved instrumental in transforming the dancer-model into a movie star. Although they courted from the start, they did not marry until 1952, when she turned eighteen, because her bourgeois parents forbade it. After their marriage, Vadim sought more steady work as a reporter for *Paris-Match* and she began her film career the same year in the black and white comedy, *Le Trou normand*, which generated the first publicity articles about her.

But her career was formed as much on the beaches at Cannes in the early years, where the starlet became known to the photographic corps. Bardot laid extensive groundwork for her fame in the movies through her yearly appearances at the Cannes Film Festival between 1953 and 1957. Bardot's first appearance at the festival in 1953 coincided with the end of shooting of the Franco-American co-production *Act of Love* directed by Anatole Litvak in which she played a minor role alongside major stars Kirk Douglas and Dany Robin. In these earliest Cannes images, she is almost too childlike to foreshadow the sultry sexpot she would become in the eyes of the media, but the iconography of spontaneity and motion associated with paparazzi culture is also part of the early Bardot imagery. The French public may have first known Bardot through fashion shoots and then reassociated her with film culture through the medium of photography. Cannes photography, however, differed from the frozen glamorous movie star photography of the studios. At Cannes, Bardot transformed this "on-the-fly" photography of leisure culture into a "starlet" photography. Bardot's rising fortunes then transformed the paparazzi photograph into the new star iconography. *Le Figaro littéraire* mocked the early press interest in Bardot and the opportunism that Cannes seemed to embody by reporting that American photojournalists at Cannes in 1953 eagerly chased down the young Bardot, asking her "Êtes-vous *famous?*"[75]

Between 1953 and 1957, Bardot became a fixture at Cannes. Many of the Bardot photos were taken on the beach and emphasized youthfulness: bikini shots with Kirk Douglas (see fig. 2.14) or dancing with Caron, or mobbed by her "fans"—little boys at the start (fig. 3.1). As her fame grew, she was photographed in more ritualized images, made as though they were spontaneous, like getting off the *Train Bleu*, which arrived in Cannes from Paris at six in the morning, or preparing for the official posed image with Minister of Justice François Mitterrand (fig. 3.2). As television journalists began to cover the festival, she seemed made for their broadcasts because she would hold photo shoots in which she would pop out of boxes (figs. 3.3 and 3.4), run, skip, or dance; moving stars were essential for this fledgling medium of quickly made moving pictures.

These images helped define Bardot because their unplanned composition (there are people in the background and photos of other photographers, see fig. 2.15) stressed spontaneity. The photos' messy structure makes no attempt to crop out other photographers in the shot and reminds the

3.1 Bardot stopped by young fans in Cannes, 1955. Courtesy: Courtesy: Kobal Collection / Hawkins, Bob.

3.2 At the Festival in 1956, with the young and good-looking finance minister, François Mitterrand. Courtesy: Corbis.

3.3–3.4 Bardot and motion. Popping out of a box at press gathering at the Cannes Festival, 1957. Courtesy: Corbis.

viewer just how many people were taking her picture at once (see fig. 3.5). Unlike the official work of Hollywood studio photographers who defined "glamour" photography such as George Hurrell, the art of photographing Bardot resided in showing up and jostling the other photographers for a desired angle.[76] By seeing other photographers in pictures of Bardot, viewers are additionally reminded that others are also looking, and that the viewer is part of a legitimately gawking crowd.

Bardot's fame was so tied to the paparazzi that, even as early as 1963, filmmaker Jacques Rozier offered an analysis of her relation to the hounding shutterbugs in a short film made during the shooting of Godard's *Le Mépris*, when Bardot and the cast and crew arrived in Capri to film. The picture reveals Bardot swarmed by photographers and crowds while being preyed upon by men with cameras hidden in bushes and on cliffs. The film, which is ultimately an exposition of the difference between authorized and unauthorized picture taking, depicts the photographers as opportunistic hustlers and Bardot as a victim. It, however, also offers behind-the-scenes

3.5 Photographers at work, here with Austrian actress Maria Schell at the Cannes Festival, 1957. Courtesy: Huffschmitt/ Sipa.

images of Bardot on the set of *Le Mépris*, and thus indulges the same audience desire to see Bardot unposed and spontaneous.

The film's focus, then, is more precisely on why Bardot became such an important target of the menacing and harassing photographers. In what appears to be a mock newsreel voiceover played within the film (which sounds remarkably like the voice of well-known cinema telejournalist François Chalais), we are informed, "the entire world photographs the Arc de Triomphe and the Eiffel Tower, and the whole world photographs Brigitte Bardot." The voiceover continues: "Why this camera mania? It is not just BB the actress that fascinates the crowds, but BB in real life."[77] The visuals that accompany this are a still of Bardot with wind-blown hair looking directly into the camera, followed by a shutter-click to the letters BB in capitals, which flash as voiceover says her name: "BB works as well in a newspaper headline as on a movie marquee, and for some years now, Brigitte Bardot has played nonstop the role of . . . BB." The film cuts to a magazine image of Bardot posing between two large B's (fig. 3.6). This is followed by about forty-five seconds of still shots from weekly magazines, connecting the fame of Bardot the movie star to her image in the press.

The rest of the movie narrates difficult circumstances on the set during the film shoot between the paparazzi and Bardot. The film provides an anatomy of the paparazzi's vital equipment: a 300mm telephoto lens with 3.5 aperture (which facilitated taking pictures from as far as 150 meters away), a Vespa, a pair of legs, endurance, a flash, and their secret weapons patience and stubbornness (fig. 3.7). The photographers are interviewed by Rozier about a clash they had in town with Bardot and her entourage, in which they claim that they are the real victims as they were physically abused, simply

3.6 Image between two letters. From Rozier film, *Paparazzi*, 1964.

3.7 Title image of Rozier film, *Paparazzi*, 1964. Note wide angle lenses of the paparazzi.

because they tried to get a photo, which is how they make a living. Rozier juxtaposes their indignity with the media coverage of the clash itself, which portrays Bardot in an unflattering manner. The photographers lament their difficult work conditions in which they risk their lives to snap a photo. They envy the easy circumstances of Jicky Dussart, Bardot's production photographer, because he has unfettered access to the star.

Finally, they explain that the best photo of Bardot is one of her in a bikini. The bikini did not just offer more flesh for the waiting audience of these photos. The bikini also became the sign of Bardot caught off guard. Further, the images that circulated of Bardot from the beach and her habit of sunbathing subsequently became a mass cultural ideal of pleasure around the world. Only a few years after Bardot frolicked on the beach at the festival and made a film shot on location in Saint Tropez, she bought La Madrague, her beachfront estate there. In another interesting connection, France and America developed parallel beach cultures: across the world on the Pacific Coast of the United States, the "surf" sound of Jan and Dean and the Beach Boys emerged as cornerstones of the Southern California beach culture in the early 1960s.[78]

Thus, Bardot's celebrity was of an intermedial and transnational nature. It was propelled forward by changing circumstances in photographic technology, the diffusion of an increasing number of photo-oriented color weekly magazines, and the way these changes helped renew and revitalize a sagging film industry worldwide. Bardot's fame also coincided with a certain critical reflection about stars. In 1957, Roland Barthes published *Mythologies*, his examination of mass culture in which he sought to unmask the bourgeois ideology embedded in the star system. In the same year, sociologist Edgar Morin published *Les Stars*. Although Barthes and Morin cannot account for the popular taste for Bardot, they can go some way toward explaining her contemplation by the likes of Simone de Beauvoir and filmmakers such as Rozier, Malle, and Godard, whose films did not just feature Bardot but contemplated her stardom. Bardot's celebrity coincided with the emergence of this new-style European photography and the intellectualization of stardom. In this way, she became famous for being famous. Her Frenchness mattered because the paparazzi emerged in Europe, especially at Cannes, and because French intellectuals who first pondered stars, pondered Bardot.

WHILE IT IS the conventional wisdom that Bardot burst into superstardom with the release of *And God Created Woman* in France in December 1956, this seems true only in hindsight. Although such a narrative works as part of the mythology of celebrity and its notion of overnight fame, it has been perpetuated in part because of the film's surprise success in United States, which established Bardot's exportability. [79] Judging from materials written before the film was even made, Bardot already was a celebrity. For example, by early 1956 the UFF newsletter noted that the magazine *Der Test* proclaimed her the "top star" in Germany. In the next newsletter they described her "dizzying climb," which they attributed to the last year and her "journalistic side that put her at the top of the list." [80]

Talk of coming to the United States inevitably followed. During the spring of 1956, Maternati wrote to Cravenne in Paris to tell him that he had seen Raoul Lévy, Bardot's producer, in Cannes and both intended to come to New York at the end of June, which would have been directly after the shooting of *And God Created Woman* in Saint Tropez. (The trip never happened.) [81] By the summer of 1956 and thus before the screening of the film in the United States, the FFO was already reporting back to Paris that an article had appeared about Bardot in the *New York Herald* and that the September issue of *Real* also planned to feature her. They reported that "Brigitte Bardot seems to be taking here and interests the journalists. We are often asked about her and we have sent out quite a lot of materials in response." In the same letter, Maternati also asked Paris to send more photos of her in a variety of poses. [82]

When *And God Created Woman* opened in Paris in December 1956, Bardot had already made sixteen films that had already positioned her as an international star. *Act of Love* was a Franco-American coproduction, *Helen of Troy* was an American picture shot in Italy, and *Tradita*, was a Franco-Italian coproduction. In 1955, she also starred in her first English-language production opposite Dirk Bogarde, *Doctor at Sea*. Bardot's formation as an international star also relied on growing French interest in exporting their films, especially the development of UniFrance and their strategic implantation in New York, spurred on by fortunes of the festival in Cannes. But if the way had been paved for Bardot, this did not guarantee she would emerge a star.

French films gained popularity in the American market just ahead of Bardot's obtaining more important roles in her films. What Bardot's films have in common with *Rififi* and *Diaboliques* is that they are commercial films with inherent exportability. There were also many other such films from France between 1956 and 1957. One could argue that all these successful films were Americanized French films but that confuses "American" film with "commercial" film in the same way that "foreign" film in America had always been collapsed into the category of "art" films. The commercial nature of Bardot's films during those two years, apart from the Franco-Italian co-production *Mio figlio Nerone* (*Nero's Mistress*), was that she played "modern" girls living in contemporary France. This quality alone, according to *Variety*'s European reporter, Gene Moskowitz, would be essential to the bankability of French films in the United States: "More clear exposure to the reality of contemporary French society will at least open up new international outlets."[83] Moskowitz implied that French filmmakers had been out of touch with their own contemporary culture; foreign viewers wanted to somehow "see" France in French films.

The quality of Bardot's films themselves is not a sufficient explanation for their success even if they had been good. They were launched in an environment where critics and theater owners in the United States alike were hungry for French product that might please American audiences. Into this same environment, the French film industry was making a systematic effort toward expansion and, in the evaluation of the trade papers, more successfully than any other country. Lastly, investment in European production in the form of what one might consider "silent" coproduction by American companies emerged in this period. *And God Created Woman* received financing from Columbia Pictures. The studio agreed to give Vadim and producer Raoul Lévy the production money once they had a confirmed and bankable star in the film. They were able to persuade the very popular German star, Curd Jürgens, to give them two weeks of his time to make the film, although they had neither a script nor a role for a sophisticated forty-something man. When Columbia's financing came through, Vadim and Lévy wrote in a part for Jürgens and could, as a result of the increased budget, make the film in Eastmancolor and in Cinemascope which they considered essential "production values" that had already been used in several of Bardot's other films.

And God Created Woman opened in France in December 1956 to a mediocre box office and with a decided lack of enthusiasm from mainstream critics. The star's physicality stood out. One reviewer even called the film *Symphonie Charnelle* (Carnal Symphony) a pun on the earnest French Resistance movie starring Michele Morgan, *Symphonie pastorale* (Pastoral Symphony).[84] It became, however, a favorite among the younger critics associated with *Les Cahiers du cinéma*.[85] The majority of mainstream critics in France derided the film for the same reasons that the young *Cahiers* crowd celebrated it: for being so much a product of its time and as a representation of a generation. As Robert Chazal, the critic for *Paris Presse* observed, it was "a film as important as a Sagan novel through which to better understand contemporary youth."[86] Sagan was the wildly successful eighteen-year-old novelist

Françoise Sagan, whose *Bonjour tristesse* had caused a sensation when published in 1954 and whose car accident the same year also habituated the French public to the elision of real life and fiction among young women artists (one of the characters in the novel suffers a fatal car crash). That elision also became one of Bardot's trademarks.[87]

And God Created Woman and its star (Jürgens, the film's original star, insisted Bardot be granted that status after screening the film) were seen to incarnate contemporary culture and represented a French society "in motion" on the cusp of modernization, and in that way seemed to break with the classical French cinema's focus on traditional and historical subjects, attributes of the so-called tradition of quality cinema that would become the style to innovate beyond for the New Wave critics. This quality in *And God Created Woman* caught the eye of the young critics of *Les Cahiers du cinéma* and of François Truffaut, in particular. Of Bardot, he proclaimed that "she inaugurated a new moment in the cinema" and declared that she was in the midst of saving French film despite the nasty critics and audiences alike who complained about her states of undress and her poor delivery of lines.[88] Claude de Givray wrote in *Les Cahiers*, "She is one of the hopes of the French cinema. BB, a product of our times, is allowing our age to appear on the screen."[89]

It is worth noting that these critics had also seen her earlier that year in *Cette sacrée gamine* (*Naughty Girl*), written by Vadim and directed by Michel Boisrond, former assistant to the well-known director René Clair. That film, shot in Eastmancolor and Cinemascope, contains many of what became the "formulaic" essentials of a Bardot film. Within a minute of Bardot's presence on the screen, her character, named "Brigitte," has disrobed from sailor shirt to bikini, dived in a swimming pool, and been called a "baby" by her father. She has so distracted the gardener that he starts hosing the pool (whose phallic significance is only matched by its wink to film history's famous first "comic short" *L'arroseur arrosé*) and responds to her father's comment, "A baby like that has always been my dream." She will eventually drive a convertible, walk around in a towel and a Greek tunic and dance to mambo (in a prison cell, no less), and perform a dream-sequence ballet that contains elements from a number of American musicals (see figs. 3.8–3.14).[90] Bardot also demonstrates a natural way with animals (a parrot) in the film and finally becomes the irresistible object of a man's desire.

Though *And God Created Woman* did not grab French audiences, the sheer volume of films Bardot made that year certainly kept her name on theater marquees and also in the press. In addition, the number of French films exhibited in the United States that year outpaced all foreign language production among the releases in 1957, which subsequently drew greater interest in films from France. Before *And God Created Woman* even played in the United States, Bardot had been seen there during the summer of 1957 in *La Lumière d'en face* (*The Light across the Street*) and in *En effeuillant la marguerite* (*Please, Mr. Balzac*). While neither film was particularly well reviewed, Bardot had begun to capture the attention of the American press. For example, *Esquire* included an article about her that previewed *And God Created Woman*, featuring a two-page spread of her naked body, bottom up, from the film's startling opening moments. A caption teases that the "ten-times-life-sized shot may be used as a Times Square billboard." While the article mocks the film, saying it is "badly written and badly directed . . . and badly acted," the Cinemascope Bardot bottom distracts viewers from the film's artistic deficiencies, the magazine reasoned. The article also tries to essentialize the film as something French while establishing a transatlantic youth culture: "It deals with the subject of French young and it has somewhat the same fascination of Francoise Sagan's sad college students and the neurotic rebellion of James Dean."[91]

The surprise of *And God Created Woman* was its box office success in the United States, which critics had not predicted, although the FFO had. In an advance review of the film, *Variety*'s Gene Moskowitz forecast "just average" U.S. market for the film and had no inkling that the film would begin a run in late October 1957 that would make it the largest grossing foreign language film in the United States up to that time.[92] Critic Bosley Crowther appreciated the film as a vehicle for Bardot's performance, noting that "she is undeniably a creation of superlative craftsmanship . . . [it is a] completely single-minded little picture. . . . She is a thing of mobile contours—a phenomenon you have to see to believe."[93] But Crowther's review was mostly unimpressed and did not send readers to the theater.

From the start, however, the FFO anticipated success, and watched the film's box office with eagle eyes. In a report written only days after the movie opened in New York, Maternati wrote to Paris about the film's success there: "this film is beating the Paris box office." In the same note, he also mentioned that a *Life* magazine article in that month's issue featured both Bardot and the film.[94] The box office success of the film preoccupied the FFO for the rest of the year, as the film began to open outside New York in dubbed as well as subtitled versions.[95] The film did well in the usual places such as New York, Boston, Washington, and Los Angeles, but it also played for more than a year around the country. Between March and September 1958, it did twenty-five weeks of steady business in Kansas City, Cleveland, and

3.8–3.14 From *Cette sacrée gamine* (The Naughty Girl), 1956; (3.8) BB in bikini, with the *arroseur arrosé;* (3.9) behind the wheel of a convertible; (3.10) in a towel; (3.11) dancing in prison; (3.12) in a dream sequence referencing *Gentlemen Prefer Blondes;* (3.13) in a dream sequence referencing *The Pirate;* (3.14) in a dream sequence with candy-colored balloons and dancing in a generic Technicolor musical.

Detroit.[96] At Squirrel Hill Theater in Pittsburgh, it broke all existing records for money, attendance, and length of run, which had previously been held by *Marty*, which the Bardot film was doubling straight down the line.[97]

Its popular success provoked the usual moral indignation. It had, needless to say, already offended the Catholic Church whose Legion of Decency had already given it a "C" classification. "The theme and treatment of this film, developed in an atmosphere of sensuality, dwell without relief upon suggestiveness in costuming, dialogue and situations. In the field of motion picture entertainment the extent and intensity of the objectionability of this picture constitute an open violation of Christian and traditional morality."[98] In addition to being condemned by the Catholic Church, parts of the film that displayed Bardot's nude body while reclining on the ground or lying in bed were eliminated by the New York censors. In other cities such as Philadelphia and Chicago, the film sometimes encountered attempts to prevent its showing. At the Squirrel Hill in Pittsburgh, the exhibitors suspended screenings during Holy Week so as not to offend the public.[99] These efforts only helped its business. In March 1958, Maternati noted that the film was doing about $100,000 a week combined in major cities across the United States, and that while there were many censorship threats, they did the film little harm. He described to UFF Paris that the film had been banned in Philadelphia, then put back in theaters, then banned again. At the time of the report, the case was before the State Supreme Court but the mayor of Philadelphia strongly condemned the attempted censorship.[100]

Banning Bardot became a favorite topic of columns and articles. For example, newspaper columnist Dick Williams asked in the spring of 1958, "Should We Ban Brigitte Bardot?" Although he published a young man's defense of Bardot, he gave more space to her female critics: "I'm sick, sick, sick of hearing about Brigitte Bardot. Every time I pick up a newspaper or go by a theater marquee there she is, blasted all over the place with her stringy, unkempt hair, her plunging necklines, her bare feet, her vapid eyes and her half-opened mouth. She looks like she never takes a bath or irons her clothes. Her personal life is nothing to admire. Her casual attitude toward marriage is both shocking and immoral."[101]

One journalist summed up what seemed to be the position of many: "*And God Created Woman* is one of the most insistently lascivious, sex-obsessed films of all time."[102] Not all reviewers found the film quite so shocking. While the critic for *Time* joked that "the language she speaks can be understood without subtitles," he remarked that the film bore a great resemblance to a Hollywood movie's treatment of sex: "In the hard sun of the Riviera her round little rear glows like a peach, and the camera lingers on the subject as if waiting for it to ripen. . . . If sex is the object, there is just as much to be seen in almost any Hollywood film and in promulgating Brigitte as a full-blown enchantress, the French have clearly sent a girl to do a woman's job."[103] Within the first month of the film's release in the United States, *Variety* marveled at its box office success and suggested that "really successful imports must be cured more towards sex than art," while also suggesting sex was not enough, as there had been any number of sexy films from Europe before this film and none had produced the box office splash of the Bardot film.[104]

And God Created Woman exploited Bardot's easy sexuality, but there were other appeals in the film. The film's visually undisruptive and commercial look was familiar to American audiences. What may have been striking was that this fairly ordinary slick middlebrow product, in color and widescreen, had been made in France in 1956 and viewed in the United States in 1957. In other words, its French origin allowed it greater latitude with sex because it did not require the approval of the Production Code but American audiences could integrate its visual style rather easily. In an interview many years later, Vadim spoke explicitly about the American influences on the film. He said that he had been inspired by Elia Kazan's use of CinemaScope to "broaden" emotions along with the picture. He also chose Eastmancolor, which was usually used for realistic "serious drama" but was beginning to be employed more widely in the United States. Finally, Vadim's script jettisoned the theatricality in dialogue he and audiences associated with French films in favor of the more spontaneous and natural dialogue for which Bardot became famous.[105]

If the film offered a visual style that resonated with contemporary filmmaking in the United States, its self-conscious engagement with France as a "modern" place all its own pervades the film. The film opens with a shot of a white convertible sports car in which the playboy millionaire, Caradine, is first seen in front of a beautiful view of the coast in Saint Tropez. This is immediately followed by his offer of a toy version of a red Simca convertible to Juliette, the Bardot character (fig. 3.15). The film also features youthful, contemporary music—records, radios and jukeboxes that play both French pop music and the more exotic "cha-cha-cha."

The narrative delineates the modernization of the south of France. The film's tenuous plot (cooked up by Vadim and Lévy in only two weeks) revolves around the scheme of the cosmopolitan playboy's plan to buy the shipyard of the Tardieu family to build a hotel and a casino. The water and coast are everywhere in the movie (and the widescreen format encouraged many coastal and port views) and while Saint Tropez still has a sleepy look, the film's message is clear: the Côte d'Azur is ready for tourism, the last sleepy town is about to get its casino. Saint Tropez promises what Juliette announces she loves to Michel, her young husband in the film played by Jean-Louis Trintignant: water, the sun, warm sand, food, and music. The music is cosmopolitan and racy: the film's last fifteen minutes features a dancing Bardot, mesmerized by the samba beat (although some scholars have referred to the musicians as African, they are clearly Afro-Brazilians, playing the hip music at the time; see figure 3.16).

3.15 Red Simca. *Et Dieu créa la femme*, 1956.

3.16 With Brazilian musicians, *Et Dieu créa la femme*, 1956.

The film embodied a certain contemporary sensibility aside from these signs of the times. For example, in the film's English-language trailer, Juliette is dubbed "the young girl of today." Her character also emphasizes this contemporanity expressly in the film when she exclaims to her older playboy, Caradine, that "the future was invented only to spoil the present." Bardot had earlier impressed director Robert Wise for these very qualities when he cast her in *Helen of Troy*. He described her as having a "beat generation look" and encouraged Fox to sign her to a contract.[106]

And God Created Woman codified qualities that had been in several of her earlier films and that would become a set of standard devices in many of her subsequent films. For example, in *Une Parisienne,* which she made right after *And God Created Woman,* Bardot is pictured at the film's start happily cruising down the Champs Elysées in a red convertible sports car, very much like the toy one from the earlier film (fig. 3.17). Throughout this light comedy, her home is a modern 1950s setting with streamlined furniture and wall-to-wall carpet (figs. 3.18). She dances several times in the movie and pops in and out of towels (fig. 3.19) (and in and out of bed), demonstrating an unusually predatory sexuality for a young woman from a fine family. If that were not enough, her character, the daughter of the prime minister, is even named "Brigitte," which she was also named in *The Naughty Girl.*

And God Created Woman's success in America then made Bardot exceptionally well known in France and initiated one of the major framings of Bardot: she could be packaged as Frenchness, possibly better suited to the American than the French audience. For Simone de Beauvoir, the American interest in Bardot spoke well of American culture, which she credited with having a more "modern" sense of female sexuality, although it was far from a culture that was beyond feminist reproach. In 1959, Beauvoir wrote an article for *Esquire* in which she attempted to explain (to American men) why "Brigitte Bardot is disliked in her own country."[107] At the outset, she identifies Bardot's export value as "important as Renault automobiles." She goes on to declare her the "new idol of American youth . . . and a great international star" (32). There are two major axes of interpretation in Beauvoir's essay. The first has to do with the creation of a new kind of eroticism and the second with a new kind of celebrity, both based in a heightened materialism and corporeality.

Bardot, she argues, is a resolutely modern version of the "eternal female," and thus offers a novel kind of eroticism to which the cinema had deliberately turned in order to reignite viewer interest in the movies (34). Although she mentions the continuing allure of the grand physical charms

3.17 Opening sequence in red convertible on the Champs Elysées, *Une Parisienne*, 1957.

3.18 Modern home in *Une Parisienne*, 1957.

3.19 Bardot in towel, again, *Une Parisienne*, 1957.

of Monroe, Loren, and Lollobrigida, Beauvoir identifies the novelty of the "erotic hoydens" of the modern cinema: the youthful persona of such actresses as Audrey Hepburn, Françoise Arnoul, Marina Vlady, Leslie Caron, and Brigitte Bardot. Because women had gained socially in relation to men, Beauvoir argues that the era of the woman-child reestablishes the differences that foment desire. She describes the type as the merging of the "green fruit" and the "femme fatale." This type, she argues, is more appealing in the United States than in France because of a more progressive attitude on the part of American men.

Caught in an eternal present, Bardot represents the perfect innocence of childhood. She is entirely unstudied, "natural," and impetuous in ways that repeat the juvenile qualities in the myths of femininity. But the audience knows that she is in fact no child. Instead, she is amoral in an intense and winning way, enveloping the era's emergent youth culture more generally, and disturbing the rear-guard as an "expression of the immorality of an age" (36). The natural sensuality of Bardot is frank, which Beauvoir contrasts to Marlene Dietrich's sultry "mystery." There is nothing mysterious in Bardot. No artifice, no poses. Her stardom is terrestrial, not divine. Bardot's "visage has the forthright presence of reality" (36).

This quality, Beauvoir suggests, produced a new kind of celebrity. Rather than the remoteness of the star, rather than the woman on a pedestal, Bardot is as much hunter as prey, not the object of bottom pinching and patronizing male teasing. Bardot rarely "settles into a state of immobility. She walks, she dances, she moves about" (36). She is a new kind of star for a new kind of American culture. Beauvoir attributes this shift in "star" quality to the views of American men. The sexual equality that Bardot's behavior affirms has been recognized in America for a long time, she argues. While Beauvoir concedes that Americans still had a long way to go, they at least granted equality between the sexes in theory, which she says was lacking in France (38).

But Bardot was also "American" in another way, although Beauvoir let readers see her implication in the text rather than claiming it outright, which may have been out of discretion given the article's placement in *Esquire*. Beauvoir notes Bardot is "deplorably materialistic and prosaic." Vadim, she claims, "reduces the world, things and bodies to their immediate presence" (36). Beauvoir finds in Vadim's style an abstraction that turns Bardot's episodic displays of sexuality into performances that turn the spectators into dispassionate voyeurs. A few years later, the writer André Maurois, writing for *Playboy*, also repeated the importance of her direct, "nonspiritual" carnality. For him, the Bardot myth was one "of fleeting desire, rapidly aroused, quickly forgotten; of a physical love barely touched by sentiment."[108]

The mobility, carnality, physical "presence," and materiality of Bardot also helped narrow the gap between life and art that characterized the Bardot myth. Vadim contended all along, "She does not act, she is," and historical conditions of the film and media business facilitated this myth.[109] The sheer volume of press coverage, the growing aggression of the paparazzi, the lack of a studio controlling access and information about the star, and her dramatic and ever-changing personal relationships (while being directed by her husband Vadim during *And God Created Woman* she became involved with her leading man, Jean-Louis Trintignant, who was married to someone else) seemed to make Bardot's real life indistinguishable from the dramas and comedies she played. Bardot's films were elided with Bardot's life, which is why the likes of Simone de Beauvoir sought to explain her.

The fact that France was as associated with sex as much as art played into the Bardot myth, but her success in America also depended on long-term American interest in France. The American press spun a variety of familiar puns and clichés. For example, Bardot became known in the United States as the "Eyeful Tower." *Life* hailed her arrival and joked, "Not since the Statue of Liberty has a French girl lit such fires in America, and Brigitte Bardot does not just stand there like a statue. She moves, she wriggles, and her clothes are as often off as on."[110] Media coverage in the United States described a "French invasion" there. As we have already seen, she graced the cover of *Look*'s first issue of 1958 with the headline "Brigitte Bardot Conquers America."

Bardot herself maintained a dialogue about the United States. When interviewed, she said she loved American actresses such as Marilyn Monroe but not Bette Davis so much. She also noted that she really liked American films, but she was not ready to say whether she would shoot in the United States.[111] She appeared on *The Today Show with Dave Garroway* in April 1959, when he went on location to France for a week. She apparently recited Shakespeare and commented that it was her first visit to the Eiffel Tower. When Garroway remarked that he thought French people went up there every day, she replied, "No, only Americans come up here every day."[112] In the American imagination, the fin-de-siècle Eiffel Tower and Bardot herself were among top contenders as iconic representatives of France.

Bardot's fame in America took the film industry by storm. By February 1958, only four months after the opening of *And God Created Woman* in New York, the trade press announced that a bidding war had erupted in

Hollywood. Columbia had won her services with those of producer Raoul Lévy for a three-picture deal (all in a row for Columbia) at $225,000 for her and $125,000 for him.[113] Exhibitors, eager to cash in on the phenomenon, bought and released *The Night Heaven Fell* and *Une Parisienne* and also played even older Bardot films, such as *Manina* and *La Mariée est trop belle (The Bridal Night)*, all of which did excellent business in the summer of 1958 in New York and Los Angeles.[114] By the summer of 1958, the media saturation concerning Bardot was so complete that *New York Times* film critic Crowther wrote to Josette Lazar in the Paris office, "No thanks on a piece about Bardot. We've had enough of that lady—for now!"[115]

Some French officials in the United States examined their "international star" with a degree of apprehension. Only months after *And God Created Woman*'s run in New York, French government officials delighted at the success of the film in the context of an increasing interest in French film in America while at the same time wringing their hands about whether Bardot herself was an appropriate "face of France."[116] The consul general in New York presented the two sides of the issue in a report to the French ambassador in Washington:

Next to our known traditional activities such as fashion, gastronomy and art there is also the existence of a modern industry. . . . Since I arrived in New York, I can vouch for the fact that French films are well placed among foreign films. . . . Of these films, it is the one entitled, *And God Created Woman*, which stars Brigitte Bardot, which has the greatest success. In fact, it was the most successful foreign film at the box office in New York in 1957. . . . I am sorry to say that it is "porno" that attracts the ingenuity of our producers who are cultivating the taste for it among Americans who are usually repressed and because of this always eager to see representations of a sexual nature.[117]

For the FFO, on the contrary, Bardot proved that their expansion in the United States had been well worth the effort. Maternati wrote to Paris in the spring of 1958 that Bardot had been featured in *Esquire, Look, Life, Coronet, Holiday,* and *Harper's*. He even intended to send his assistant, Donald La Badie, back to France to gather more materials and photographs of Bardot to feed to the American press.[118] The office retitled their publication "Letter from France" and called the April–May 1958 issue "Brigitte Bardot: The Birth of a Star." "In the history of French cinema," it boasted, "there certainly has never been a personality of comparable export value. . . . She has, in fact, become as much a star of the newspapers as of films, since she is already a household word to people who have not yet had the opportunity to see her on a theatre screen." The newsletter describes the centrality of *And God Created Woman* because through it, Bardot "emerged as an absolutely distinctive presence. . . . she has moved since then onto the screens and front pages of the world to become the No. 1 international star." Columbia planned more productions, including a musical costarring Frank Sinatra called *Paris by Night* (it was never made; he refused to work in France and she refused to come to America), and a film version of a Pierre Louÿs novel *Aphrodite*, with Ava Gardner and Marlon Brando under the direction of Elia Kazan.

As her fame grew, she continued to make light comedies, most of them with flimsy plot and clothing, but she also ventured into "family" entertainment in such films as *Babette Goes to War,* which producer Lévy hoped would be the first of a series of Babette movies in which she kept her clothes on. Her fame and box office strength drew producers and directors to her; costars were more apprehensive. She began to work with directors and actors of the traditional French cinema such as Claude Autant-Lara, who directed her with Jean Gabin and Edwige Feuillière in a film version of a Simenon novel *En cas de malheur* (*Love Is My Profession*) (1958), Julien Duvivier in *La Femme et le pantin* (*A Woman Like Satan*) (1959), and Jean-Henri Clouzot in *La Vérité* (*Truth*) (1960).

At the same time, her fame in the press took on an even more intensive beat as she went through a series of lovers and finally married her *Babette* costar Jacques Charrier and became pregnant. So stalked was she by the press that it was determined she would have to give birth in her apartment. When their son, Nicolas, was born in late January 1960, Charrier went downstairs to pop champagne with the press. Eight months later, her marriage on the rocks, she attempted to commit suicide on her twenty-sixth birthday, which made headlines around the world. Only three months earlier, she had announced her retirement from filmmaking: "As far as cinema is concerned, BB is dead."[119] She remained, however, the most famous person in the world. An article in *France Soir* in February 1961 reported that the Institute of American Statistics revealed that Brigitte Bardot was the most cited name in the dailies across the world in 1960.[120]

Although she complained about working so hard and felt mercilessly hounded by the press, she recovered and returned to making films. Bardot mattered to too many people: French producers and directors, young film critics, and old diplomats. The Cannes Film Festival would spend years in search of another star who might repeat Bardot's successful launch from their own beaches. Her triumph gave the FFO in New York proof that they had had an impact on the American market. She gave independent exhibitors a real boost at their box offices and American audiences a contemporary and sexy reinterpretation of *la gaieté française*. Tabloid readers eagerly followed her personal dramas, which were made more vivid by the snapshots of an increasingly aggressive paparazzi. Bardot represented French youth and seemed to restore France's place as an international producer of contemporary mass culture.

This boom in the commercial fortunes of French film in America would soon bust. Bardot's career in the movies and the strong international commercial market for French films ended as the New Wave she ushered in took shape. While cinephiles still cherish the contributions of the group of French filmmakers who rocked the film world at the dawn of the 1960s, general audiences in the United States would have little of it. Instead, they were offered what must have been a horrifying sight in more ways than one: Brigitte Bardot, motionless in a crashed red sports car, dead. Jean-Luc Godard killed Bardot and her myth at thirty, literally and figuratively, in his 1963 film, *Le Mépris (Contempt)*. If Brigitte Bardot made the New Wave possible, the aesthetic triumph of the New Wave around the world replaced the middle-brow slick color films of Bardot as the carriers of Frenchness. The embrace of the New Wave by intellectuals in France and abroad guaranteed France a major role in the development of film "art." By the end of the New Wave, French film had transformed into a luxury item, and "popular" French film more or less disappeared outside of the Hexagon, other European markets such as Italy, and in the Francophone world.[121]

OUR UNDERSTANDING OF the New Wave has, until recently, been prisoner to the articulate pronouncements of its most celebrated practitioners, such as François Truffaut, who initially advanced the notion of film as a personal expression and who railed against the high production costs that kept newcomers out of the film business. The New Wave's eloquent proponents accomplished a good many things: they championed new practices in filmmaking (facilitated by faster film stock, which allowed the use of hand-held cameras and exterior shoots in natural light), codified new modes of narrative, and empowered a young generation who imagined themselves as "artists." Between 1958 and 1964, roughly 120 first-time French directors made feature-length films. Perhaps more significantly, the New Wave gave an enormous boost to those who wrote about film, helping transform the amateur practice of cinephilia into a legitimate aesthetic discourse of film criticism. The groundwork laid by their mentor, André Bazin, helped develop the academic study of film.[122] The new film critics were not the first to write seriously about film (think, for example, of James Agee) but their timing fostered an explosion in writing about film at a critical moment. By the 1950s, film was finally old enough to have a history. Hollywood was changing enough to suggest that the studios might not survive the challenges of the Paramount decrees; television marked the beginning of a new era in entertainment; and universities were undergoing enormous expansion in the Western world, leaving room for changes in the curriculum. A generation of youth would both consume mainstream commercial culture and help shape the formation of a new counterculture in the West.

But if the French New Wavers championed writing about film, they also did so at the very moment that the French had a special purchase on the film world in the person of the globe's most famous star: Brigitte Bardot. Although the early writings by the young critics who became the directors of New Wave films celebrated both Vadim and Bardot, scholarly assessments of the New Wave have been more shaped by the values left in its wake.[123] Scholars have tried to interpret the "New Wave" label as a coherent movement, seeking formal qualities and aesthetic principles among its films, and have focused on the work of individual directors.[124] But that approach has recently given way to more historical and sociological frameworks.[125] The New Wavers were themselves part of a broader cultural innovation and experimentation in which the *nouveau roman* also revitalized fiction. Young intellectuals in America read translations of such authors as Alain Robbe-Grillet and Eugène Ionesco and attended the films of Truffaut and Godard.[126]

But to fully understand the history of the New Wave, we need to consider the strides France had made in its export market in the late fifties, and the eventual commercial failure that the New Wave represented. The writers for the *Cahiers du cinéma* who would become directors were first and foremost cinephiles with a passion for Hollywood film. It is essential to emphasize the transatlantic circulation that produced the New Wave. It was a French movement, inspired by a love of Hollywood film, which would later help influence and revitalize American film by the end of the 1960s. The New Wave inspired both *Bonnie and Clyde,* a project that had even been in the hands of François Truffaut for a while, and the New American Cinema that followed on its heels.[127] The New Wave's influence also extended far beyond its resonance on American shores, as young and undercapitalized filmmakers from all over the world picked up cameras and began to make movies.

The timing of the New Wave coincided with the return of Charles de Gaulle to the presidency of the newly formed Fifth Republic, and to internal changes relating to the government's cultural policies. An internal change within the French system of film subsidies that coincided with the immediate post-Bardot period ended up deemphasizing commercial film. When the CNC was founded in 1946, it established a system of loans with the Crédit National that amounted to an advance on box office receipts for up to 25 percent of the cost of production. In addition, the CNC handed out subsidies for future production with money earned from taxing tickets in order to stabilize and encourage steady output from producers. Producers naturally favored the hand-outs as opposed to the loans but this automatic state subsidy, regardless of quality or need, came under scrutiny in 1959 when the French minister of culture André Malraux applied "cultural" criteria to film and fought to move it out of the hands of the finance minister Antoine Pinay, who had already questioned the subsidy by asking why film, rather than groceries, received such special treatment.[128] *Esquire* even managed to note Pinay's quip: "I am removing the subsidy on movies because I see no reason to finance Bardot's thighs, for the sight of which millions seem quite happy to pay."[129] The new system relied on selecting films for subsidy that met a standard of quality, thus devaluing commercial viability as the primary criterion for investment. This gave French filmmakers freer range to produce noncommercial films, although the sums were so paltry that it particularly encouraged low budget productions.

But the New Wave also built on Bardolatry and that connection seemed the most relevant way for it to be framed outside of France in the early 1960s, especially as the American press tried to describe the phenomenon. An article in *Esquire* in early 1962 explained the New Wave to Americans:

Bardot was the spark of a great fire which began to flame in the late Fifties and which has become known as La Nouvelle Vague. The New Wave is the most exciting art form of the Sixties, an integral part of the intellectual and cultural life that keeps Paris supreme among the world's great cities, as an experimental crucible of creation. It all began with Bardot and a film called *And God Created Woman*. Its first box office returns barely paid off the distributors. Its one hope was in a small group of avant-garde critics who hailed it as a masterpiece. Truffaut, Jean-Luc Godard, Claude Chabrol—three young critics who have since become important names in the movies—said in 1956: "Bardot symbolizes a new side of a new French generation, the postwar freedom and sexual independence of women." This statement—hotly debated in the group of the Cahiers—caught the ear of the big daily newspaper reporters. It made lively copy and soon hundreds of thousands of people of course had to see this movie about sexual independence. *And God Created Woman* became one of the all-time top money earners of French cinema.[130]

This summary has many factually false elements, not the least of which is that the film became a top money earner of French cinema; it became the top money-earner of the French cinema in the United States but did much less business in France in its first run. That said, what this 1962 article (two and a half years into the New Wave) managed to do was to turn Bardot into "art" and restore to Paris its status as "experimental crucible of creation" in American eyes. This transformation speaks to a willingness on the part of the American press to appreciate French filmmaking, despite its lack of commercial appeal.

Truffaut, however, did not set out to reject commercial success. In fact, despite the critical acclaim for *The 400 Blows*, a 1960 New York Critics' Award and an Oscar nomination for best screenplay, his commercial failure plagued him.[131] Truffaut's careful cultivation of his "difference" from other cinema (notably American cinema) finally began to reap actual profits with 1973's successful release of *La Nuit américaine* (*Day for Night*), a tribute to American cinema's ability to heighten reality ("nuit américaine" in French means the shooting of nighttime scenes during the day with a special filter). Whether one agrees or disagrees with the notion that his cinema was "different," he became one of the most commercial of the New Wave directors and the darling of American film intellectuals (as much for his writings on Hitchcock as for his films), but not until long after the New Wave's failure to function as a popular exportable cinema.

The New Wave seemed to be over almost as quickly as it began in the United States. Only a year and half after Truffaut's *400 Blows*, critics were declaring it dead: "The New Wave has already subsided in France; the enthusiasm for it has begun to wane. What it did show was that several young people could conceive and make movies with individuality and effectiveness, that they could sometimes find new subjects and sometimes handle old subjects in a way that they looked new."[132] While critics such as Andrew Sarris championed the New Wave and helped establish its bulkhead among intellectuals and academics, more popular publications such as *Esquire* were satisfied to have Bardot's commercialism recast as art and were ready to give up on the New Wave as early as 1960.

French film interests were not. UniFrance initially positioned the New Wave with caution. When they could, they carefully emphasized continuity between the New Wave and Bardot because they valued her commercial success in the export market. When the Cannes festival gave legitimacy to Truffaut, UniFrance chose not to underscore the relative youth of the filmmakers of the New Wave but rather their status as newcomers to the film industry.

The newsletter muffled any critique that the New Wave launched against traditional French filmmaking (which had been its platform in their rejection of the *cinéma de papa*) and instead situated them as "a new movement [that] heralds the further glory of a legendary cinema tradition."[133] UniFrance hoped that whatever the New Wave would produce, it would extend the positive trend begun in 1955 and keep the American market for French export as healthy as it had become. It failed. What the New Wave could not manage was big box office. Even the Bardot films made by New Wave directors—Louis Malle's *Vie privée* (*A Very Private Affair*) (1961) and Jean-Luc Godard's *Le Mépris* (*Contempt*) (1963), both attempts to exploit her fame and mythology—were commercial and critical failures at the time.

Representatives of the French film industry became alarmed. Where once UniFrance had felt it had been directing a successful renewal of French film abroad, the wake of the New Wave left them deeply unhappy. Cravenne warned in the annual report of 1965: "If it wants to survive, French film has to change back and to draw the spectators of tomorrow, the mass audiences, it has to be accessible to all . . . we need to make films that are designed for the general public, but which preserve the trace of French taste."[134] In an internal report about the French industry in North America, its author worried that French cinema was not distinct and that Bardot was still the only well-known French actress, suggesting that the New Wave had failed to build sufficient momentum:

The only actress that everyone knows is Brigitte Bardot—even if Jeanne Moreau, Jean-Paul Belmondo and several others are known and favorably reviewed. Brigitte Bardot reinforces a well-known image of France with Americans: for them, French film is generally risqué, provocative and morally unwholesome. . . . Moreover, the cliché that sees Paris as one big Pigalle [sex zone] and the Côte d'Azur as one big nudist camp is held by Americans. . . . it must be said that the youth hold these notions less frequently than their elders; for them a French film is more an intellectual film, a film with a message.[135]

Like the French diplomat who earlier worried that the French would be too associated with selling sex, this report fretted about the racy image of France. But it also reveals the impact of the New Wave (French films are intellectual films) but at the expense of the commerce that had been established by selling sex through Bardot. In the end, the report suggested that the "intellectual" label would not serve the French cinema at the American box office since it also concluded that Americans sought entertainment in their cinema.

Even American foreign film advocates Lillian Gerard (programmer of the Paris Theater) and Robert Griffith (head of MOMA's film library) complained that the New Wave, by the end of the 1960s decade, had come to dominate the discussion in intellectual circles. Griffith wrote to Gerard on September 29, 1968 complaining of sensationalism: "Eileen Bowser quotes Godard to the effect that the movies must now go through a flamboyant period. That tells a lot, I think. Perhaps they must; the trouble is, his work strikes his elders, some of them, as, not flamboyant, but pallid—formlessness, intended to shock—but to shock whom? The philistines? Are they any left? No, the shocks are directed at young (and the arrested) who think themselves unshockable. But they smile on all efforts to shock their elders—taking the will for the deed—and so swell the box office."[136]

Gerard's response back to her friend on October 3, 1968 is somewhat intolerant of the entire current of French cinema, which she traces back to Bardot. More than anything though, her letter takes the opportunity to snipe at the New Wave crowd of the *Cahiers:* "How right you are about the shock tactics of Godard and his followers. It all started with Vadim's *God Created Woman,* one scene in particular, where Bardot deliberately defies the adults in the family and storms out with a 'je m'en touche.' Here was an ordinary melodrama, with a longhaired unwashed girl of good contourism who brought down the French intellectuals on their dirty knees. How the French and the *Cahiers du cinéma* worship success!" Griffith replied the next week (October 10, 1968) in an interesting retort that acknowledges at some point Gerard must have applauded the commercialism of French filmmakers: "You are inconsistent—which is, of course, the unpardonable sin. In conversation you upheld the French for bending their talents to viable commercial use, while castigating their American avant-garde counterparts for failing, or refusing, to do the same. Now you say 'How can the French and the *Cahiers du cinéma* worship success?' Wiggle out of that one, I'd like to see you." Although the trail of the correspondence ends there, I would suggest that her position is not as contradictory as Griffith makes it out to be. She also cared deeply about the commercial viability of French film in America and had seen that it had begun to succeed in the United States. Griffith notes that elsewhere she had celebrated the commercial cinema associated with Vadim. However, in 1968, from the vantage point of years of a New Wave that had already fizzled at the box office, Gerard seems to be looking back and bemoaning the entire experiment.

But this exchange took place in the long shadows cast by the commercial failure of Louis Malle's *Vie privée* and Godard's *Le Mépris.*[137] The latter, shot in April and May 1963 in Capri and Rome, was neither a small budget nor a particularly "personal" film despite Godard's status as a New Wave director. Produced by the Italian Carlo Ponti and American Joseph E. Levine, and based on Alberto Moravia' s Italian novel *A Ghost at Noon*, *Le Mépris* is especially interesting as an attempt to make a big-budget, international "New Wave" film. Bardot's presence in the film gave all those involved in the project very high hopes. She was the biggest star in the world at the time: her willingness to play the part of the "contemptuous" wife Camille helped secure funding. The film marks an important moment in the trajectory of Bardot as a French export for both its self-conscious references to her fame and its indictment of the milieu that produced it. Godard's film is both a celebration of filmmaking and a condemnation of its system, in which an arrogant (American) producer (played by Jack Palance, speaking English the entire film) disrespectfully undermines the work of a "great director" (played in the film by Fritz Lang, speaking in French, German, and English).

Although Godard had to be convinced by the producers to add the film's opening scene (which begins with Bardot face down asking her husband (and the audience) to dissect her body, part by part), he also transformed the producers' formulaic interest in her nudity into a riff on the fetishism attached to Bardot's stardom. This leitmotif is repeated throughout the film: she is bare-assed on fuzzy rugs as the camera slowly pans her legs; she is wrapped in towels and sheets and goes in and out of bathtubs (figs. 3.20–3.21). She sunbathes nude in Capri; she jumps in the water and swims away from her husband. Aside from her trademark nudity, the film's main setting, the Roman apartment in which the couple's relationship unravels, shares the same contemporary design of many of the earlier Bardot comedy sets (*Une Parisienne,* in particular).

Bardot's persona and its vapidity are alluded to throughout the film. Lang recites the following to Bardot and her writer-husband who has been called in to fix the film's script: "Each morning, to earn my bread. I go to the market where lies are sold and, hopeful, I get in line with the other sellers." Camille approaches him and asks, "What's that?" He answers, "Hollywood." Then, he admits that it is a piece of a ballad from "poor BB," which is followed by a pregnant pause until her husband looks up and asks, "Bertolt Brecht?" and Lang replies, "Yes." The producer then enters the conversation, continuing the obvious subtextual references to Bardot. He mentions an actress they were in the midst of casting for their production: "she agrees to take off her clothes Tuesday morning eight o'clock on the beach." Lang then launches into a riff about reality as poetry (in homage to New Wave

3.20–3.21 In towel, naked, *Le Mépris*, 1963.

mentor André Bazin's philosophy of film) and then Prokosch, the producer, turns to Camille to ask her why she doesn't say anything. She answers, "Because I have nothing to say." The camera pans her face and then cuts to the movie theater marquee: "Silver Cine," as if to underscore that in this cinema Bardot actually says nothing both literally and figuratively.

The film concludes with its most overdetermined reference to Bardot's iconography. Camille has left her husband Paul and returns to Rome with the American producer. She rides with him in his red convertible despite the fact that they can barely communicate since they do not even speak the same language. Nevertheless, he manages to ask her what she thinks of him and she says: "Get into your Alpha (pause) Romeo. We'll see about that later." They drive away and the film cuts to a note from Camille to her husband, "Take Care. Farewell. Camille." We hear a car crash and the film cuts back to the car where the viewer finds Palance and Bardot dead, the red convertible having been hit by a truck. The camera lingers on her bloody face, as if Godard wants the audience to contemplate the death of Camille as the murder of Bardot, the destruction of the icon of the red convertible, and the audience's infatuation with her, known at the time as Bardolatry (fig. 3.22). Fi-

3.22 BB dead in the red convertible, *Le Mépris*, 1963. Compare to earlier BB images.

nally, having killed the producer and the great movie star, the film's final scene cuts to Godard's real hero, Lang, the director shooting his film of *The Odyssey*.[138]

Camille/Bardot's death in the red sports car is also a symbolic death: it stands for the French New Wave's "symbolic" and perhaps even accidental murder of France's exportable commercial cinema. Godard snuffed out Bardot, along with the "man" responsible for her in the first place: an idiotic American producer. But this cinematic death of Bardot at the hands of the New Wave director was no mere metaphor. Bardot played the role of the great French export of the postwar era that helped spark the New Wave, but neither she nor the New Wave sustained the development of a French commercial cinema of international proportions that producers and audiences around the world envisioned as the start of the 1960s. Yet rather than think in terms of the success or failure of French "national" film, Bardot's career locates Frenchness as an exchange commodity rather than as a characteristic of a national film culture. While promoting Frenchness in the persona of Bardot, the Franco-American partnership also helped internationalize the film business after the war. Through their partnership, the filmmaking map would shift to a global scale in which multinational casts and location productions around the world would emerge as a cosmopolitan alternative to film as a national product.

Thus, the Bardot phenomenon cannot be explained by recourse to the general cultural historical terms that argue that her youth, beauty, and sexuality offered respite in a repressed world. Nor can her popularity be understood as a function of the opening of the American market to foreign film that resulted from the American product shortage after the Paramount decrees. Her fame emerged from and sustained a complex web of interconnections between France and America in the 1950s in and around the movies. In short, America wanted and needed Bardot as much as France did. Yet, Bardot's career in films more or less ended with the New Wave. She quit the movies and pursued a career as a recording artist with great success in France. With the end of her film career, she receded into the national market, so famous for having been a famous French person that she ended up as the model for a 1970 sculpture of Marianne, the symbolic incarnation of France (fig. 3.23).

Bardot made only one visit to the United States as a movie star: to promote another Louis Malle film, *Viva Maria* (1965) made as a star vehicle for Bardot and Jeanne Moreau, the great New Wave actress. In an interview with journalist Pete Hamill, she foreshadowed the end of her career. Once the real person had actually set foot on American soil, the films stopped coming. "I am Brigitte Bardot. And that Brigitte Bardot, the one I see in the magazines and the newspapers, the one up on the movie screen, that Brigitte Bardot will never be sixty. . . . Don't you agree?"[139] BB retired entirely from the world of entertainment in 1973, at the age of thirty-nine, the only French superstar of the postwar era.

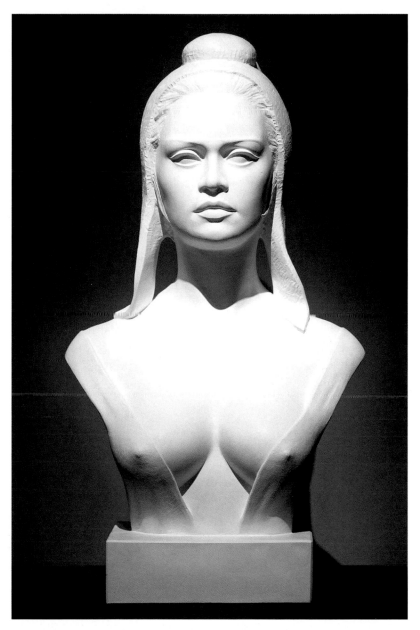

3.23 Bardot as Marianne, the incarnation of France. Sculpture made in 1970. Photo taken in 1996. Courtesy: Adenis/Sipa.

THE COSMOPOLITAN

FILM *From Around the World in Eighty Days* to Making Movies Around the World

IN ITS 1946 annual report, the Motion Picture Association of America proclaimed the global appeal of film, articulating what Hollywood hoped to achieve at the time: to reach all the world's spectators. "Because the moving, talking images on the screen have all the immediacy and vitality of life itself, film spectators all over the world come into each other's presence and live together in the same reality. The community of film spectators is a symbol of the world community yet to come."[1] That same year, in the wake of war, Hollywood resumed a steady distribution of its films abroad. But beyond that, the MPAA boldly claimed that film would create rather than simply reflect the world community yet to come. As we have already seen, nations and nationness played a complicated role in film culture during the post-war period and were constructed and deployed in often unpredictable ways: Frenchness could mean something particular to filmmakers; a film festival in Cannes could both help to launch a French superstar and internationalize film culture by decentering Hollywood without excluding it. The French-American film connection after the war also helped foster and create a context for the "cosmopolitan" film culture of the 1950s and 1960s.

During this period, European and American filmmakers turned their attention to "the world" as a place for production, as an unlimited market and as a concept to be thematized in their films. If Hollywood had once served as a magnetic geographic center for filmmakers, the postwar era witnessed a decentering of production, explained at the time by both the press and people within the industry as film's "internationalization." This chapter examines this internationalist rhetoric in relation to the changing nature of film production itself and in the emergence of the "hybrid" films made as a result of this practice that themselves self-consciously thematized the idea of a unified, transnational "world." Thus cosmopolitanism in cinema was not simply Americanization through film. It was instead a key moment in the construction of film as a global cultural practice.

The cosmopolitan film represents both a mode of production and a film's self-conscious relation to its own status as somehow reaching beyond nations and national identity in search of a global consciousness and cosmopolitanism, especially in their attempts to get beyond the nation as essential limit to identification. The film cycle consisted of a hodgepodge of films—some of which were commercially successful, others of which were positively received in critical terms or have survived to become integrated into an "auteur'" canon as with the films of director David Lean. Cosmopolitan films do not constitute a genre since they do not systematically share conventions that would allow them to be meaningfully classified that way.

But they also cannot be sufficiently explained by describing the structure of their financing. One could possibly describe them as coproductions but that term is neither a sufficient explanation of the economic globalization of cinema, nor can the economic organization of film stand as the "proof" of its internationalization. Identifying the economic practice of coproduction is only to begin to describe one aspect of the cosmopolitan cinema.

Cosmopolitan film refers to the overlap of a certain mode of production (independent, location-shooting and/or shooting outside Hollywood, an "international" cast) with the thematic preoccupation of the globe or internationalism. They were hybrid films that reflected an attempt to "think and feel beyond the nation." Many of the epics made during the period, for example, fit into the category but not all the cosmopolitan films are epics (for example, the James Bond pictures, Jules Dassin's *Never on Sunday,* or the comic-thriller *Charade*). By naming the cosmopolitan films, recognizing their hybridity in national and generic terms and historicizing them within changes in film production and as part of the broader postwar culture of "internationalism," fostered as we have seen, by an interesting partnership between Paris and Hollywood, we identify an important moment in the history of film as a global practice.

The cosmopolitan film cycle emerged as part of the broader transatlantic developments in film already described in this study. When contextualized in relation to the flourish of popular Frenchness films, to the career of Brigitte Bardot and to the rising box office of foreign film in the United States, we can see how and why the route between Hollywood and France helped to forge a global film culture. But this chapter also argues that the film cycle has a very precise history in which the success of Mike Todd's 1956 adaptation of the Jules Verne novel *Around the World in Eighty Days* played a critical role in the cycle's development. Todd's only feature film defined the qualities of the cosmopolitan film cycle in terms of production, visual codes, and themes, yet it remains singular in its combination of those attributes. Almost entirely omitted from the history of film, except when embarrassed comments are made about the fact that is was awarded the best picture Oscar of 1956, its remarkable commercial and critical success also helped shape the history of the cosmopolitan film as others sought to imitate many of its elemental ingredients to reproduce its box office popularity.

Late in the 1960s, as the first wave of cosmopolitan films seemed to subside, economist Thomas Guback studied the internationalization of cinema and contended that it would inevitably lead to the "homogenization" of culture. As he put it, "the finished product will reflect universal idioms at the expense of national ones. . . . What is happening is the extension, on an international scale, of industrial production applied to culture."[2] His sense of this phenomenon was categorically negative: "So many of the new international films border on dehumanization by brutalizing sensitivity, often deflecting attention from reality. They count on developing audience response with synthetic machine-made images. Their shallowness and cardboard characters are camouflaged with dazzling colors, wide screens and directorial slickness."[3] Guback's position is characteristic of the retrospective analysis of what many observers at the time called film's "international" trend. In fact, there are few groups of films as denigrated as these, described by French screenwriter Jean-Claude Carrière as "middle ocean pictures." Carrière called them "those films which sought to be both European and American at the same time and which ultimately were neither, but just good for throwing into the middle of the ocean."[4] Earlier, in 1963, a study by Jean-Claude Batz shared the French director's disdain for international production: "The internationalization of the market demands the internationalization of film content, a hybridity in intellectual view, the triumph of places in common, ideas accepted by large numbers of people, the banality of millenarian ideas. . . . in a word, international co-production consecrates a cultural potpourri."[5] Another journalist, writing in disgust at the state of the film industry he observed while at Cannes in the late 1960s, wrote that the movies had retreated into an "increasingly international no-man's land."[6]

Since then, scholars have had trouble making sense of these films. Peter Lev described the Euro-American cinema of the period, which he identified as big-budget English-language films made by European art directors intended to please a sophisticated international audience.[7] He also connected the films to the Cannes Film Festival, identifying it as the leading showcase for the international art film. Lev's emphasis on a commercialized art cinema, however, leapfrogs over the more explicitly big-budget and commercial Euro-American cinema under consideration here. Although he mentions that such films as *Never on Sunday* had an important launch in Cannes, he neglects to mention the big-budget extravaganzas, *The Fall of the Roman Empire* and *Doctor Zhivago*, played at Cannes in opening and closing night galas.

Rather than be dismissed as a cultural potpourri, these films deserve reconsideration for what they can tell us about how film transcended national idioms and how and why the decade of the mid-1950s to mid-1960s seemed to generate these sorts of films in rapid succession, mostly to great commercial success and sometimes accompanied by contemporary critical acclaim.

Film's internationalism had prewar roots in Hollywood. The industry's official rhetoric insisted that the success of Hollywood product abroad arose from its integration of universal themes and issues. The MPAA boasted that Hollywood had long represented the world's stories: "no other picture-making country in the world ranged so far, thematically and geographically, for its story material, backgrounds and locales. Hollywood's perennial practice of drawing on world literature, world history and the world's arena for its inspiration and material provided cogent reasons why U.S. movies continued to enjoy public support in theatres around the globe."[8]

There can be little doubt that the Hollywood filmmaking community had, indeed, drawn broadly—perhaps not from the entire world but certainly from European literature, art and history. European-born personnel, from directors to actors and editors, had worked assiduously in Hollywood during the expansion of the studios. The experiment with multilingual films in Joinville in the early sound era also produced an intense sense that film would "internationalize" as much as sound hardened national differences.[9] Producer Walter Wanger could reasonably refer to Hollywood as a "veritable celluloid Athens" while trying to persuade the government that the film industry had much to offer as a model for American leadership after the war.[10] In fact, Wanger boasted of the internationalism of the film industry, which poised it for a great role in diplomacy: "we have never been nationalistic. No one has ever been able to say that Hollywood did not want talent because it was English, French, Italian, German or Russian. There has never been any nationalistic thinking on subjects or castings and our pictures are still the most popular in the world. We have more international content in our pictures than is to be found in the films of any other country."[11] A decade later, in 1960, the Motion Picture Academy explained in a report, "While Hollywood is still the film center of the world, we know that ours is an international business. We are producing for the peoples of the world as well as for the American people. A global industry calls for global activity and global thinking."[12]

The increasing sense of the movie business as international did not simply come from imagining a worldwide audience. The Paramount decrees of 1948 weakened the Hollywood studios and inaugurated the first era of "runaway production." *New York Times* film critic Bosley Crowther observed the phenomenon with great interest and asked his paper to send him to Europe in 1960 to report on what he thought was the most important new trend in cinema production: "The whole European area is right now coming along with the greatest challenge to Hollywood as the prime locality of film production that the old glamour town has ever known. . . . The big thing today and for the future seems to be this internationalization of the production of films."[13]

Crowther was not alone in his interpretation of the changes in filmmaking. By 1964, the trade press was already explaining the causes of the phenomenon rather than merely describing it: "Reasons for making motion pictures abroad: demand by present day audiences for unqualified realism; need to make motion pictures with universal appeal because of increasing dependence on foreign market; lower production costs abroad for scenes in spectaculars requiring use of thousands of extras; and the need to maintain the strength of world-wide distribution organizations through cooperative arrangements with foreign film interests."[14] In short, by the mid-1960s global filmmaking had become recognized as the order of the day. When Paul Lazarus, executive vice president of Bronston Pictures, flew from Spain, where he was involved in the production of *55 Days at Peking*, to address the meeting of independent theater owners, he explained what he dubbed the "worldwide concept in picture production." He announced that his boss, Samuel Bronston, believed in "making your pictures where they should be made. . . . No community, no country holds the exclusive patent on good film-making." Bronston Pictures attempted to provide a regular supply of family features to reestablish the theater as a familial recreational center. They sought to create films "too big, too colorful, too elaborate" for television, and make films "equally acceptable and suitable on the broadest international base, not particularized by any national interest."[15] In other words, runaway production for Lazarus offered a positive agenda, and cannot be understood merely as a bric-a-brac response to a variety of difficult circumstances in filmmaking.

While taking note of the phenomenon, many observers at the time derided the internationalization of motion pictures because they believed that it was motivated by economic rather than authentic artistic interests. Crowther spoke of the decline of the particular and peculiar film of national idiosyncrasies in favor of the "all-purpose entertainment film."[16] Yet he was also open to the notion that the films were not simply an economic expression in cultural form. He noted that the economics of international coproduction may have instigated the phenomenon but that the results were a "curious sort of hybridization of the motion pictures of the Western world."[17] This new form of production generated a range of films, some of which were commercially successful, others of which were not. By taking a closer look at the structure of cosmopolitan film production and by examining the films themselves, we can better understand the internationalization of the film industry and what visions of globalism actually looked like in film. This story begins with an American theatrical impresario directing the worldwide production of a French story about a shrinking globe.

ALTHOUGH MANY FACTORS contributed to the development of the cosmopolitan film cycle, one filmmaker and one film constituted an important starting point: Mike Todd's *Around the World in Eighty Days*. In May 1957, this film sensation inaugurated the tenth annual Cannes Film Festival. The festivities included the appearance of Phileas Fogg's balloon in the skies over the Croisette and the arrival of the film's producer Mike Todd with his new wife Elizabeth Taylor dressed in tiara and ermine, in her grey, monogrammed Rolls Royce (fig. 4.1). The evening showcased the European premiere of a film that had already been taking the United States by storm for over six months.

4.1 Mike Todd and Elizabeth Taylor, opening night at Cannes, 1957. Courtesy: Corbis.

Mike Todd made only one feature film in his lifetime, financed it almost exclusively with personal funds (thereby owning almost 80 percent of the movie), and died while it continued to play on screens around the world. Yet, the story of Mike Todd's *Around the World in Eighty Days* is an essential element in the history of the cosmopolitan film. Todd and his film stand as an example of the changes in the film industry that facilitated the production of cosmopolitan films. But more important, the scope of the film's economic and critical success also spurred important developments in film production, which helped drive the film cycle.

That Todd, a man with virtually no education and even less cultural capital, would turn to a story by the famous French author, Jules Verne, first published in 1873, attests to the long-lasting international fame and popularity of both the author and his tale. According to his son, Mike Todd, Jr., the story was the first book his father ever read. Like many of Verne's stories, *Around the World in Eighty Days* enjoyed great sales in serial form and then as a novel not only in France but also in England and America. Like other Verne stories, it was adapted for the stage (in 1874) and served as material for early screen adaptations as well.[18]

Todd's involvement with the Verne story began in 1946 with a proposed theatrical collaboration with Orson Welles, who had already produced a radio version of the tale in 1938 for his Mercury Theatre.[19] Todd came to this theatrical production with a reputation as one of the most successful stage producers of the previous five years. The son of Jewish immigrants from Russia and Poland, he was raised in Minnesota and had an early career in construction, where he developed a reputation as a high-stakes gambler. By 1946, Todd had achieved his great aspiration: to become an American showman in the tradition of Florenz Ziegfeld. He burst onto the theatrical scene at the Chicago World's Fair in 1934, where he produced the "flame dance," which offered crowds a spectacular version of a burlesque strip in which a woman dressed as a moth attracts a flame and burns her costume off. A few years later, he was known for such hits as *The Hot Mikado* (starring Bill Robinson), *Harvey, Something for the Boys* (starring Ethel Merman), and for his Theatre Café in Chicago, which featured Gypsy Rose Lee in what Todd imagined as an American Folies Bergères show for the whole family.[20]

Orson Welles and Mike Todd shared a vision of creating a theatrical "fairy tale for adults" by bringing the Verne story to the stage in musical form. The two imagined an over-the-top production that would rely, like many other Todd productions, on spectacular stage effects. They hired Cole Porter, with whom Todd had already worked on three productions, to write the score. Their collaboration began in February 1946 but ended only months later when Todd walked away from his $40,000 investment because he could not abide Welles's inability to actually write a script. As Todd explained on Tex and Jinx McCreary's radio show: "I have one superstition in show business. I do like to read a script."[21] Welles then turned to the director, producer, and head of London Films, Alexander Korda, to provide the financing for the production, in exchange for which Korda was given the rights to the film. The stage production ran eight weeks in late 1946, and ended in financial failure.[22]

The intervening years brought many changes to Mike Todd's career, while plans for a film project based on Verne's novel were discussed in a variety of filmmaking circles simultaneously. What made those years so interesting for Todd's career were the same things that put *Around the World* on the agendas of other filmmakers as well: the advent of widescreen, the preference for location shooting, independent production, international casting, and "globalism" as a point of view. In short, Todd's career and his film embodied a central point in the confluence of these different aspects of 1950s and 1960s filmmaking that are key elements of the cosmopolitan film.

CINERAMA WAS THE first of these confluent aspects. Cinerama is the name of the pioneering form among the 1950s innovations in widescreen technology whose novelty and scale would provide unprecedented spectacle at the movie theater. Because widescreen threatened to devalue the holdings in studio film libraries and possibly even make those films obsolete, it should come as no surprise that men from outside the film industry were responsible for the innovation that became known as Cinerama, but its investors also came from outside Hollywood.[23] Novelty for its own sake may have been the impetus for the development of film as a medium, as historians of early film have shown, but it became even more attractive as film would have to lure its shrinking audience out of their houses and away from their televisions in order to get them back into the theaters. Fred Waller, the inventor of water skis and the man who had successfully used multicamera technology to help train aerial gunners in World War II, has been credited with inventing Cinerama. The format approximated the depth of human vision and used three cameras and three projectors to fill a huge and deeply curved screen with the Cinerama films. Sound engineer Hazard Reeves joined the project and succeeded in stoking the interest of the well-known radio commentator, lecturer, and journalist Lowell Thomas.

Almost thirty years before, Thomas had made the travelogue *With Allenby in Palestine and Lawrence in Arabia* and toured with the film, giving lectures and turning T. E. Lawrence into a celebrity.[24] In 1950, Thomas was still up to the same sort of sensational journalism. This time, he had caught the attention of Todd because of an expedition that Thomas and his son made to Tibet on the heels of the Chinese Invasion there. The son had planned to do a lecture tour based on the trip, and Mike Todd, casting about for projects, thought he could promote the tour. He proposed to kick it off by holding the first of the film lectures in Madison Square Garden before a crowd of thousands. Having seen the Thomas footage, which he liked, Todd worried that even blowing up the 16mm film to 35mm would not work in a space as vast as Madison Square Garden. He shared this concern with Thomas, who invited him to see a demonstration of a project with which he had recently become involved: projecting films on the largest screen ever built.[25]

Lowell Thomas brought Todd into Cinerama. Todd saw dazzling footage of a rollercoaster ride and was convinced that Cinerama would revolutionize the filmgoing experience. He and Thomas became business partners with an exclusive license to exploit Cinerama. Next they needed to make a movie. Before he hooked up with Todd, Thomas had promised his friend, the celebrated documentary filmmaker Robert Flaherty, that he could produce and direct the first Cinerama feature. According to Mike Todd, Jr., while Flaherty worked on the concept for a film, Todd kept an opportunistic eye on the news, looking for potential opportunities to film sequences for the Cinerama movie. After observing the missed opportunity to film General MacArthur's return in the ticker tape parade in New York, Todd packed up Flaherty and crew and sent them to Chicago where MacArthur would next be welcomed at Soldier Field. The filming took place in April 1951 in a torrential downpour. Flaherty developed pneumonia and died in July. Todd stepped into the creative breach.

Todd turned Flaherty's death into an opportunity to gain experience as a globe-trotting filmmaker. The film would become *This Is Cinerama!* a travelogue of visions of Europe and America, which introduced the process to the general public. Moving beyond General MacArthur, Todd next thought the film could present cultural festivals around the world. He and the Cinerama crew went on location to Edinburgh, Salzburg, Vienna (where they botched a shoot), Venice, and Milan. Although he was able to assemble an impressive set of location shoots, as he and the crew watched the footage, Todd became increasingly concerned with the flaws of the system: seam lines, fuzzy edges, and what was probably the greatest insight into the limits of mere spectacle by a man known for his brilliant exploitation of it: "You can't spend your life on the roller coaster. Someday someone's going to want to say, 'I love you,' and the seams are going to get in the way."[26] Cinerama films could be best exploited in episodic travelogues, magnificent landscape, and locomotion, and the effect remains with us today in IMAX films.[27] But Todd believed that the films would need to develop their narrative capacities if the format were to have any real impact. In short, he did not believe that travel and spectacle would be enough.[28]

Todd wanted the board of Cinerama to invest in perfecting the process. The board did not want to be told what to do by Todd, who was in bankruptcy at the time. When *This Is Cinerama!* made its debut in September 1952, the Cinerama board of directors had already bought out Todd, seeking to divest themselves of his tarnished financial reputation as the company went public. The film ran 122 weeks and grossed $4.7 million in New York alone.[29] Todd seized the opportunity to move forward on improving the process. While the studios battled it out in the aftermath of Cinerama with a variety of widescreen formats such as CinemaScope and VistaVision, Todd believed that it was possible to get "Cinerama" to come out of one hole, employing both a single lens and a single camera. He went to the leading optics engineer of the time, Dr. Brian O'Brien, to solve the problem.[30]

The result of Todd's idea and O'Brien's science became known as "Todd-AO" (standing for O'Brien's American Optical company), a process that appeared so promising that the new company was able to persuade the holders of the hottest entertainment property of the era to make their Broadway show into the first Todd-AO film. They signed Rodgers and Hammerstein to make a screen version of their wildly successful musical, *Oklahoma!* Unfortunately for Todd, the arrangement granted the composers artistic control over the project, and Todd, while holding financial stakes in the process that deepened his own pockets, had to shop around for his own vehicle to produce, which would become the second film made in Todd-AO.

Todd bounced around Europe during this period looking for projects to make in Todd-AO. When he had earlier been making the rounds in Europe shooting Cinerama, he met Alexander Korda in London. Todd contacted him again in 1954 and they agreed to coproduce *Richard III* with Laurence Olivier in Todd-AO. That is, until Todd realized that he would not have artistic control if he worked with Olivier. He then tried to convince John Huston to reshoot *Moby Dick* in Todd-AO. Huston said no. He next set his sights on making *War and Peace* and went to Russia to enlist the government to participate in this unprecedented Cold War thawing project. Todd believed the message would be antiwar, which was sorely needed for an exceptional Russian-American coproduction. When the Russians seemed reluctant, he went to Yugoslavia. General Tito consented to use his army for filming, and it seemed he would move ahead until the Russians started making noises that they had decided to make their own film version of the Russian epic.

In the meantime, Todd returned to London and asked Korda for advice. It was then that Korda offered him *Around the World in Eighty Days*. He explained that he had invested in the Welles stage production in exchange for the film rights and that Welles had even shot a few scenes in Africa and Italy.[31] Not even a year earlier, *Variety* had reported that Cy Howard and Alexander Korda would produce the film, starring Alec Guinness as Phileas Fogg.[32] Reports differ as to whether Todd and Korda agreed that Korda would produce and direct the English shoots or that he would simply have nothing to do with the project. In November 1954, *Variety* announced that Mike Todd had bought the rights and all treatments and scripts from Korda for $240,000.[33]

But Welles, Korda, and Todd were not the only people interested in the story. Stanley Donen apparently spent the better part of 1948 trying to convince Arthur Freed to do an MGM musical based on the Verne story.[34] In the spring of 1953, John Mock wrote an interoffice memo to director William Wyler that explains the film rights to the Verne story.[35] The memo explains that the story was in the public domain in the United States, would become available in Europe in two years, and that Korda had had something to do with the rights, although he was not sure that was still the case. He also mentioned the stage version by Welles and said it would, of course, still be under copyright.

Classic tales are always kicking about the filmmaking community but the interest in such tales also seems to reemerge in particularly meaningful historical moments. *Around the World* was an ideal vehicle for this moment in filmmaking, which may help explain why several producers and directors independently pursued it. The success of Todd's film was also a sign of the times. The enormous global profits of *Around the World* resulted from its status as an exceptional film marketed in exceptional ways. Yet the story and the film's mode of storytelling, casting, location shooting, and scale of production bear further examination. *Around the World* became an important event at the box office and thus encouraged the development of a mode of filmmaking that would be imitated for years to come. In fact, reviews at the time lauded the singularity of the achievement while anticipating copy-cats. As one critic noted, "the only slight criticism I could possibly make of Mr. Todd's offering is that there are sure to be imitations of it, imitations that can't possibly be as good."[36]

NO HOLLYWOOD STUDIO invested in the film's production. Only a few years earlier, Todd had come to Hollywood and ended up buying and los-ing the Del Mar horse track, which did not leave a favorable impression with the men in the movie business. Yet Hollywood powerhouse Joseph Schenck, who had been president of United Artists and cofounder of Twen-tieth Century Pictures with Darryl Zanuck, befriended Todd. Schenck lent Todd money on a regular basis, invested in Todd-AO, and brought in George Skouras (president of United Artists theaters, which Schenck had founded. Skouras's brother Spyros was head of Twentieth Century Fox at the time). Todd's other sources of finance were personal. He regularly borrowed money from Lorraine Manville, the asbestos heiress. With help from these private investors, *Around the World* would eventually be made for slightly more than $6 million, and financed otherwise entirely by Todd (with money from the sale of his piece of Todd-AO) and the personal loans from these few Todd friends. Short on money late in the shooting, Todd struck a distribution deal with United Artists that reduced his personal stakes in the movie to approx-imately 80 percent. This personal gamble, first on Todd-AO and then with *Around the World* paid off in unprecedented ways. It has been claimed that *Around the World* made more than $65 million in its first two years of dis-tribution worldwide. But Mike Todd himself would never live to reinvest, spend, or lose that money; he died in a plane crash in March 1958.[37]

Films made on the scale of *Around the World* are usually referred to as ep-ics, although until the widescreen productions of the late 1950s to the mid-1960s, few comedies had been made on an epic scale. The film is neither an epic, nor a comedy, nor a mere travelogue, however. Todd, in any event, was determined to think outside the generic categories constructed by Holly-wood. His Todd-AO process would reconceive not only the experience of the audience, but also the films themselves. Todd was a showman, and films in Todd-AO would be shows. This meant elevating the exhibition and be-ing dedicated to the art of the pitch. In a speech he gave at Harvard Busi-ness School in the spring of 1957, he explained, "I think showmanship is about the most important single thing dramatizing the sale of merchandise in business. . . . showmanship is probably the most important thing in public life."[38]

Todd insisted on elevating the exhibition environment. In a notorious battle with exhibitors, Todd refused to allow popcorn to be sold at the screenings of films in Todd-AO. "My fight against selling popcorn in the theatre is really more a question of principle and I am not going to relax this policy regardless of the pressure put on me. I am insisting on this policy because I want to demonstrate that occasionally a show comes along that does not have to depend on popcorn to satisfy the customers. Many exhibitors have pointed out to me that popcorn saved the industry. I say that shows saved the industry."[39]

In the place of popcorn, the theater sold "commemorative albums," which Todd called "hardcover books." "This type of book," he explained, "and the penetration that comes from the customers taking these hardcover books home with them can sell a show and even an industry much better than a discarded pop-corn bag."[40]

WHEN MIKE TODD warned his Harvard audience "you can't fake it," he meant that film audiences had become so discerning that filmmakers had to deliver quality products. He also believed that the more knowledgeable and well traveled the audience became, the more location shoots would replace studio fabrications, as the audience's greater knowledge of the world would produce an inability to see "the real" in studio settings. Finally, he had invested in the notion that Todd-AO provided the best way of capturing the world's beauty. Although his belief in the wisdom of the audience may seem to be mere showmanship and guff, his actions confirm his sincerity. For example, when *Around the World* premiered, Todd sat in the audience and observed several responses, including clapping at a scene as if it had ended when it had not. Todd went back to California with the film and recut it to better match the audience's reading of the scene. He insisted to his Harvard audience that spending $500,000 to improve the film was more effective than spending $500,000 to advertise a flawed product.

Not only did he promise a photographic hyperrealism that respond to audience expectations, but he also stressed that the shows needed to be marketed as events. In the very year that Todd made *Around the World in Eighty Days*, one of the great directors of the silent and classical studio era, Cecil B. DeMille, was busy digging more deeply into the arsenal of movie magic tools on the Paramount lot by devising an unparalleled number of special effects to remake one of his own films, *The Ten Commandments*.[41] Mike Todd, on the other hand, believed in exploiting the world as a spectacle. While De-Mille toiled in Hollywood, Todd arrived in Chinchón, Spain, where he hired the town's entire population of 6,500 residents to play extras at a bullfight. Both productions were enormously successful, especially at the box office. Yet critics complained that DeMille's film was a stagy and old-fashioned Victorian theatrical while they lauded Todd's film as novel, fresh, innovative, and ultimately worthy of many awards, including the Academy Award for best picture.

Todd's grandiose vision and the scale of the film's production projected the notion that to be part of the film was to become a part of filmmaking history and that the film's significance could also be attributed to its vast scale. The film's publicity claimed it "shattered records and precedents with Toddian profligacy."[42] This material noted that the movie had been shot in 140 actual locations, as well as in six Hollywood studios and studios in England, Hong Kong, and Japan. It boasted having filmed 68,894 persons, establishing 2,000 camera set-ups and designing 74,685 costumes. The film's budget also expanded over time from a projected $3 million to more than $6 million. At times, simply to make payroll during the film's production, Todd had to hunt down friends with deep pockets such as Lorraine Manville and Al Streslin, who worked in "construction and real estate." Streslin ended up with 1.8 percent ownership in the film, which paid off his almost $250,000 in loans rather handsomely.[43]

Because Todd was first and foremost a producer, he understood his achievement in those terms: producers were the "authors of all action."[44] The scale of the project would be one of his great accomplishments. While making the movie, he also made a film documenting the making of the film, suggesting that he imagined that the film would be so important that people would have an interest in understanding how he did it. As he explained, "When I first started the picture, I had this idea. I knew it was going to be [a] very difficult task, so I thought I'd start a film called *Object Impossible*, because all the wire guys said I must fall on my face. . . . I had this idea of doing a documentary about the making of the picture and I have some wonderful shots."[45] The documentary unit is even credited in the published materials relating to the film credits. In his speech at Harvard, Todd called the documentary an "hour and a half trailer" and spoke of possibly using it for educational purposes at Cannes or a film school.[46] The film was never actually made, although the extensive footage of the shooting of *Around the World* was used in a television special called *Around the World of Mike Todd* in September 1968 and written and produced by his son, Mike Todd, Jr. While production stills were a common feature of the studios, Todd's documentary may be the first example of an explicit "the making of" movie, and it suggests the importance Todd attached to the scale of the production and its international reach as one of its great accomplishments.

The scale and scope of Todd's casting reflected his desire to signify the film's global reach. Aside from the vast numbers of extras employed for the making of the film, Todd sought out an array of well-known film and stage actors who would play what Todd eventually called "cameo roles." His notion of the cameo was that it would be "a gem carved in celluloid by a star." Todd legitimated the onslaught of famous names by explaining that the film's story was about "four people who go traveling. When you go traveling you meet a lot of people. It's that simple."[47] Trade papers and his son's biography describe how Todd cajoled the vast number of stars—such as Frank Sinatra and the famous French comic Fernandel—into appearing in the film by using the other stars he had already signed as leverage to get them to sign on. Todd was most desperate to cast Marlene Dietrich as the madam in a San Francisco brothel, so he offered to shoot the sequence without a contract and subject it to her approval at what was close to a $250,000 bet that she would agree to print the scene. She did.

The cameo roles brought actors from the past into the present: Buster Keaton, Gilbert Roland, Joe E. Brown, Beatrice Lillie. Lillie and other performers such as Noel Coward, Red Skelton, and Hermione Gingold were not exclusively known as movie stars. Finally, featuring such actors as Charles Boyer, Peter Lorre, and Dietrich foregrounded the stable of "international" stars that already resided in Hollywood. Critics appreciated the cameos and found the game of spotting the famous "bit players" an entertaining diversion. Robert Griffith noted that "the remarkable thing is that so few of them are really important as themselves, so perfectly do they lend color, vitality and authenticity to Mr. Todd's mighty spectacle."[48] Another noted, "It's a neat trick and it comes off socko."[49]

If Todd's film would physically travel around the world, his central cast would also be drawn from around the world. The cast represented an international eclecticism. He decided immediately on David Niven to play the English protagonist, Phileas Fogg, with the cool, precise detachment that Verne had written into his spoof of the English character. Casting an

Englishman to play an Englishman in a film in English seems perfectly un-original. But the casting of Mario Moreno, better known as Cantínflas, as Phileas Fogg's French valet Passepartout, turned out to be a stroke of genius. Cantínflas was at the time the greatest star of the Mexican cinema, though he had never before appeared in an English-language film. His casting was both idiosyncratic and difficult to achieve, but it later proved to yield great returns. Todd had earlier met Cantínflas and his manager Jacques Gelman while vacationing in Mexico with the actress Evelyn Keyes (with whom Todd had been involved for the several years before and during the filming). Keyes knew Cantínflas from her experience making films in Mexico. Cantínflas was a nimble, physical comic who has been regularly compared to Charlie Chaplin. Todd considered him "the greatest performer I have ever in my life had the experience of being connected with" and insisted that "his comedy is universal, because it's based on pathos."[50] He had never made an English-language film, although he had been entertaining offers for years, because he refused to adapt his character to the interests of foreign producers and because he was also known in Mexico for a verbal patter that he knew would be lost in translation.[51]

Cantínflas made sense as Todd's choice in several ways. Todd was, no doubt, thinking about a box-office draw for targeted sectors of the world-wide audience. In fact, Todd agreed to pay the Mexican star a percentage of the gross box office in Spanish-speaking territories. Cantínflas also topped the salary scale for the film as its highest paid performer, suggesting that Todd also respected and recognized him as a star, treatment which might not have come as easily from a mainstream Hollywood producer embedded in a system that had for the most part denoted a star's value mainly within the Hollywood context.

Casting Cantínflas shaped the film's episodes in important ways. As Ernest Anderson, who worked for Todd, wrote in a letter to John Huston at the end of April 1955:

Coming in from the airport, I gathered the director will be John Farrow, Harry Tugand is writing the script, Cantínflas plays Passepartout and David Niven, Fogg. And, says Mike, wait'll you see the bullfight scene. Knowing that Spain or Mexico were never locations for 80 days and since Mike's dialogues were so frag-mentary and sporadic as we drove in, I quite innocently asked, "What's the name of the picture? Mike says, "what are you a wise guy or something? Around the World in 80 Days." So I guess they are interpolating some of Cantínflas' block comedy numbers. The picture goes into production June 6.[52]

The film did not start its production in June, but two months later for its ninety-two days of shooting.

Cantínflas played Passepartout as a "Hispanic" Latin and not a French one. The character's name and origins remained opaque in the context of the film. In the hands of Verne, Passepartout's Frenchness anchored the story as an observation of both the world and the imperturbable British, seen from the French point of view. The fact that the story was French in origin but played otherwise suggests the porous way in which French culture could be easily assimilated into a generalized "Western" culture.[53] In casting Cantínflas, Todd must have been thinking about the various "spectacular episodes" of physical comedy he would film that did not rely on dialogue, thus facilitating the translatability of the film worldwide.

Other casting choices also would have been unlikely studio choices. The role of Inspector Fix, Fogg's nemesis, went to a well-known English character actor with a well-known drinking problem: Robert Newton, who died right after the film was shot. Finally, Todd decided, two weeks before shooting was scheduled to begin, to cast Hollywood newcomer Shirley MacLaine in the female lead as the British-educated Indian Princess Aouda, who joins Fogg and Passepartout for the second half of their journey. None of the production materials suggest that Todd ever considered hiring an Indian actress but, it must also be said that in this way the film repeats Verne's literal elevation of Aouda through her "whitewashing" since the novel describes her as "white as a European."[54]

And yet, in other ways, the film's global aspirations were many. Its comprehensive quality suggests an encyclopedic kind of globalism. Yet it also integrated elements of many cultures to project the image of covering the globe in its content. One effect of this "kitchen sink" approach was that reviewers pondered the nature of the film as such. At a moment when the very value of films and filmmaking seemed up for grabs, this film that was not a film (Todd called it a "show") appeared to reviewers as something that could help "save" the film industry. "In any formal, disciplined sense *Around the World in Eighty Days* is hardly a movie at all, but it is a wonderfully entertaining grab bag of treats and surprises produced on a scale reminiscent of Cecil B. DeMille and the Emperor Nero. It is a spectacular show."[55] *Newsweek* struggled to label the film and so described it as "a travelogue, a circus, a costume piece (1870s), a review, a two-reel comedy, and an all-star revival."[56] A week later, in an article that attempted to account for the phenomenal attention the film seemed to be getting, *Newsweek* this time cited one review that insisted that it was "A movie so new that nobody could describe it."[57] The hybrid nature of the production was part of the film's critical interest. Jacques Doniol-Valcroze paused on the paradoxical nature of the transnationalism of the production: "The film is made by Americans who show America from the critical perspective of an Englishman . . . all of it invented by a Frenchman."[58]

If the film's hybrid quality struck the critics, they also applauded the film's comedic elements: the witty vignettes written by S. J. Perelman, who had penned scripts for the Marx Brothers; the "British" blasé attitude of Phileas Fogg in the face of remarkable sights and adventures; and the physical comedy of Cantínflas. "It is delightful entertainment and a grand spoof with plenty of delicious satire on the English and on movies themselves."[59] The novel's original characterization of Phileas Fogg was a French spoof on English restraint and obsessions about time and precision. The film played this to the hilt: Fogg never looks out a window in all his travels and seems blasé about the remarkable beauty of the sunsets seen from the boat, never admires the marvels of the American Western landscape, never appreciates the picturesque quality of the Asian ports. By playing it as comedy, the film also spoofed the nineteenth-century novel's bet as a bold dare. How else could a film about the impossibility of traveling around the world in eighty days be made in 1956, when one could travel the world in fewer than eighty hours?

The film winked at the history of the movies. Parodies of an early Western's train attack and rescue (fig. 4.2), of an adventure film's rescue of a maiden in distress (Fogg and Passepartout save Princess Aouda from sati, the ritual burning of a widow on her husband's funeral pyre in India), of the Marx Brothers (a buffet mime between Cantínflas and Red Skelton in the San Francisco saloon) drew spectators into a familiar idiom, while their placement as episodes facilitated the audience's recognition that this was part of the joke. These comic opportunities not only winked back at silent film. Geared for a worldwide audience, *Around the World in Eighty Days*, cleverly integrated visual gags to broaden the film's appeal to audiences who could then follow the action without reading the subtitles. Thus, while the droll dialogue could appeal to a certain sector of the audience, the film never turned on the dialogue and easily moved forward without it. Todd had in Cantínflas a physical comic who would entertain audiences without saying a word: he would dance Flamenco, fight bulls (fig. 4.3), shoot Indians, perform in a Japanese circus, ride an ostrich, and tour Japanese temples, all without speaking.

4.2 Cantínflas / Passepartout as cowboy. The Western episode from *Around the World in 80 Days*, 1956.

4.3 Cantínflas / Passepartout as bullfighter, *Around the World in 80 Days*, 1956.

Of course the big scale of production matched the notion that the world itself was big (all those people and places), but it also suggested that film would make the world not so much smaller as more accessible. Todd knew that location shots would display the virtues of Todd-AO. But the film's globalism was quite literal, and shooting covered thirteen different countries and 140 locations.[60] The locations would deliver not only a punch of realism that exploited the Todd-AO process but would also serve as the best travelogue ever seen. Initially, skeptics raised doubts about the project of location shooting a film that was set in 1872. It was one thing to shoot on contemporary European locations as they had for *Three Coins in a Fountain* (Rome) and *Summer Madness* (Venice), but another thing altogether to use locations to shoot a historical film like *Gigi* or *Moulin Rouge*. As Todd explained, "most people said it was impossible to capture 1872 on location today, because of all the signs, Coca-Cola signs and telegraph poles."[61] But Todd insisted on shooting in every country depicted in the film to achieve authenticity in the film's look and feel. When discussing on-location extras in a radio interview, he insisted that "people act, react different in different countries. . . . In that Greco scene—you know, you've got to have Spanish people. In the bullfight—they, they act different, scream and they, they're all—they're just different and—it looks—it's more real."[62] In fact, Todd believed so much in the authenticity of the location extras that he fired his original director, John Farrow, when Farrow attempted to coach the Spanish extras.[63]

There were those who, having seen the film, doubted the success of this location strategy. One of the film's rare tepid reviews (in the *Nation*) noted that the close-ups had all been staged because the action is supposed to be some eighty years ago and there are few corners of the world today where a jeep or a neon sign wouldn't spoil the illusion."[64] This comment is, however, false. For example, in Japan, Passepartout visits a large Buddha on location and even steals an apple from his altar. The Paris arrival is also shot in the streets of Paris and provided one of the great location stories from the film's production. Although Todd's crew had earlier paid off the local police to post "no parking" signs for the Sunday morning shoot, this did not prevent forty disobedient French people from parking anyway. Todd arrived with his own tow trucks, ready to take them away. When the French police refused to tow the cars, Todd did it himself, causing an uproar, which was facilitated by the fact that Todd had also invited the French press to attend the shooting of the sequence and they, instead, reported the towing of the cars. To make matters worse, the next week, his crew climbed up to the top of Nôtre Dame to shoot a sequence of the balloon ride for which they used a smaller-scale model flying by the cathedral and over the roofs of Paris. The sequence was shot as the French police chased the camera crew (figs. 4.4 and 4.5). The Paris police prefect warned that he would not allow the city to be turned into a film set and would be more vigilant about granting permissions to shoot on the streets of the French capital. Thus, while the spectacular vistas and sunsets and the aerial views of the countryside would exploit Todd-AO, the other location shots contributed to the overall achievement of the production's grand scale.

The hard work of the London, Paris, and Yokahama street shoots prevented the film from being a mere travelogue of beautiful sunsets and aerial shots (although there is no shortage of panoramic views in the film either) (fig. 4.6). The film's spectators also watched landscapes of India and the American West through a train window. In these scenes, Fogg remains blasé and often simply plays cards; it is Passpartout who serves as the audience's double. When the audience assumes the tourist gaze, we are looking through the eyes of the simple and likable Passpartout as opposed to the

4.4 Paris, 1956 becomes 1872, *Around the World in 80 Days*, 1956.

4.5 The view from Nôtre Dame, *Around the World in 80 Days*, 1956.

4.6 Views at sea, designed to show-off Todd-AO, *Around the World in 80 Days*, 1956.

haughty and distant Fogg. This might have seemed like a gamble with Euro-American audiences, hardly used to imagining seeing the world through the eyes of a "Mexican." Todd wisely banked on the universality of the clown in casting Cantínflas to occupy the position that would most assume the audience's gaze. In the same way that Chaplin had functioned in an "every-man" role worldwide, so would Todd use Cantínflas's skills as a great mime to universalize his perspective.

If the film attempted to display a catalog of cultures, its globalism can be understood in its literal and constant representation of the globe. The film depicted a trip around the world and thus featured not merely travel itself but also many modes of transport, as if to counteract the fact that the audience was, in fact, going nowhere. Almost every vehicle for transport imaginable circa 1872 appears in the film: bicycle, balloon (not in the novel), train, elephant, royal barge, steamboat, ostrich, rickshaw, horse, stage coach, sailmobile, sidewheeler, handsome cab, an Asian junk with red sails. These mechanisms of transport emphasize the novelty of the mobility of the modern world that such a journey underscored when Verne wrote the novel at the end of the nineteenth century.

The film begins, however, with a prologue that makes the globe itself one of the film's subjects in a fairly explicit manner. Prologues were not unusual for "roadshow" movies and often set the stage for films in a preachy and pompous way.[65] For example, Cecil B. DeMille comes out from behind a red velvet curtain to begin *The Ten Commandments* with a speech about "the birth of freedom."[66] *The Agony and the Ecstasy* begins with a fifteen-minute tour of St. Peter's and a lecture on the work of Michelangelo. The prologue of *Around the World* connects the past to the present, flaunting our own prog-

4.**7** Edward R. Murrow in his study, globe on right. *Around the World in 80 Days*, 1956.

ress as well as the possible dangers of the shrinking world, and seems to turn what will be a comic adventure film into something of importance, reflecting Todd's sense that the film itself was making history. The picture opens in a square, 35mm image of America's great television news journalist, Edward R. Murrow, sitting at a desk, surrounded by bookshelves in the background and a globe conspicuously placed to the right of the desk (fig. 4.7). The choice of Murrow suggests an immediate identification with internationalism as he was a well-known wartime correspondent in London. His association with American liberalism and a "truth" effect had become synonymous with "news" on television by the time the film was being made. The camera cranes into a medium shot of Murrow, who identifies Jules Verne as a fantastic fiction writer whose predictions had become fact: "flying machines, submarines, television, rockets." Yet, Murrow explains, not even Verne's fertile imagination could shrink the earth to the point it had reached in 1956. He then shifts to a discussion of another of Verne's stories, about a trip to the moon, and introduces "the authentic genius" Georges Méliès and his film *A Trip to the Moon* made at the turn of the century. Todd bought what was probably the best existing copy of the film from the Méliès family. The silent film plays for about three minutes, with Murrow narrating the action and with the introduction of the movie's theme music, which audiences will later hear played over and over again throughout the film. This musical connection links the cinematic past with the present and in that way repeats the Frenchness films pattern of turning to France as America's past.

　　Also like those films, the prologue underscores the medium's progress when it cuts away from the silent pictures of fin-de-siècle France as Murrow describes the characters as about to "return to earth, a minor planet, where fiction lags behind fact." At this point, the image goes from black and white to color and (in the dead center of the screen) displays a missile in the desert preparing for launch. While the missile remains in the center of the frame, the frame expands at the sides, as the film goes from the 35mm format to

70mm in widescreen, using the Todd-AO cameras, while the soundtrack features a countdown followed by a launch. The audience witnesses the wonders of Todd-AO in the context of the impressive launch (figs. 4.8–4.11). Images of the missile are followed by images of the earth taken from the inside of the missile. Murrow, however, grows solemn in tone, mitigating any triumphal assumptions by warning, "Speed is good only when wisdom leads the way" and that the earth's future would be "determined by the collective wisdom of the people who live on this shrinking planet."

The prologue functions as more than a narrative mechanism to ease viewers into the film's historical setting. In fact, a different prologue was initially shot that simply sketched the continuity between past and present by grouping the cameo players on an airplane in small vignettes. Niven and Cantínflas in that version were seated together and the former, with the blasé attitude that characterizes Fogg, ignores all the chaos of the loading of the plane and opens his book, *Around the World in Eighty Days*. Todd envisioned this prologue as a chance to feature the films' star power at its start while beginning the cameo recognition game.[67] Sometime between then and the film's opening in late October, Todd replaced this with the more serious prologue featuring Murrow, Méliès, and the missile launch, which obviously took advantage of the Todd-AO process. But it did more than that. By showing the Méliès film, Todd placed his film in the context of the medium's origins in Europe and then connected that history to notions of a shrinking globe. Murrow reminds the viewers that Méliès had put the earlier Verne story about a trip to the moon onto film, "35 mm just like you are watching now." This would, only minutes later, underscore the novelty and innovation of the 70mm process as a watershed for film: from 1900 to 1956 and from Todd-AO forward.

The images of planet earth from the rocket are replaced by a cut to Murrow's hand on the spinning globe (fig. 4.12). He reminds us that learned men used to think the world was flat. He pauses and changes tone: "Jules Verne's classic already had a sense of a shrinking world back in 1872," and the film dissolves to London in 1872 and the changing of the guard, the first of the travelogue scenes enhanced by Todd A-O. Each location also featured a variety of crowd scenes that usually included parades and dances and some sort of locally associated activity: in London, we view the changing of the guard; in Paris, people strolling in front of the Tuileries; in Spain, a flamenco dance and a bullfight; in India, a parade that includes music and dance; in Hong Kong, a parade with dragons and fireworks; in San Francisco, a political rally with musical fanfare and fireworks. This repeating pattern not only turned

4.8–4.11 Expansion of the image from 35mm to 70mm. *Around the World in 80 Days*, 1956.

4.12 Murrow's hand on the globe. *Around the World in 80 Days*, 1956.

people into cultural displays, akin to the exposition culture Todd knew so well, but also attempted to universalize the human experience: everyone has music, dances, parades, only the themes and colors change. The film sought to put the globe's diversity on ready display while drawing attention to the structural similarities of the human experience. In this way, we see a 1950s vision of globalism in keeping with Edward Steichen's blockbuster Family of Man photography exhibit that opened at the Museum of Modern Art the year that Todd was filming.[68] That exhibit has since been analyzed extensively in negative terms. Blake Stimson has recently summarized that view that says the exhibit functioned as "a sort of humanist Trojan horse sneaking American-dominated economic globalization and political hegemony past restrictive political boundaries in the belly of a maudlin cultural embrace." Stimson rightfully has taken another look at the exhibit and asked about the significance of a liberal ideal of a single global identity in the 1950s and the role photography played in shaping it.[69]

Like the Family of Man exhibit, *Around the World in Eighty Days* achieved both commercial and critical success in its initial American release. Although United Artists bought the film's distribution rights, Todd determined the unusual terms of the initial two-year release: the film would play only ten times a week in 125 theaters in cities selected by Todd. United Artists would advance him $4 million and take only a 10 percent distribution fee, as opposed to the customary 30 percent for the road show before the film went into general distribution. UA would also get 10 percent of the film's profits.[70] It is virtually impossible to determine the film's profits except to be sure that slightly less than 80 percent of those profits went directly to Mike Todd. A window into its San Francisco run gives us a sense of its staying power. It opened there at the Coronet Theater in January 1957 (three months after the New York and Los Angeles premieres) and played ninety-five weeks until the end of October 1958, grossing $1,756,453 and $985,000 in rental fees.[71] The rental earnings for the film during 1957, according to *Variety*, were $16,200,000 domestic.[72] According to one source, it grossed $65,000,000 in its first two years of worldwide release.[73] When Elizabeth Taylor, Todd's widow, sold the film's rights to Warner Brothers in 1982, *Variety* reported that it was the fourth highest grossing film of all time.[74]

Hollywood also responded to the film on Oscar night. The film was nominated for eight Oscars and won five for best color cinematography, film editing, music score, screenplay and, finally, best picture, prevailing over nominees *Giant*, *The King and I*, *The Ten Commandments*, and *Friendly Persuasion*.[75] At the ceremony in March 1957, whose set featured a globe sitting atop a reel of film, the president of the Academy announced that film was "truly a global medium." Todd grabbed the top honors. Literally. He leapt out of his seat and towards the stage so quickly that he had to return to kiss his wife Elizabeth Taylor. His acceptance reminded Hollywood of just how big he and his film were: "I'm especially thrilled, this is my first time at bat. I'd like to thank you on behalf of the sixty-odd thousand people who worked on this show."[76]

Only a few months later, Todd, Taylor, and *Around the World* appeared at the 1957 Cannes Film Festival, eagerly solicited by the festival's organizers. What better film to open the festival than a spectacular presentation of a well-known tale by a Frenchman that explicitly linked the cinema to the shrinking of the world?

While *Around the World* emblematized many of the recent developments in Hollywood, its very success also fueled the cosmopolitan cinema that would take off on the heels of its vast commercial triumph. By foregrounding the history of a single film, we have been able to look at the various contexts that shaped cosmopolitan films and filmmaking. Embedded within *Around the World* are the historical changes that had a particularly important impact on films, such as increased travel and ideas about the "Family of Man." The film also is a telling example of the shifts in the industrial organization of the film industry itself (such as independent, footloose production). Its 70mm Todd-AO format captures film's heightened competition on the American market for leisure dollars. Finally, the film was tailor-made for what was in the 1950s clearly becoming a fundamental hub of the international film business: the Cannes Film Festival, which functioned as both an international publicity machine and a market for film distribution. Yet the critical and financial acclaim of the film also had an impact on filmmaking itself as filmmakers sought to replicate the film's success.

SAM SPIEGEL'S OSCAR acceptance for best picture for *Bridge on the River Kwai* evinced the new globalism in filmmaking and its further decentering of Hollywood power. "The soundstages of Hollywood have been extended in recent years to the farthest corners of the world," said Spiegel. "No land is inviolate to the glare of our camera. Yet it is fitting and proper that people the world over are waiting for a decision which only you in this community are able to render."[77] Worse pandering would be hard to find. Spiegel, an independent producer, had always had rocky relations with the Hollywood filmmaking community. In fact, his career as an independent producer, and the increasing number of films made entirely outside of Hollywood such as his *Bridge on the River Kwai*, stood as evidence of the declining power of Hollywood-based filmmaking. But his comment also underscores the notion that Hollywood in the 1950s managed to radiate outwards physically while maintaining a seemingly coherent identity in the face of the world. Although Spiegel's language suggests a sort of Hollywood imperialism—"No land is inviolate to the glare of our camera"—his films were hardly proof of Hollywood's extended gaze. Rather, his comments suggest the increasingly porous national boundaries of well-financed filmmaking in the West.

The loosening of the studio system encouraged what was then being called "runaway production"—a term that itself implied that production was naturally based in Hollywood. The reasons for making films outside of Hollywood were complex. Even at the time, observers were trying to explain its causes. As early as 1953, an article in *This Week* by Louis Berg called "Movies on the Move!" noted, "the film industry is going global." The phenomenon extended beyond Hollywood: the French star, Michèle Morgan, who left France during the war, had repatriated but was shooting a film in Vera Cruz, Mexico, while Fernandel, the French star, was in Chicago shooting *Public Enemy Number One* with Zsa Zsa Gabor, of Hungary and Hollywood—"proof that the movies are on the move not only from Hollywood, but all over the place and in every direction."[78]

Incentives for footloose production included being able to spend studio assets and profits that had been frozen in Europe (this had also contributed to the Frenchness films). In addition, a new tax law remitted American income taxes for anyone working abroad seventeen out of eighteen consecutive months. This was a boon to independent production companies, and stars such as Kirk Douglas and his company Bryna Films immediately set out to take advantage by making films such as *Act of Love* (1953) and *The Vikings* (1958) in Europe. This dodge would also be taken to new heights when, in 1958, *Suddenly, Last Summer,* set in New Orleans, was shot in England and on the Costa Brava in Spain because of Elizabeth Taylor's complex salary and tax shelter schemes.[79]

Production by nominally American companies in Europe doubled between 1950 and 1957 and the proportion of American films filmed abroad went from 5 percent to 15 percent, according to one source.[80] Most of the filming initially took place in Italy, France, Germany, and Spain, although the most spectacular examples were locations in Ceylon (Sri Lanka) for *Bridge on the River Kwai* and Jordan for *Lawrence of Arabia.* Those locations were hardly vehicles for saving money, as they were difficult, time-consuming, and grueling.

The dispersion of blacklisted and other left-leaning personnel abroad during the 1950s also created a pool of professionals who were available and needed to work abroad. For example, screenwriters such as Dalton Trumbo (*Roman Holiday, Exodus, Spartacus*), Michael Wilson (*Friendly Persuasion, The Bridge on the River Kwai,* and *Lawrence of Arabia*) and Carl Foreman (*Bridge on the River Kwai*) could work for producers under easier cover when production was going on outside the United States. Director, actor, writer, and producer Jules Dassin moved to Europe in 1950 after being named by Edward Dymtryk as a Communist. There he made the highly successful film *Rififi Chez les Hommes.* Later, he met and married Melina Mercouri and made the successful "multilingual" film *Never on Sunday* in 1960. Betsy Blair, who left both her husband Gene Kelly and the United States in 1957, worked in French movies and eventually moved to England and married the Jewish Czech-born "English" director of such films as *Saturday Night and Sunday Morning,* Karel Reisz.

If in the 1920s and 1930s Hollywood had drawn the world's talent to it (in part because of the instability and anti-Semitism of Europe during that period), the reverse happened in the 1950s and 1960s when talent left Hollywood to work with independent production and its multinational financing, crews, locations, talent, even languages. A closer look at the phenomenon suggests that to describe it as a regime of "coproductions" is not sufficient. Coproduction may well describe the multinational origin of a film's financiers but companies, not countries, were often doing the investing. For example, American-based studios such as Columbia and United Artists had a propensity for investing in productions made abroad, but usually through an independent producer. Sam Spiegel's Horizon Pictures received financing from Columbia to make both *The Bridge on the River Kwai* and *Lawrence of Arabia.* MGM financed the Italian Carlo Ponti to make *Dr. Zhivago.*

Many of the producers and directors of the cosmopolitan films were cosmopolitans themselves in the sense that they were people born in one place who eventually made their home in a different place, or even in several places. Many of them were polyglot European Jews who had bounced around because of Hitler's rise. Directors such as William Wyler (born in France of German-Jewish origin) and Otto Preminger (born in Austria) were part of the émigré tradition that shaped the studios before World War II. Lesser known among directors were people such as Andrew Marton, the Hungarian-born quintessential second unit director who worked mostly for the studios directing big location shoots such as *King Solomon's Mines*, the chariot race in *Ben-Hur*, the production numbers in *Cleopatra* and *55 Days in Peking*. Even Terence Young, the British director of the early James Bond movies, was born in Shanghai.

Polish-born Sam Spiegel, who lived in Austria and Palestine before coming to the United States, left and never returned to Hollywood because of his shady dealings. Instead, Horizon Pictures, the company he originally formed in partnership with John Huston when they made *The African Queen*, operated out of London, with American financing largely from Columbia Pictures. Samuel Bronston, the Rumanian-born producer, began his career working for MGM and Columbia in France before he set out on his own and helped establish Spain as a shooting location for English-language films in 1961–64, during which he produced *King of Kings*, *El Cid*, *55 Days at Peking*, and *The Fall of the Roman Empire*. In France, Belgian-born Raoul Lévy, worked in Mexico for his cousin, the Russian-born, French-raised producer Jacques Gelman (the very same Gelman who was Cantínflas's agent) before returning to France where his films, including *Et Dieu créa la femme* and the explicitly multinational *The Fabulous Adventures of Marco Polo*, were financed by Columbia and MGM.[81]

The casts of these films were often as multinational as the production crew. In European coproduction ventures, films might feature a star from each country as in the 1952 *Fan-fan la tulipe*, which starred Frenchman Gérard Philippe and Italian Gina Lollobrigida. The cosmopolitan film, on the other hand, did not operate in such formulaic "package unit" terms in part because independent production facilitated the assembly of a cast and crew that could be drawn from a wide pool of talent. The films usually had a requisite American star: William Holden in *Bridge*, Anthony Quinn in *Lawrence*, Charlton Heston in *El Cid*. The films favored Anglophone actors. While the films did not have a nationality, they did have a language: English. Even then, dubbing actors became more common during the cosmopolitan film moment. For example, Claudia Cardinale was dubbed in *The Pink Panther*, Ursula Andress in *Dr. No*, and Gert Frobe in *Goldfinger*. Other linguistic strategies included multilingualism on screen, as in *Never on Sunday*, which featured Dassin playing an American speaking English, the bilingual Mercouri in both Greek and English, and subtitles for English translations of the Greek actors. *Le Mépris*, Godard's engagement with cycle of the "cosmopolitan" film produced by the Italian Carlo Ponti, the American Joseph E. Levine, and the Frenchman Georges de Beauregard, underscores both the possibilities and limits of this form of multilingualism with its hodgepodge of translations and subtitles.

The transnationalism of production, settings, and subjects produced a new kind of star. If the *après-guerre* witnessed a flurry of European settings in American movies, the war itself produced the mobility of such stars as the Hungarian Gabor sisters, Zsa Zsa and Eva, and, more famously, Belgian-born and London-dwelling Audrey Hepburn. During the heyday of the studios, the relationship between a star's origins, cultural context, and roles had been quite complex. Charles Boyer, for example, became a Hollywood actor, as did both Garbo and Dietrich, although their origins outside the United States contributed to their allure as stars. In contrast, Maurice Chevalier, who in his day was one of the best-paid performers in Hollywood, milked and exploited his Frenchness despite the fact that he remained, one could say, actually more cosmopolitan than other non-American born actors by going back and forth between France and America rather than simply quitting France for Hollywood. Decades later, Brigitte Bardot became an international star but never set foot in Hollywood.

Historical epics, a subset of the cosmopolitan films, facilitated international casting since they required not only casts of thousands but also great suspension of disbelief in the first place. British actors such as Alec Guinness (English) and Stephen Boyd (Irish) often played Romans, and Canadians such as Christopher Plummer were also able to play a variety of nationalities precisely because non-American origins combined with anglophony facilitated his familiar "otherness." Actresses such as Sophia Loren could be more comfortably believed as the emperor's daughter in *The Fall of the Roman Empire* or as Jimena, the wife of *El Cid*, than in more contemporary roles that required less suspension of disbelief and thus where her Italian identity would have been more of a problem.

No actor seems to have ridden the cosmopolitan film wave better than the man born as Michel Chaloub, who became known as Omar Sharif. As he put it in his memoir, *L'éternel masculin*, "I live abroad. I am never at home where I am."[82] Sharif grew up in a French-speaking household, in Alexandria, Egypt, where he attended French and then English schools. He attended a British university in Cairo, after which it was assumed he would join his father in his lumber business. Although he claims to have been raised a Catholic, and it has been said his family was also Lebanese, rumors have also circulated that he was actually an Egyptian Jew. By the time he was in his early twenties, he could speak French, English, and Arabic—although in his memoirs, written in French for the French market, he insists on his cultural identification with France.[83]

Sharif's career in Egyptian movies began with a boom. He changed his name to one he considered more "Oriental" that could be easily spelled and said. He married the co-star of his first film, Egypt's premier film actress, Faten Hamama. Their film, *The Blazing Sun*, directed by the Egyptian-born and Pasadena Playhouse–trained Youssef Chahine, played at the Cannes Film Festival in 1954. The film earned a special mention by the jury and the young and beautiful "Omar el Cherif," as some of the French press called him, became a much photographed and talked about newcomer at Cannes. He would become a regular and in 1966, he would again be featured as part of the festival's headliners when *Zhivago* opened the festival that year (fig. 4.13).

Sharif's first Hollywood screen tests came when William Dieterle saw his face on a poster advertising *The Blazing Sun* while he was in Cairo scouting locations for his upcoming film, *Joseph in Egypt*. The project was shelved along with Sharif's screen tests. It was not until 1960, when Sam Spiegel began to search for Arab actors (for *Lawrence of Arabia*) that Sharif came to his attention. Although Sharif eventually won the role of Sherif Ali, it was only after Spiegel had run through three other swarthy European actors, (the German Horst Buchholz, and two Frenchmen, Alain Delon and Maurice Ronet). Spiegel signed Sharif to a seven-film-contract between Columbia and Horizon, though Columbia did not like the seven-year gamble with an actor virtually unknown outside the Middle East and France. Spiegel understood that you no longer had to be tested and proven in Hollywood to have a lucrative career in the movies.

Sherif Ali was the only Arab role that Sharif played in his career in the cosmopolitan cinema. During the peak of his stardom between 1960 and 1968, he played the king of Armenia in *The Fall of the Roman Empire*, a Spanish civil war exile in *Behold a Pale Horse*, the title lead in *Genghis Khan*, a German in *Night of the Generals*, the Austrian archduke Rudolph in *Mayerling* (a film made in both French and English), a Jew in *Funny Girl*, and, probably most

4.13 Omar Sharif at Cannes Film Festival, 1960s. Courtesy: BIFI, FIF.

famously, Yuri Zhivago (complete with straightened hair and taped eyes to make them look more Russian) in the 1965 film *Dr. Zhivago* directed by David Lean.[84] His good looks and his accent evoked a general sense of foreignness to audiences who simply didn't know better. (One might also argue that Sharif's roles stand as evidence of the limited number of parts for Arabs in English-language cinema.) But Sharif also carefully cultivated this sense of indeterminate cultural identity. The only parts he would never play were "Anglo-Saxon" roles. As he put it in his memoir, "I speak six languages the same way, with an accent that allows me to seem like a foreigner without exactly defining my origins, something that has served me well in my career."[85] His multilingualism, combined with the variety of roles he played, contributed to his construction as the "international actor, Omar Sharif," as one French reviewer called him.[86] Unlike the Frenchness films, which drew deep lines of affinity across the Atlantic between France and America by underscoring nationality, the cosmopolitan films thrived on stars such as Sharif and on a hodgepodge of actors from many nations who seemed "unmarked" enough to play any number of nationalities.

The mobility and travel discussed earlier in *Around the World* became a staple of the cosmopolitan films whose narratives often began by establishing that the story begins in different places, although the plot will eventually have people from those places converge. For example, *The Pink Panther* begins with a fantasy Indian backstory and cuts to contemporary scenes in Paris, Rome, and Los Angeles. By the end of the film, everyone is at a ski lodge in Cortina in the Italian Alps. While audience demand for location shooting no doubt helped fuel cosmopolitan filmmaking, the practice also reflected the abilities of those making the films to actually work around the world. Studios had always sent second units to film establishing shots abroad, and each time such a crew went abroad, it also took a variety of shots to be stored in a studio's stock images library.[87] Prior to the 1950s, filming on foreign locations was rare. There had been extraordinary projects such as MGM's *Trader Horn* (1931), which was the first time a studio took principals to Africa; the next was almost twenty years later in late 1949 when MGM filmed *King Solomon's Mines* in color in Nairobi.[88]

Studios and cameramen liked to boast about the feats accomplished while shooting on location and those challenges began to be integrated into the films' publicity materials. Trailers touted the locations, from the Norwegian fjords in *The Vikings* (1958) to the ports of Cyprus and Israel in *Exodus* (1960). Although it was impossible to film *Doctor Zhivago* in the Soviet Union in 1965, producer Carlo Ponti and director David Lean produced the film's winter scenes in Finland, as close to the Russian border as they could get. They also rebuilt Moscow and the Russian steppe in the studios and suburbs outside Madrid.[89]

As jet travel began to extend transatlantic voyages within the reach of the middle classes beginning in 1958, the movies kept a step ahead by going to even more exotic locations: Jamaica and Istanbul in the first two James Bond films, Greenland in *Savage Innocents*, the Jordanian desert in *Lawrence of Arabia*, and the jungle of Ceylon (Sri Lanka) standing in for Thailand in *The Bridge on the River Kwai*. But jet travel also enabled these location shoots themselves and the peripatetic quality of the cosmopolitan film production, as cast and crew could travel far distances more quickly, and daily work could be shot, developed, and sent back for evaluation.[90] For example, during the shooting of *Bridge* in 1956–57, David Lean lived in a hotel within a short drive of the prison camp set where he shot much of the film. By the

1960–62 shoot of *Lawrence of Arabia*, cast and crew flew into the desert each day; O'Toole and Sharif were even given a plane to go to Beirut on the weekends to enjoy the women and drinking binges they could have there.[91]

If jet travel made it easier for cast and crew to participate in the location shoots, the films also foregrounded travel as a theme—across time and space. The films were more than travelogues that take you elsewhere, they underscored the journey itself. Like *Around the World*, which featured a variety of Victorian modes of transport, the cosmopolitan films set in the present—such as the James Bond films, the Pink Panther movies, the comic whodunit *Charade*—feature hip hotels and airports that signal both a contemporary feel and luxury in travel. For example, *Charade*'s opening scene was shot at a brand new luxury hotel in the French Alps, complete with indoor pool (fig. 4.14). In *Dr. No*, James Bond arrives in Jamaica at the state-of-the-art airport on which the camera dwells seemingly gratuitously (fig. 4.15). In *Goldfinger*, the 1954 Fountainebleau Hotel in Miami Beach, known at the time as the ultimate in modern luxury, is the setting for the film's opening minutes (fig. 4.16).

Travel is also prominently featured as a theme of the epics within the cosmopolitan film cycle. The bridge that will span the River Kwai and facil-

4.14 Hotel in Megève, with indoor pool, *Charade*, 1963.

4.15 Sparkling and new, the airport in Kingston, Jamaica, *Dr. No*, 1962.

4.16 Fontainebleau Hotel, Miami Beach, *Goldfinger*, 1964.

4.17 Goggles in trees after motorcycle accident, *Lawrence of Arabia*, 1962.

itate rail travel from Rangoon to Bangkok is the main element in that film; in *Lawrence*, Colonel Lawrence rides camels, jeeps, blows up train tracks, and meets his end by falling off a motorcycle, an accident chronicled in the film's opening sequence. The motoring goggles suspended in a tree (fig. 4.17) point to the irony that a man who could so ably ride camels through the scorching desert would meet his end on a modern and convenient mode of transport in his own serene English countryside. The films even portrayed elaborate travel in antiquity. In *The Fall of the Roman Empire*, the first spectacular scene features a summit of leaders of the provinces of the Roman Empire, from the king of Petra to Egypt to Judea to Britannia, each arriving on horseback or by chariot to assemble in front of Marcus Aurelius.

The films also heighten the audience's awareness of geography by displaying maps and making reference to transnational experiences. *Lawrence of Arabia*'s flashback begins with an image of T. E. Lawrence painting a map (fig. 4.18). In *Dr. No*, when Bond visits M, the set includes a large map on the wall of Moneypenny's office and a prominently featured globe in M's office (figs. 4.19 and 4.20). The meaning of the maps is reinforced by the films' internationalism and transnational consciousness. In the Bond films, Honey Ryder, the daughter of a scientist, has lived all over the world; Dr. No is the child of a German missionary and a Chinese mother. The organization he represents, SPECTRE, which is an invention of the film series, is an international organization that transcends the East-West divisions of the Cold War.[92] In fact, SPECTRE, which stands for Special Executive for Counter-Intelligence, Terrorism, Revenge, and Extortion has no headquarters and in that way mimics the film industry itself. In *Bridge on the River Kwai*, when the British assemble the team to blow up the bridge, a young Canadian joins them, acknowledging how perfect he is for the mission by saying that his presence is in keeping with the "international nature of the outfit." This sort

4.18 Lawrence drawing map, *Lawrence of Arabia*, 1962.

4.19 In M's office with globe on the left, *Dr. No*, 1962.

4.20 Map across the wall in Moneypenny's office, *Dr. No*, 1962

of international team figures in part of Marcus Aurelius's vision of the Roman Empire in *Fall*. He explains:

you do not resemble each other, nor worship the same gods. You are the unity, which is Rome. Two hundred years ago, Gauls were our fiercest enemies and now we greet them as friends. . . . We come now to the end of the road, here within our reach, golden centuries of peace . . . wherever you live, whatever the color of your skin . . . will bring the supreme right of Roman citizenship . . . no longer provinces or colonies but Rome everywhere, a family of equal nations . . . that's what lies ahead.

Although it would be simple to see Rome as a stand-in for an emerging American empire, the statement is fraught with the much broader "family of man" rhetoric of the period. This same perspective is alluded to in *Bridge*, as the two commanding officers Nicholson and Saito, the former held prisoner by the latter, salute each other as they share a sense of accomplishment at the completion of the bridge.

These films had no vested interest in the American empire per se. Rather, they articulated a vision of transnationalism that matched a postwar internationalist idealism with what mattered to filmmakers with big-budget pictures. They were also commercially driven to create the globe as a whole in order to establish it as a marketplace.

This view itself is not global but is very much attached to an Occidental culture that posed identity itself as potentially enigmatic and thus up for question. James Bond insistently declares his identity: "Bond, James Bond." In *Lawrence*, the issue of the protagonist's identity is at the heart of the story. The film poses the question of identity and manages to offer both the usual host of clichés about the Middle East and what anthropologist Steven Caton rightly identifies as a much more complicated text: an allegory about anthropologists and cross-cultural identification, a film at once imperialist and aware of the limits of imperialism. "Who are you? Who are you?" a British man screams across the Suez Canal to T. E. Lawrence, dressed in his Arab garb. By raising identity itself as an issue, the films may have opened themselves up to broader identification among their transnational audiences.[93]

As a group, the films above survey some of the myths, legends, and cultural continuities that had been part of the story of civilization in the West. After *Around the World in Eighty Days*, audiences that watched the cosmopolitan films would have also seen, between 1956 and 1966 alone, a range of Biblical and Ancient histories: *The Ten Commandments* (1956), *King of Kings* (1961), *The Greatest Story Ever Told* (1962), *Barabbas* (1962), *Ben-Hur* (1959), *Spartacus*

(1960), *Cleopatra* (1963), *The Fall of the Roman Empire* (1964). Then there were the myths, legends, and events of a "civilization" narrative: *Genghis Khan*, *The Vikings*, *The Adventures of Marco Polo* (1965), *El Cid*, *The Agony and the Ecstasy* (1964), *War and Peace* (1956), *55 Days at Peking*, *Khartoum* (1966), *Lawrence of Arabia*, *Exodus* (1960), and *Doctor Zhivago*. Taken together, these films reiterated and helped construct a canon of important texts, events, and legends for audiences worldwide that are sometimes international, sometimes transnational, all globe-trotting and in that way "global" cultural products. Rather than serve any one nation, these films surely engaged in a triumphant Occidentalism by creating a popularized canon of Western civilization in film. In its own moment and now later seen through the prism of our increasingly globalized film production, the cosmopolitan film cycle underscores that producers also took on the messy business of representing a hybrid culture designed to be projected on screens around the world.

The development of films as that hybrid culture cannot be reduced to the postwar developments of increased travel and tourism nor to the internationalism of organizations such as the United Nations, nor to the ideology of Occidentalism taking aim at Communism during the Cold War nor can they be thrown off as meaningless function of an expanding market or expansionist marketing. The cosmopolitan cinema that arose in the mid-1950s embraced mobility across national borders and boundaries at the level of financial investment in production, in the act of filmmaking itself, in using multinational casts, and in telling stories that foregrounded both travel and the world itself as a theme and object. The films are a cultural potpourri whose very incoherence underscores their attempt to represent cultural hybridity and transnationalism. They are the "bastard" children of an odd union of Hollywood and Paris, conceived (to continue the metaphor) in the shade of the Promenade de la Croisette in Cannes. The films and their narratives "traveled" in ways that have made them obscure as a film cycle and also obscured their important role in the development of "global" film practice.

Around the World in Eighty Days is now largely forgotten for many reasons: Todd never made another film; the film loses much of its visual power when not projected in 70mm let alone in Todd-AO. In addition, today's audiences probably cannot suspend enough disbelief to accept Shirley MacLaine as an Indian princess or the Mexican Cantínflas as a Hispanico-Gallic Passepartout. Their characters make no sense in the terms of identity and identity politics that have developed since the 1960s and they could be easily dismissed as absurd at their most benign and offensive and racist at their worst. Yet this film and the cosmopolitan cinema shed light on a cinematic imaginary of the 1950s and 1960s when film seemed like an ideal medium to help advance a brighter future in which the destructive forces of right-wing nationalism would be surpassed by an idealized and more "cosmopolitan" world. Although this may now seem like a naïve pipedream as a way of imagining relations between people the world around, it still makes business sense for the movies. What else can explain the 2004 Disney remake of *Around the World in Eighty Days* starring Jackie Chan as Passepartout?

Conclusion

WHETHER IN ITS uncanny capacity to capture the past for future generations; whether in its profound ability to shape the consciousness, experiences, and beliefs of those living in the present; whether in its vastly influential set of social practices dedicated to its consumption; whether in the enormous sums of financial and human resources dedicated to its production and distribution, film matters in the context of any history of the twentieth century. We can understand why movies matter by looking at why and how a certain set of influential films and their related institutions generated and re-generated a set of images and clichés that became a mass cultural entertainment to form a "global imaginary." While I was writing this book, two of the films discussed within its pages were re-made: *Moulin Rouge* (2001) and *Around the World in Eighty Days* (2004). Movies are, of course, frequently remade, but the new versions of these films highlight how important the French fin-de-siècle and its visual culture have been in shaping the cinematic century. At the very least, I was encouraged by the fact that I was clearly not the only one thinking about Frenchness films from the 1950s at the start of the twenty-first century.

Moulin Rouge opened the 2001 Cannes Film Festival, of course. Director Baz Luhrmann explained why he chose to make a film with a Belle Epoque Parisian setting: "I had really wanted to do an 1890's musical because I thought it would be a great way of looking at our millennial moment. The popular culture of the twentieth century basically grew out of that moment in time."[1] Luhrmann's view echoes the 1950s Frenchness films in ways that suggest that we still connect with the Parisian Belle Epoque. Luhrmann's own concept and his use of Belle Epoque "popular culture" defies national categorization and operates instead at the level of an imagined global "our." The Australian-born director locates Paris as the birthplace of a cosmopolitan popular culture.

The new *Moulin Rouge* rehearses the origins of film as did the 1950s Frenchness films. It opens with the parting of a red curtain, which exposes a flickering image of an early film, complete with an intertitle announcing Paris, 1899. Later, during the film's operatic medley of love songs between the young playwright Christian and the courtesan with whom he has fallen in love, Satine, we get a view of the face of Méliès' moon from his 1902 *Voyage dans la lune* (shown also in Todd's *Around the World*). With the wink to the sepia-toned world of 1900, the new millennium's *Moulin Rouge* underscores the connections between film and fin-de-siècle Paris. But to that connection, it adds a new set of allusions. The film abounds with references to 1950s movie musicals, refracting through yet another lens the same resonant set of Belle Epoque images. Aside from the obvious repetition of John Huston's title and Toulouse-Lautrec's prominence in the film, *Moulin Rouge* contains important visual references to other 1950s musicals as well. The initial love scene between the couple features them dancing magically in the clouds above Paris, with the Eiffel Tower poking through; Christian grabs an umbrella and dances like Gene Kelly in *Singin' in the Rain*; the lovers' dance evokes the quai by the Seine between Kelly and Leslie Caron in *An American in Paris*; Nicole Kidman's first entrance as Satine has her performing "Diamonds Are a Girl's Best Friend" from the 1953 Marilyn Monroe classic, *Gentlemen Prefer Blondes*. Made as it was in 2001, however, its musical numbers also reflected both the quick-paced editing of MTV and the frenetic fantasy of Bollywood film musicals, and received much praise for its updating of the musical genre. But the film is as much self-consciously historicist as it is newfangled. It traces a line between Paris and Hollywood and adds Indian musicals—our contemporary "signification" of a global cinematic culture.

Like *Moulin Rouge*, the remake of *Around the World in Eighty Days*, updates both the Verne story and the Todd film. In the 2004 version, Phileas Fogg becomes an inventor seeking to make a flying machine—rendering entirely explicit what is latent in the 1956 film—that air travel will shrink the globe in ways Verne had not even anticipated. The spectacular scenes are no longer travelogues but martial arts numbers featuring Jackie Chan as Passepartout, a choice that parallels Todd's casting of Cantínflas–both being famous actors from big non-Anglophone markets. The female traveling companion (and love interest for Fogg) is no longer the Indian princess rescued from the funeral pyre by the good imperialists, but rather a proto-feminist French woman who aspires to be a painter. She is prevented from achieving her goals by fin-de-siècle sexism, so she decides to travel with Fogg and Passepartout. The trio beats the clock in Fogg's homemade airplane.

Unlike the new millennium *Moulin Rouge*, the contemporaneous *Around the World* remake was a commercial failure. Unlike Luhrmann's film, it is simply a period comedy that makes no interpretation of either the Belle Epoque in which it is set or the famous Todd film that precedes it. Perhaps by choosing to remake but not refer to the other versions of the film so detached it from the set of long recognized clichés of Frenchness and modernity that it simply did not work. The Kung Fu numbers operated as random spectacle instead of working to construct a continuous cinematic culture as did the use of Indian musicals in *Moulin Rouge*.

Also in 2004, the annual movie issue of the Sunday *New York Times Magazine* devoted itself to the phenomenon of the contemporary globalization of film, although it made no mention of the *Around the World* remake.[2] It featured articles about film festivals; a short profile of Pierce Brosnan's stint as James Bond; a feature about Bollywood; a genealogy of the "foreign film" as art film; an article about DVDs; another about a Hong Kong Chinese actress fluent in English, Maggie Cheung; and an article called "What Is an American Movie Now?" whose subtitle answered, "The Blockbuster Hollywood Films the World Sees Aren't about Here   or Even Made Here—Anymore." Everything that is old is new again, though the magazine certainly reflected no awareness of the past repeating itself. While technologies for distributing films, such as DVDs and the Internet are new, the globalization of film long predates the cultural influence of Bollywood and Hong Kong, as this book has argued. The issue's title—Us and Them: What Globalization (Here and There) Has Done to Films—coyly recognizes that "globalization" is also transforming identity and ideas about space. This book has tried to address some of the contemporary issues about globalization, identity, and film by historicizing the phenomenon and reversing the terms of the question: rather than ask what "globalization has done to films" it has asked what films have done to promote globalization.

This study has interrogated and put into historical perspective three of the key assumptions about the recent globalization of culture. The first is the assumption that the Americanization and globalization of culture are the same phenomenon. Few would dispute the importance of American political, economic, and military dominance after World War II; yet this study has proposed that cultural forms have a logic and function that do not merely reflect the world, but independently help to shape it. Culture works in ways that are particular and semiautonomous in the sense that culture cannot be reduced to something else. In this way, America might have had tremendous political and economic power and Hollywood may even have benefited from that power, but Hollywood itself is no mere "instance" of American hegemony.

The second assumption has to do with the peculiarly global imaginary generated by film and filmgoing. Sean Cubbitt has recently argued that the contemporary film audience is constituted by an address to its universality. "Cinema . . . aims not for endurance but for extension: to universalize itself in space, rather than to secure itself in time."[3] Similarly, Charles Acland has suggested that there has been a recent speeding up of the "felt internationalism" of cinematic culture.[4] Although I do not dispute the notion that cinema is somehow "more global" today than it was once was, "felt" internationalism has always been part of film culture from its inception. This book identifies a moment in that history when Frenchness prominently represented and invoked internationalism. Hollywood, in particular, found a patrimony in Frenchness; this cliché of nationality had the historical complexity to offer both a fantasy of cultural specificity while being familiar enough and universalizing enough to stand in for something general in the 1950s.

The last assumption about globalization and film this book revises is the relationship between France and America. France has been seen as the archetypical government and people resisting cultural homogenization (especially when they are not the hegemonic power) and thus opposing American influence. France of late has stood as a beacon of cultural protectionism in the name of sustaining cultural diversity in the face of Americanization. It has been thought that the fact that France has the most successful and influential national film industry in Europe is owed to their unrepentant protectionism.[5] Yet this study has drawn a different portrait of the cultural exchange across two continents. It is one of strategic and enthusiastic partnering between two symbolic capitals: Paris and Hollywood, both of whom embraced a cosmopolitan approach to film and whose partnership and relations played a major role in film's subsequent and further globalization. By looking at the cultural interaction between Paris and Hollywood after the war, we have seen that a strong national identity and identification in culture can coexist with and even be fostered by an investment in cooperation with other nations.

Few would dispute the global cultural prominence of Paris in 1900. But Paris in 1900 was Paris before the physical and moral devastation of World War I; Paris before the Depression of the 1930s; Paris before Fascism in Italy and Germany; Paris before Hitler triumphantly visited the Eiffel Tower in June 1940; Paris before the Allies liberated it in August 1944; Paris before decolonization denied it the confidence of a radiant imperial capital. Yet through and despite its rocky political and economic history in the twentieth century, Paris has remained an important physical and imagined space of world cultural production, both high and low, especially when it comes to the cinema: the fin-de-siècle cultural form that helped define the twentieth century. This book suggests that Paris has been able to maintain that place without economic dominance and despite the losing strategy of cultural protectionism. The people in and around film in France used what they had: cultural capital. France had an upper hand with American culture producers who had a longstanding (and partially fantasy-based) relation to France. (Has any other culture inspired an equivalent to Gershwin's "An American in Paris" or Gene Kelly's ballet set to that music?) But the long-term association of Paris with "internationalism" and the French investment in the notion of their culture as universal and cosmopolitan helped them carve out a unique role in the promotion of film culture that reached far beyond the nation as a rubric for the production and even the consumption of film. The Cannes Film Festival contributed to the subsequent rise of film festivals, but through its sophisticated mix of press, prestige, and trade it has remained the undisputed center of international film culture and trade, extending "Paris" to a physically remote location on the Mediterranean. By creating an international showcase for films, the Cannes Film Festival helped shape the economic and cultural fortunes of filmmakers around the world, including in France and America. But Cannes was never anti-Hollywood, and Hollywood gave the festival a helping hand.

This sort of mutual aid and public display of a shared film culture also contributed to the expansion of the market for foreign-language films in America. Despite an entirely insignificant French immigrant population in America, French film witnessed a huge boost in the 1950s, reaching even beyond the niche of New York intellectuals and into middle-American drive-ins. Brigitte Bardot's "conquest of America" was at once about her films, but extended far beyond them. In no time, as a phenomenon produced by an international celebrity culture, she became famous for being famously "French," made possible through the recycling of the Belle Epoque clichés of French gaiety and open sexuality. In Bardot, the Can-Can girl's show of the leg became the naked body sun-bathing in *And God Created Woman*.

Finally, we return to the production of Mike Todd's *Around the World* as a point of convergence and reconfiguration. Once again, we see a line drawn between 1950s filmmaking and Paris, circa 1900 in both the selection of the Verne novel and the pride of place given to the 1902 Méliès movie. But *Around the World* was very much of its own time. Film historians have focused on the dichotomy between Hollywood studio productions and highbrow, mostly "European" art cinema in a way that has disconnected both *Around the World* and the cosmopolitan film cycle it helped create from the way film history has been written. That is, until recently, when cinema audiences and scholars alike began to contemplate the contemporary "globalization" of culture.

In our current phase of globalization, cultural hybridity may be commonplace in such films as *Kung Fu Hustle* and *Crouching Tiger, Hidden Dragon* but its development in film culture predates the contemporary globalization of culture. In fact, this book argues that film has served an important role in the cultivation of a global imaginary with a specific history. In that history, the 1950s can be seen as an important moment in which film culture developed a global perspective while governments were engaged in making a Cold War. Although Charles de Gaulle always thought of France as offering a middle ground in that battle, he may have been less successful in cultivating that road than in trying to protect the culture that produced Brigitte Bardot. This book has argued that France and Frenchness played an important role in contributing as much to its internationalism and globalization as to the development of nationalism and protectionism. Hollywood continues to operate as the capital of "the world republic of film" and now there are equally busy "frequencies" across the Pacific as those established earlier across the Atlantic. But the image of the Hong Kong Chinese Jackie Chan as a French valet in a film remake of a 1950s blockbuster based on Jules Verne's late nineteenth century novel suggests that Frenchness lingers on in the global cinematic imaginary in an elemental way. To "get around the world" in a cultural sense you may still have to go by way of Paris. Now, that's so French!

Notes

INTRODUCTION

1. Richard Kuisel, *Seducing the French* (Berkeley: University of California Press, 1994), and Kristin Ross, *Fast Cars, Clean Bodies: Decolonization and the Reordering of French Culture* (Cambridge: MIT Press, 1995).

2. See Philip H. Gordon and Sophie Meunier, *The French Challenge: Adapting to Globalization* (Washington, D.C.: Brookings Institute Press, 2001).

3. Harvey Levenstein, *Seductive Journeys: American Tourists in France from Jefferson to the Jazz Age* (Chicago: University of Chicago Press, 2000); Harvey Levenstein, *We'll Always Have Paris: American Tourists in France since 1930* (Chicago: University of Chicago Press, 2004). See also an excellent study by Christopher Endy, *Cold War Holidays: American Tourists in France* (Chapel Hill: University of North Carolina Press, 2004).

4. R. R. Palmer, *Age of the Democratic Revolution: A Political History of Europe and America, 1760–1800*, 2 vols. (1959, 1964; Princeton: Princeton University Press, 1969); Patrice Higonnet, *Sister Republics: The Origin of French and American Republicanism* (Cambridge: Harvard University Press, 1988); *Sister Revolution: French Lightening, American Light* (Faber and Faber: New York, 1999); Jacques Rupnik, Denis Licorne, and Marie-France Toinet, *The Rise and Fall of French Anti-Americanism*, trans. Gerry Turner (New York: St. Martin's Press, 1990), Jean-Philippe Mathy, *Extreme-Occident: French Intellectuals and America* (Chicago: University of Chicago Press, 1993) Philippe Roger, *The American Enemy: The History of French Anti-Americanism*, trans. Sharon Bowman (2002; Chicago: University of Chicago Press, 2005).

5. Richard Kuisel, *Seducing the French* and Kristin Ross, *Fast Cars, Clean Bodies. Decolonization and the Reordering of French Culture* (Cambridge: MIT Press, 1995). Citation from Ross, p. 10. Ross's book is as much about French modernization and decolonization as it is "Americanization." That said, despite her superb identification of texts one might consider as examples of "French mass culture" she ultimately distances France from the production of mass culture.

6. See Leora Auslander, *Taste and Power: Furnishing Modern France* (Berkeley: University of California Press, 1996), Lisa Tiersten, *Marianne in the Market: Envisioning Consumer Society in Fin-de-siècle France* (Berkeley: University of California Press, 2001); Marjorie Beale, *French Elites and the Threat of Modernity, 1900–1940* (Stanford: Stanford University Press, 1999), Nancy J. Troy, *Couture Culture: A Study in Modern Art and Fashion.* (Cambridge: MIT Press, 2003), Susan J. Terrio, *Crafting the Culture and History of French Chocolate* (Berkeley: University of California Press, 2000), Kolleen Guy, *When Champagne Became French: Wine and the Making of a National Identity* (Baltimore: Johns Hopkins University Press, 2003).

7. Vanessa R. Schwartz, *Spectacular Realities: Early Mass Culture in Fin-de-siècle France* (Berkeley: University of California Press, 1998). See also Charles Rearick, *Pleasures of the Belle Epoque* (New Haven: Yale University Press, 1985) and *The French in Love and War: Popular Culture in the Era of the World Wars* (New Haven: Yale University Press, 1997); Rhonda K. Garelick, *Rising Star: Dandyism, Gender, and Performance in the Fin de Siècle* (Princeton: Princeton University Press, 1998); Regina Sweeney, *Singing Our Way to Victory: French Cultural Politics and Music during World War I* (Weslyan: Weslyan University Press, 2001); Jean-Pierre Rioux et Jean-François Sirinelli, *La Culture de masse en France de la Belle Epoque à nos jours* (Paris: Fayard, 2002), Dominique Kalifa, *La culture de masse en France, 1860–1930* (Paris: Editions La Découverte, 2001), Marie-Emmanuelle Chessel, *La publicité: Naissance d'une profession. 1900–1940* (Paris: CNRS Editions, 1998), Concetta Condemi, *Les Cafés-concerts: Histoire d'un divertissement* (Paris: Quai Voltaire, 1992); Jean-Yves Mollier, *Le Camelot et la rue: Politique et démocratie au tournant des XIX et XX siècles* (Paris: Fayard, 2004), Ginnette Vincendeau, *Stars and Stardom in French Cinema* (London: Continuum, 2000).

8. Gabrielle Hecht, *The Radiance of France: Nuclear Power and National Identity after World War II* (Cambridge: MIT Press, 1998); Michael Bess, *The Light-Green Society: Ecology and Technological Modernity in France, 1960–2000* (Chicago: University of Chicago Press, 2003); Andrew Feenberg, *Alternative Modernity: The Technical Turn in Philosophy and Social Theory* (Berkeley: University of California Press, 1995); Annette Fierro, *The Glass State: The Technology of the Spectacle, Paris, 1981–1998* (Cambridge: MIT Press, 2004).

9. See especially Herman Lebovics, *Mona Lisa's Escort: André Malraux and the Reinvention of French Culture* (Ithaca: Cornell University Press, 1999); Herman Lebovics, *True France: The War Over Cultural Identity, 1940–1945* (Ithaca: Cornell University Press, 1994); and Tony Judt, *Past Imperfect: French Intellectuals, 1944–1956* (Berkeley: University of California Press, 1994).

10. Anne McCauley, *Industrial Madness: Commercial Photography in Paris, 1848–1871* (New Haven: Yale University Press, 1994); Maurice Samuels, *The Spectacular Past: Popular History and the Novel in Nineteenth-Century France* (Ithaca: Cornell University Press, 2004); Adrian Rifkin, *Street Noises: Parisian Pleasure, 1900–1940* (Manchester: Manchester University Press, 1993); Dean de la Motte and Jeannene Przyblyski, *Making the News: Modernity and the Mass Press in Nineteenth-Century France* (Amherst: University of Massachusetts Press, 1999); Jonathan Crary, *Techniques of the Observer* (Cambridge: MIT Press, 1990); and especially Jonathan Crary, *Suspensions of Perception: Attention, Spectacle and Modern Culture* (Cambridge: MIT Press, 1999); Dennis Philip Cate, Andre Mellario, Sinclair Hitchings *Color Revolution: Color Lithography in France, 1890–1900* (Layton, UT: Gibbs Smith,1978), Charles Rearick, *Pleasures of the Belle Epoque* (New Haven: Yale, 1985); Richard Thomsom, Philip Dennis Cate, and

Mary Weaver Chapin, *Toulouse-Lautrec and Montmartre* (Washington, D.C., National Gallery of Art, 2005).

11. Richard Abel, *The Red Rooster Scare: Making Cinema American, 1900–1910* (Berkeley: University of California Press, 1999).

12. John Trumpbour, *Selling Hollywood to the World: U.S. and European Struggles for Mastery of the Global Film Industry* (Cambridge: Cambridge University Press, 2002).

13. Akira Iriye, *Global Community: The Role of International Organization in the Making of the Contemporary World* (Berkeley: University of California Press, 2002), p. 62. See also Akira Friye, Cultural Internationalism and World Order (Baltimore: Johns Hopkins University Press, 1997).

14. David Held and Anthony McGrew, eds., *The Global Transformations Reader: An Introduction to the Globalization Debate,* second edition (Polity Oxford, 2000 and 2002), p. 18.

15. In fact, Italy had interesting and important films relations with both France and America during the period. Saverio Giovacchini is currently working on Italy and transnationalism.

16. What became famous was the Chartier-Darnton debate over whether Frenchness exists. The debate began around Robert Darnton's book, *The Great Cat Massacre* (New York: Basic Books, 1984). Roger Chartier criticized Darnton in "Texts, Symbols and Frenchness," *Journal of Modern History* 57, n. 4 (1985):682–95. Darnton replied to Chartier in "The Symbolic Element in History," *Journal of Modern History* 58, n. 1 (1986):218–34. See also by Dominic LaCapra, "Chartier, Darnton and the Great Symbols Massacre," *Journal of Modern History* 60 n. 1 (1988): 95–112, and James Fernandez, "Historians Tell Tales: Of Cartesian Cats and Gallic Cockfights," *Journal of Modern History* 60, n. 1 (1988): 113–27.

17. The literature on the globalization of media culture is vast. A most basic and "popular" primer on the subject is Thomas Friedman, *The Lexus and the Olive Tree* (1999; New York: Anchor Books, 2000). See also, Anthony D. King, *Culture, Globalization and the World-System* (Minneapolis: University of Minnesota Press, 1997); John Tomlison, *Globalization and Culture* (Chicago: University of Chicago Press, 1999); Arjun Appadurai, *Modernity at Large: Cultural Dimensions of Globalization* (Minneapolis: University of Minnesota Press, 1996).

18. Paul Gilroy's important book *The Black Atlantic* (Cambridge: Harvard University Press, 1993) describes the important axis of race in the modern Atlantic. Victoria de Grazia, without citing Gilroy, refers to the development of the "White Atlantic" of Europe and America but the recent histories of race in America and imperialism and postcolonialism in Europe make it impossible to conceive of either Europe or America as "white."

19. Victoria de Grazia's *Irresistible Empire: America's Advance through Twentieth-Century Europe* (Cambridge: Harvard University Press, 2005) is the most important recent study of the twentieth-century Atlantic. See also, Jean-Philippe Mathy, *Extreme-Occident: French Intellectuals and America* (Chicago: University of Chicago Press, 1993), Jacques Portes, trans. Elborg Forster, *Fascination and Misgivings: The United States in French Opinion, 1870–1914* (Cambridge: Cambridge University Press, 2000). See also important studies of Germany and America: Mary Nolan, *Visions of Modernity: American Business and the Modernization of Germany* (Oxford: Oxford University Press, 1994), Uta G. Poiger, *Jazz, Rock and Rebel: Cold War Politics and American Culture in a Divided Germany* (Berkeley: University of California Press, 2000), Heide Fehrenbach and Uta G. Poiger, eds., *Transactions, Transgressions, Transformations: American Culture in Western Europe and Japan* (New York: Berghahn Books, 2000).

20. Christopher Endy, *Cold War Holidays: American Tourism in France* (Chapel Hill: University of North Carolina Press, 2004), p. 11; Richard Kuisel, "Americanization for Historians," *Diplomatic History* 24, n. 3 (Summer 2000): 509–15.

21. See Leo Charney and Vanessa R. Schwartz, eds., *Cinema and the Invention of Modern Life* (Berkeley: University of California Press, 1995); Davis Nasaw, *Going Out: The Rise of Public Amusement* (New York: Basic Books, 1993); Lauren Rabinovitz, *For the Love of Pleasure: Women, Movies and Culture in Turn of the Century Chicago* (New Brunswick: Rutgers University Press, 1998).

22. This is, for the most part, the largest field of historicizing study. One can go as far back as Siegfried Kracaueur's important study, *From Caligari to Hitler* (Princeton: Princeton University Press, 1947). More recent works such as Thomas Elsaesser's *Weimar Cinema and After: Germany's Historical Imaginary* (Routledge: New York, 2000) to Ed Dimendberg's *Film Noir and the Spaces of Modernity* (Cambridge: Harvard University Press, 2004) move beyond films in interesting and complex ways that are much more like my own approach.

23. Just to name a few: Douglas Gomery, *Shared Pleasures: A History of Movie Presentation in the United States.* (Madison: University of Wisconsin Press, 1992); Richard Butsch, *The Making of American Audiences: From Stage to Television, 1750–1990* (Cambridge: Cambridge University Press, 2000); Haidee Wasson, *Museum Movies: The Museum of Modern Art and the Birth of Art Cinema* (Berkeley: University of California Press, 2005).

24. Pascale Casanova, *The World Republic of Letters*, trans. M. B. DeVoise (1999; Cambridge: Harvard University Press, 2004).

25. Margaret Cohen and Carolyn Dever, eds., *The Literary Channel: The Inter-National Invention of the Novel* (Princeton: Princeton University Press, 2002), pp. 12–13.

26. For an excellent description of the French investment as the center of universal culture and civilization and summary of that literature, see Herman Lebovics, *Mona Lisa's Escort: André Malraux and the Reinvention of French Culture* (Ithaca: Cornell University Press, 1999).

27. Casanova, *The World Republic of Letters*, p. 30.

28. Franco Moretti, *Atlas of the European Novel* (London: Verso Press, 1999), p. 186.

29. There are many studies of the Cold War and cultural diplomacy. See, recently, Frances Stonor Saunders, *The Cultural Cold War: The CIA and the World of Arts and Lettters* (New York: New Press, 2000) and David Caute, *The Dancer Defects: The Struggle for Cultural Supremacy during the Cold War* (Oxford: Oxford University Press, 2003).

30. For more on youth culture, see especially Uta G. Poiger, *Jazz, Rock and Rebels: Cold War Politics and American Culture in a Divided Germany* (Berkeley: University of California Press, 2000). See also two edited volumes, Reinhold Wagnleitner and Elaine Tyler May, eds., *Here, There, and Everywhere: The Foreign Politics of American Popular Culture* (Hanover: University of New England Press, 2000) and Poiger and Fehrenbach, eds., *Transactions, Transgressions, Transformations.*

31. Trumpbour, *Selling Hollywood to the World.*

32. Richard Abel, *The Red Rooster Scare: Making Cinema American, 1900–1910* (Berkeley: University of California Press, 1999); Kristin Thompson, *Exporting Entertainment: America in the World Film Market, 1907–1934* (London: BFI, 1985); Ruth Vasey, *The World According to Hollywood, 1918–1939* (Exeter: University of Exeter Press, 1997); and Andrew Higson and Richard Matby, eds., *"Film Europe" and "Film America": Cinema, Commerce and Cultural Exchange, 1920–1939* (Exeter: University of Exeter Press, 1999), p. 93.

33. De Grazia, *Irresistible Empire*, p. 335.

34. See Jens-Ulff Moeller and Bill Grantham, *Some Big Bourgeois Brothel: Contexts for France's Culture Wars with Hollywood* (Luton: University of Luton Press, 2000), p. 58–60. Note here that after Paramount's decision with the extension of independent exhibitors in the United States, they were the biggest advocates of screening foreign films in the United States. See also Paul Swann, "The Little State Department: Hollywood and the State Department in the Postwar World," *American Studies International* 29, n. 1 (April 1991): 1–19.

35. In 1957, 105 American films screened in France, 97 in 1963 out of a possible 125 and 140 allowed (Centre d'archives contemporaines, Fontainebleau [hereafter CAC]) 001995514, n. 18, CNC Report to Malraux).

36. See Christian Delage, *La Vision Nazie du Cinéma* (Lausanne: L'Age d'Homme, 1989) and Eric Rentschler, *The Ministry of Illusion: Nazi Cinema and Its Afterlife* (Cambridge, Harvard University Press, 1996).

37. Walter Wanger, "Donald Duck and Diplomacy," *Public Opinion Quarterly* (Fall 1950): 443–52.

38. For a general history of postwar America, see Lizabeth Cohen, *A Consumer's Republic: The Politics of Mass Consumption in Post-War America* (New York: Knopf: 2003); for car culture, see Peter Wollen and Joe Kerr, eds., *Autopia: Cars and Culture* (London: Reaktion Books, 2002); for film, television and visual culture, see Karal Ann Marling, *As Seen on TV: The Visual Culture of Everyday Life in the 1950s* (Cambridge: Harvard University Press, 1988), Lynn Spigel, *Make Room for TV: Television and the Family Ideal in Postwar America* (Chicago: University of Chicago Press, 1992) and especially Jon Belton, *Widescreen* (New York: Columbia University Press, 1992).

39. Colin Crisp, *The Classic French Cinema, 1930–1960* (Bloomington: Indiana University Press, 1997); Heide Fehrenbach, *Cinema in Democratizing Germany: Reconstructing National Identity After Hitler* (Chapel Hill: University of North Carolina Press, 1995); Gian Piero Brunetta, *Storia del cinema italiano dal 1945 agli anni ottanta* (Roma: Editori Riuniti, 1982); Melvyn Stokes and Richard Maltby, *Hollywood Abroad: Audience and Cultural Exchange* (CB, FI: London, 2004); and Geoffrey Nowell-Smith and Steven Ricci, eds., *Hollywood and Europe: Economics, Culture and National Identity, 1945–1995* (London: BFI, 1998), which is an important volume for the present work as the editors take the transatlantic exchange as a given.

40. In a 1960 report prepared in the wake of the coming of the Common Market in Europe, France derived 31.2 percent of its profits from export within Europe as compared with Germany at 15.18 percent and Italy at 15.22 percent. Yet, at the same time, French films had 68.8 percent of its own market compared to Germany at 84.82 precent and Italy at 84.78 percent. In short, while French film held a strong position within Europe it also was more open within France to foreign film.

CHAPTER ONE

1. Rick Altman, *The American Film Musical* (Bloomington: Indiana University Press, 1987).

2. Gaylyn Studlar, "'Chi-Chi Cinderella': Audrey Hepburn as Couture Countermodel," in David Desser and Garth S. Jowett, eds., *Hollywood Goes Shopping* (Minneapolis: University of Minnesota Press, 2000), 159–78; Dina M. Smith, "Global Cinderella: *Sabrina* (1954), Hollywood and Postwar Internationalism," *Cinema Journal* 42, n. 4 (Summer 2002): 27–50; and Pierre Verdaguer, "Hollywood's Frenchness: Representations of the French in American Films," *Contemporary French and Francophone Studies* 8, n. 4 (2004): 441–51.

3. *Time*, May 19, 1958.

4. Irwin Wall, *The United States and the Making of Postwar France, 1945–1954* (New York: Cambridge University Press, 1991), Serge Guilbault, *How New York Stole the Idea of Modern Art* (Chicago: University of Chicago Press, 1983).

5. Jon Belton, *Widescreen Cinema* (Cambridge: Harvard University Press, 1992).

6. William Keylor, "'How They Advertised France': The French Propaganda Campaign in the United States During the Break-up of the French-American Entente, 1918–1923," *Diplomatic History* 17, n. 3 (Summer 1993): 351–73.

7. T. R. Ybarra as cited in Harvey Levenstein, *Seductive Journey: American Tourists in France from Jefferson to the Jazz Age* (Chicago: University of Chicago Press, 1998), p. 275.

8. Foster Rhea Dulles, *Americans Abroad: Two Centuries of American Travel* (Ann Arbor: University of Michigan Press, 1964); Shelly Baranowski and Ellen Furlough, eds., *Being Elsewhere: Tourism, Consumer Culture, and Identity in Modern Europe and North America* (Ann Arbor: University of Michigan Press, 2001); Christopher Endy, *Cold War Holidays* (Chapel Hill: University of North Carolina Press, 2004).

9. CAC 760009, CNC 1387. Letter to CNC from Ed De Segonzac, February 21, 1956.

10. *Hollywood Reporter*, August 28, 1951.

11. USC Special Collections, MGM Collection, Freed Collection, *Gigi* Pressbook.

12. CAC 76009, CNC 1387, "Bon Voyage."

13. CAC 76009, CNC 1461. List of films from between 1947 and 1963.

14. Peter Brunette, *Roberto Rossellini* (New York: Oxford University Press, 1987); David Forgacs and Sarah Lutton, eds., *Roberto Rossellini: Magician of the Real* (London: BFI, 2000); Sidney Gottlieb, ed., *Roberto Rossellini: Rome Open City* (New York: Cambridge University Press, 2004).

15. Hugh Fordin, *MGM's Greatest Musicals: The Arthur Freed Unit* (1975; New York: Da Capo Press, 1996), p. 98.

16. The Hollywood studios took the task of re-creation very seriously. The best-known example of this is the photos produced by the Séeberger brothers of Paris for the International Kinema Research firm who in turn sold them to the studios. See Dudley Andrew and Steven Ungar, *Popular Front Paris and the Poetics of Culture* (Cambridge: Belknap Press, 2005), esp. pp. 249–52.

17. USC Special Collections, Freed Collection, *Gigi* production note.

18. Fordin, *MGM's Greatest Musicals*, p. 482.

19. Ibid., p. 495.

20. Bibliothèque du Film (hereafter BIFI), Institut des Hautes Etudes Cinématographiques (IDHEC) Files, *Funny Face* coupures de presse.

21. CAC 760009, CNC 1387, Production List, *Funny Face* submitted to CNC.

22. Jon Belton, *Widescreen* (Cambridge: Harvard University Press, 1992), and chapter 4 of this book.

23. The Champs-Elysées were well known to Americans, especially since Eisenhower's office as head of Allied forces in Europe was there.

24. Vanessa Schwartz, "The Eiffel Tower," *Urban Icons: Multi-media Companion to Urban History* 33, n. 1 (May 2006): http://journals.cambridge.org/urbanicons.

25. For more on film's respectability in the United States after the silent era, see Haidee Wasson, *Museum Movies: The Museum of Modern Art and the Birth of Art Cinema* (Berkeley:

University of California Press, 2005), and Peter Decherney, *Hollywood and the Culture Elite: How the Movies Became American* (New York: Columbia University Press, 2005).

26. See Richard Thomson, Philip Dennis Cate, and Mary Weaver Chapin, *Toulouse-Lautrec and Montmartre* (Washington, D.C.: National Gallery of Art with Princeton University Press, 2005) and especially, Mary Weaver Chapin, "Henri de Toulouse-Lautrec and the Café-Concert: Print-Making, Publicity, and Celebrity in Fin-de-Siècle Paris" (Ph.D. dissertation, Art History, New York University, 2002)

27. Vanessa R. Schwartz, *Spectacular Realities: Early Mass Culture in Fin-de-siècle Paris* (Berkeley: University of California Press, 1998).

28. Ministère des Affaires étrangères (hereafter MAE, Quai d'Orsay), Relations Culturelles, Echanges Culturels, 126. Raoul Bertrand, Consul General, LA to minister of foreign affairs, October 27, 1953.

29. James Naremore, *The Films of Vincente Minnelli* (Cambridge: Cambridge University Press, 1993) p. 139.

30. *An American in Paris*: eight nominations, six awards, *Lili*: six nominations, one award; *Moulin Rouge*: seven nominations, two awards; *Gigi*: nine nominations (the most of its time), and won them all.

31. Simon Harcourt-Smith, "Vincente Minnelli," *Sight and Sound* 21, n. 3 (March 1952): 115–119, 116.

32. Herrick Library, Vincente Minnelli Collection, preview report, January 20, 1958.

33. Herrick Library, Vincente Minnelli Collection, *Motion Picture Daily*, April 10, 1959.

34. MAE, Quai d'Orsay, Relations Culturelles, Echanges Culturels 126, Raoul Bertrand, Consul General LA to minister of foreign affairs, October 27, 1953

35. Charles Bitsch and Jean Domachi, "Entretien avec Vincente Minnelli," *Les Cahiers du cinéma*, n. 74 (août–septembre 1957): 4–18.

36. Annie Cohen-Solal, *"Un Jour, ils auront des peintres." L'avènement des peintres américains. Paris 1867–New York 1948* (Paris: Gallimard, 2000), p. 185.

37. Hans Huth, "Impressionism Comes to America," *Gazette des Beaux Arts* 29, series 6 (April 1946): 225–52 and Alice Cooney Frelinghuysen, *Splendid Legacy: The Havemeyer Collection* (New York: The Metropolitan Musuem, 1993), p. 8.

38. See Frelinghuysen et al., *Splendid Legacy*; and *La Collection Havemeyer. Quand l'Amérique découvrait l'Impressionisme* (Paris: Réunion des Musées Nationaux, 1997).

39. Cohen-Solal, *"Un Jour, ils auront des peintres,"* p. 311.

40. Neil Harris, *Cultural Excursions: Marketing Appetites and Cultural Tastes in Modern America* (Chicago: University of Chicago Press, 1990).

41. Leo Charney and Vanessa R. Schwartz, eds., *Cinema and the Invention of Modern Life* (Berkeley: University of California Press, 1995); Jonathan Crary, *Suspensions of Perception: Attention, Spectacle, and Modern Culture* (Cambridge: MIT Press, 1999), and many of Tom Gunning's essays. See especially "The Cinema of Attractions: Early Film, Its Spectator, and the Avant-Garde" in Thomas Elsaesser, ed., *Early Cinema: Space, Frame, Narrative* (London: BFI, 1990).

42. Robert L. Herbert, *Impressionism: Art, Leisure and Parisian Society* (New Haven: Yale University Press, 1988). T. J. Clark's *The Painting of Modern Life* (Princeton: Princeton University Press, 1985), which emphasizes the connection between the production and reception of the Impressionists more than Herbert and finds more anxiety, social displacement, and anomie in the paintings.

43. MAE, Quai d'Orsay, Relations Culturelles. Echanges Culturels 126. Memo from Raoul Bertrand, Consul General, LA to MAE, October 27, 1953.

44. In fact, the collecting habits of Hollywood actors and producers is an interesting topic. Kirk Douglas owned several Van Gogh paintings, and Edward G. Robinson had a significant collection. See Edward G. Robinson, with Leonard Spigelgass, *All My Yesterdays: An Autobiography* (New York: Hawthorn Books, 1973).

45. Philip Dennis Cate and Sinclair Hamilton Hitchings, *The Color Revolution: Color Lithography in France, 1890–1900* (Santa Barbara: Peregrine Smith, 1978).

46. Fordin, *MGM's Greatest Musicals*, p. 463.

47. Leo Charney and Vanessa R. Schwartz, eds., *Cinema and the Invention of Modern Life* (Berkeley: University of California Press, 1995).

48. For more on film and art, see Angela Dalle Vacche, *Cinema and Painting: How Art is Used in Film* (Austin: University of Texas Press, 1996); Dalle Vacche, "A Painter in Hollywood: Vincente Minnelli's An American in Paris," *Cinema Journal* 32, n. 1 (Fall 1992): 63–83.

49. A. L. Hine, "Paris in the '90's," *Holiday*, April 1953.

50. In all the materials about Kelly, I cannot find his making a direct mention of *The Red Shoes*, but I find it hard to believe it played no role. In the early 1940s members of the Ballet Russes made a few films in Hollywood that remain unstudied, although they are mentioned and excerpted in the documentary, *Ballet Russes* (directed by Dan Oeller and Dayna Goldfine, 2005).

51. Michael Powell, *A Life in the Movies* (New York: Knopf, 1986), p. 661.

52. Fordin, *MGM's Greatest Musicals*, p. 321.

53. Herrick Library, *American in Paris* file. Ballet script, September 6, 1950.

54. Vincente Minnelli, with Hector Arce, *I Remember It Well* (Garden City: Doubleday, 1974), p. 230.

55. *Variety*, August 29, 1951.

56. *Time*, October 8, 1951.

57. *Libération*, May 8, 1952.

58. Donald Knox, *The Magic Factory: How MGM Made An American in Paris* (New York: Praeger, 1973), Minnelli quoted on pp. 133–34.

59. Donald Knox, *The Magic Factory*, Minnelli quoted, p. 125.

60. Herrick Library, *American in Paris* file. Ballet script, September 6, 1950, p. 2

61. John Alton, *Painting with Light*, introduction by Todd McCarthy (Berkeley: University of California Press, 1995), pp. xxiv–xxvi; and Donald Knox, *The Magic Factory*.

62. *Variety*, August 29, 1951.

63. *Time*, October 8, 1951.

64. William Pfaff, review of *An American in Paris* in *Commonweal*, October 19, 1951.

65. *Time*, May 19, 1958, p. 100–101.

66. Stanley Kauffman, *New Republic*, June 9, 1958.

67. Robert Kass, *Catholic World*, March 1953, p. 459–60.

68. *Newsweek*, February 23, 1953, p. 46–48.

69. *New York Times*, February 11, 1953.

70. Philip Hartung, review of Funny Face, *Commonweal*, April 5, 1957.

71. See Todd Haynes's *Far from Heaven* (2002) which is a tribute to 1950s Douglas Sirk melo-

dramas, for a recent association of the 1950s with this aesthetic. For an important analysis of color, see Laura Kalba, "Outside the Lines: The Production and Consumption of Color in Nineteenth-Century France," dissertation in progress, Department of History, USC.

72. Herrick Library, Oral History of Lela Simone, Rudy Behlmer, interviewer, p. 144.

73. Jean Domarchi and Jean Douchet, "Rencontre avec Vincente Minnelli," *Les Cahiers du cinéma*, n. 128 (February 1962): 3–13.

74. Charles Bitsch and Jean Domarchi, "Entretien avec Vincente Minnelli," *Les Cahiers du cinéma*, p. 13.

75. Others who have studied émigré directors in America have raised the issue of the relation between a director's nationality and the place they worked. See Thomas Saunders, *Hollywood in Berlin: American Cinema and Weimar Germany* (Berkeley: University of California Press, 1994), and Janet Bergstrom, "Jean Renoir's Return to France" in Susan Rubin Suleiman, ed., *Exile and Creativity: Signposts, Travelers, Outsiders and Backward Glances*, 180–219 (Durham: Duke University Press, 1998).

76. *L'Aurore*, September 1, 1953.

77. Special Collections, USC Library, Freed Archive, cable from Robert Vogel to Arthur Freed, August 4, 1952.

78. *Le Film Français*, December 24, 1958.

79. Special Collections, USC Library, Freed Archive, letter from E. Lapinière to Peggy O'Day, December 24, 1958.

80. Jean d'Yvoire, *Radio-ciné*, August 10, 1952.

81. Les *Lettres françaises*, December 24, 1954.

82. *Libération*, August 5, 1952.

83. *Le Figaro littéraire*, February 21, 1959, *La Croix*, February 27, 1959; *Le Combat*, March 7, 1959.

84. Eric Rohmer, *Arts*, November 20–26, 1957.

85. Jacques Doniol-Valcroze, *France-observateur*, November 28, 1957.

86. Jacques Siclier, *Radio-Ciné-Télé*, March 1, 1959.

87. *La Croix* (date hard to read), January 1, 1954.

88. *Comoedia*, December 15–22, 1953.

89. Eric Rohmer, *Arts*, November 20–26, 1957.

90. Initially, Renoir was not so eager to leave France, contrary to the received knowledge on the subject. See chapter 2.

91. Raymond Durgnat, *Jean Renoir* (Berkeley: University of California Press, 1974).

92. *New York Times*, April 17, 1956.

93. It should be noted that Renoir came late to the film project and that its conceptualization and script by André Antoine had been written for Yves Allégret to direct before Renoir was brought into the project.

94. *Libération*, May 6, 1955.

95. *L'Aurore*, May 2, 1955.

96. Jean Renoir, *Ecrits, 1926–1971* (Paris: Editions Belfond, 1974), p. 276.

97. Harvey Levenstein, *We'll Always Have Paris* (Chicago: University of Chicago Press, 2004) underscores that the plots of many of the Frenchness films include romance and sex (160–62).

CHAPTER TWO

1. MAE, Quai d'Orsay, Relations Culturelles, Cinéma, 6–8, n. 7, Brochure (1945–47).

2. There are no scholarly treatments of the history of film festivals in general. See Kenneth Turan, *From Sundance to Sarajevo: Film Festivals and the World They Made* (Berkeley: University of California Press, 2002) for a chatty memoir. On Cannes, see a fine overview, Cari Beauchamp and Henri Béhar, *Hollywood on the Riviera: The Inside Story of the Cannes Film Festival* (New York: William Morrow, 1992). After completing the research and writing of this chapter, Loredana Latil's book, *Le Festival de Cannes sur la scène internationale* (Paris: Nouveau Monde Editions, 2005) was published. She unfortunately, did not have access to the festival archives at the BIFI, which are cited extensively below, and which would have provided her with a much better view of the festival as an institution. An even more recent doctoral dissertation completed after this book and written without access to the Cannes Archives is Marijke de Walk, *Film Festival History and Theory of a European Phenomenon that Became a Global Network* (University of Amsterdam, 2006).

3. See Brian Mackenzie, *Remaking France: Americanization, Public Diplomacy and the Marshall Plan* (New York: Berghahn Books, 2005), Richard Kuisel, *Seducing the French* (Berkeley: University of California Press, 1993).

4. See Jens Ulf-Moeller, *Hollywood's Film Wars with France: Film Trade Diplomacy and the Emergence of the French Film Quota Policy* (Rochester: University of Rochester Press, 2001); John Trumpbour, *Selling Hollywood to the World: U.S. and European Struggles for Mastery of the Global Film Industry, 1920-1950* (Cambridge: Cambridge University Press, 2002); and Jacques Portes, "A l'origine de la légende noire des accords Blum-Byrnes sur le cinéma," *Revue d'histoire moderne et contemporaine* 33 (avril–juin 1986): 314–29.

5. Toby Miller, ed., *Global Hollywood* (London: BFI, 2001).

6. Bibliothèque du Film, Archives du Festival International du Film, box 856 (1939). Hereafter, BIFI FIF.

7. BIFI, IDHEC, FES 235. Note by Georges Huisman, 1957.

8. Ministère des Affaires Etrangères, Nantes. Archives des Echanges Artistiques, n. 930, Brochure, 1939, Festival International de Film. Hereafter MAE, Nantes, ADEA.

9. Archives Municipales de Cannes, 2R65, July 30, 1939.

10. Maurice Bessy, *Cinémonde*, August 30, 1939.

11. MAE, Nantes, ADEA, n. 933, mars 1964. Opening text for twenty-fifth anniversary.

12. MAE, Nantes, ADEA, n. 930. Letter from Georges Husiman to Jean Zay, November 10, 1939.

13. Archives Municipales de Cannes, 2R66. Letter from Philippe Erlanger to Pierre Nouveau, December 6, 1939.

14. Archives Municipales de Cannes, 2R66. Letter from Pierre Nouveau to Philippe Erlanger, December 9, 1939.

15. Archives Municipales de Cannes, 2R66. Letter from Georges Prade to Pierre Nouveau, January 17, 1940.

16. Marc Bloch, *Strange Defeat* (New York: Norton, 1968).

17. See Colin Crisp, *The Classic French Cinema, 1930-1960* (Bloomington, Indiana, 1993); Jean-Pierre Jeancolas, *Le Cinéma des français: 15 ans des années trentes, 1929-1944.* (Paris: Stock,

1983); and Jean-Pierre Bertin-Maghit, *Le cinéma français sous Vichy: Les films français de 1940 à 1944* (Paris: Revue du Cinéma/Albatros, 1980).

18. BIFI, FIF 857. Letter from the Action Artistiques to the Secrétaire d'Etat à l'Education Nationale et la Jeunesse, October 16, 1941.

19. BIFI FIF 857. In a note dated November 10, 1941, the comte, upon a return from Vichy, advocated for a spring 1942 event that would not be a "festival" but an "exposition international du Film" that needed to look independently instead of governmentally organized.

20. MAE, Nantes, ADEA, n. 105. Erlanger was descended from both the Comte de Camando and the Rothschilds, prominent Jewish families. Note on the reintegration of Philippe Erlanger, Conseil d'Administration of the Association Francaise d'Action Artistique, December 6, 1944. During the war, Erlanger's secretary general held his position of director general. What happened to Erlanger during the war is still unclear, although his apartment was pillaged and occupied according to the document of reintegration. In 1946, by virtue of an agreement between the Ministry of Foreign Affairs (MAE) and the Ministry of Education, the AFAA became known as the Service des Echanges Artistiques under the auspices of the Directeur Générale des Affaires Culturelles of the MAE.

21. MAE, Quai d'Orsay, Relations Culturelles, 1945–47, 0.7.1 Cinéma, December 18, 1944. Note attached to report from O. Baueur concerning "une cité cinématographique Hollywood Européan."

22. MAE, Quai d'Orsay, Relations Culturelles, 1945–47, 0.7.1 Cinéma. Letter from Henry Gendre to Pierre Souchon, April 18, 1945.

23. MAE, Quai d'Orsay, Relations Culturelles, 1945–47, 0.7.1 Cinéma. Note from the director general of cultural relations, MAE to the director of Europe, MAE, June 25, 1945, which says as much. M. Robert Bichet, Le Festival international de film. Conférence de Presse, October 18, 1946.

24. The participants were France, the United States, the Soviet Union, Sweden, Norway, Denmark, Finland, Egypt, Belgium, Holland, Argentina, Mexico, Switzerland, Greece, Canada, Turkey, China, Chili, Portugal, and Australia.

25. BIFI, FIF 857. Press release, 1945.

26. The Blum-Byrnes Accords have been the persistent fixation of French-American film historiography in postwar Europe. Essentially, the agreement prevented the imposition of any limits on American films imported into France although they did guarantee the French 30 percent screen time. See Colin Crisp, *The Classic French Cinema* (London: I. B. Tauris, 1993).

27. BIFI, IDHEC Fes 180, *France Illustration*, September 21, 1946.

28. Léon Moussinac, "Une ère nouvelle commence," *L'écran français*, September 18, 1946.

29. Emmanuel Ethis, *Aux marches du palais. Le festival sous le regard des sciences sociales* (Paris: La Documentation Française, 2001), p. 237.

30. For the earlier period, see Miriam Hansen, *Babel and Babylon: Spectactorship in American Silent Film* (Cambridge: Harvard University Press, 1991).

31. René Jeanne and Charles Ford, "Grandeur et décadence du 7e art," *Mercure de France* (August 1960): 675; article found in MAE, Nantes, ADEA, n. 930.

32. BIFI, FIF 857, various documents.

33. BIFI, FIF 910, "Note sur le 6e festival," no date.

34. Archives Municipales de Cannes, 93 w 18, 1956. "Reflexions du IXème Festival International du Film."

35. *Variety*, September 17, 1947, p. 4 and 18.

36. National Archives, College Park, NARA, RG 84, November. 16, 1951. Foreign Service Dispatch 1328. American Embassy in Paris.

37. Conseil d'Administration (hereafter CA), FIF, October 14, 1952, in CAC 960010128 (CNC 1689).

38. BIFI, FIF 910. Rapport 1953.

39. *Variety*, May 9, 1956.

40. *Variety*, May 22, 1957.

41. Toni Howard, "Whindig of the Movie Queens," *Saturday Evening Post*, May 18, 1956.

42. BIFI, FIF 963, CA FIF, July 1, 1959.

43. BIFI, FIF 856. Press release, c. 1939.

44. MAE, Nantes, ADEA, n. 930, FIF CA, July 1, 1959, "Notes sur le festival."

45. MAE, Nantes, ADEA, n. 930, February 24, 1959.

46. BIFI, FIF 879, October 6, 1949.

47. Herrick Library, Cannes Files. Report of the Executive Secretary, Motion Pictures Academy of Arts and Sciences, 1952.

48. Archives Municipales de Cannes, 93 W 18 1956, March 22, 1956.

49. Brian Mackenzie, *Remaking France: Americanization, Public Diplomacy and the Marshall Plan* (New York: Berghahn Books, 2005).

50. Cari Beauchamp and Henri Béhar, *Hollywood on the Riviera: The Inside Story of the Cannes Film Festival* (New York: William Morrow, 1992). In fact, Cannes and Beverly Hills became sister cities in 1986.

51. Kevin Starr, *Americans and the California Dream, 1850–1915* (New York: Oxford University Press, 1973).

52. BIFI, FIF 857, 1946.

53. CAC 760010/28; CNC 1689, FIF, CA, June 11, 1953.

54. *UniFrance infos*, n. 9, April 1951, p. 13.

55. Kenneth Silver, *Making Paradise: Art, Modernity and the Myth of the French Riviera* (Cambridge, MIT Press, 2001).

56. During the earliest part of the war, director Jean Renoir promoted the formation of a studio in the unoccupied zone in Valbonne, only miles from Cannes. A photocopy of a letter oddly placed among the festival's archives (FIF Box 857) from Renoir to Georges Prade dated October 8, 1940, makes clear that months after the formation of the Pétain government, Renoir was busy planning the future of French cinema rather than planning his departure from France. The future of French cinema, he argued, would distinguish itself from American cinema by shooting real exteriors in the new studios they were to set up in Valbonne. Even more provocative than his clear articulation of how a French cinema would differ from its American competition is his advocacy of establishing what would be the better business practices of the studios in the south of France: "What a terrific opportunity to finally eliminate all the scheming of the movie business (black marketeering in stars, technicians and extras, production loans, advances) and the idiocies that have infected French cinema). All the trashiness is linked to the fact that we filmed in Paris; at Valbonne, we'll have longer days, we'll gain time and we'll also gain moral and physi-

cal health." Renoir's criticism of the film business here seems reformist enough even if the language of moral and physical reform oddly echoes some of what would be Pétain's proto-Fascist talk of a healthier nation. But it is later in his letter that the great leftist champion shows his own stripes in what at the time would not have even seemed like a veiled anti-Semitic remark: "We are very ambitious and we know it. We also know that in Paris our ideas of purity and grandeur are quickly beaten down to the benefit of the hustlers of Fouquets and other places who are possibly less numerous (now) but whom I can't believe have disappeared entirely." Basically, with the corrupt Jews gone, people like Renoir would revitalize the French film industry.

57. This is noted in Silver, *Making Paradise*, pp. 86–100.

58. Alexandre Astruc cited in Claude-Jean Philippe, *Cannes, le festival* (Paris: Nathan Sipa, 1987).

59. Pierre Meunier, May 12, 1952; *Agence France Presse* in Arsenal, 4 SW 12776, p. 23–24.

60. BIFI, FIF 899. Article by Yves Bridault in *Arts*, 24 avril, 1952.

61. The television coverage, which displays many of the photographers, shows that the press was in black tie as well.

62. See Daniel Boorstin, *The Image: A Guide to Pseudo-events in America* (1961; New York: Vintage Books, 1992).

63. The story of May 1968 at Cannes is an interesting one. The young New Wave directors fought the festival administration to shut down in sympathy with events in Paris. The festival administration and many film critics were violently opposed to this on the grounds that the festival was an international event and to shut down meant being provincial. Violent disruption of a screening led the leadership to change its mind. The festival was halted after only a few days and reorganized the next year in the wake of the renovations of culture more generally in 1968. See various files, BIFI, FIF, P 112–239, 1968. See also Sylvia Harvey, *May 68 and Film Culture* (London: BFI, 1981).

64. BIFI, FIF 1033, 1966. Letter from Favre Le Bret to Françoise Giroud, May 19, 1966.

65. BIFI, CA, FIF 1033, 1966.

66. BIFI, FIF, 1033, 1966

67. These numbers are pieced together from a variety of sources within the festival archives. To underscore the relative significance of press coverage at Cannes, Venice in 1961 had 229 journalists in attendance. Nathaniel Golden report of La Mostra, Aug. 30–Sept. 3, 1961 in BIFI, FIF 991.

68. Tribute from François Chalais to Louisette Fargette, May 16, 1992, documents courtesy of Louisette Fargette, interviewed July 15, 2003, Paris.

69. Herrick Library, Cocteau as cited in BFI "Newsletter," June 1953, n. 223, v. 20.

70. This ritual suggests the title for a recent sociological study of the festival: *Aux marches du palais: Le Festival de Cannes sous le regard des sciences sociales*, under the direction of Emmanuel Ethis (Paris: La Documentation Française, 2001). There is an essay on the staircase ceremony in the volume by Pascal Lardellier that explores the ritual but does not sufficiently account for the role photographers played in the design of the Palais.

71. MAE, Nantes, ADEA, n. 933. "Rapport Moral du XVII festival" (1964).

72. BIFI, FIF 972. Nathaniel Golden, report on the Cannes Film Festival, 1959.

73. For a short history, see Pierre-Jean Amar, *Le Photojournalisme* (Paris: Nathan Université, 2000).

74. Toni Howard, "Whindig of the Movie Queens."

75. Ibid.

76. BIFI, FIF, CA, January 31, 1953, and also CAC 760010/28.

77. BIFI, FIF 952, CA, January 24, 1958.

78. BIFI, FIF 941, January 31, 1957. Favre to J. L. Jeauffre (controleur d'état).

79. BIFI, FIF 943, Frances Knecht, "Real Festival on Cannes Staircase," *Globe and Mail*, May 16, 1957.

80. Richard Dyer, *Stars* (London: BFI, 1979).

81. See the recent English translations: *The Cinema or Imaginary Man*, trans. Lorraine Mortimer and *The Stars*, trans. Richard Howard, foreword by Lorraine Mortimer (Minneapolis: University of Minnesota Press, 2005).

82. Edgar Morin, "Notes pour une sociologie du festival de Cannes," *Les temps modernes* (June–July 1955): 2273–84; p. 2273.

83. Ibid., p. 2274.

84. Ibid.

85. The most significant analyses before Morin were the much more negative interpretations by Horkheimer and Adorno and Leo Lowenthal in the 1940s. See Max Horkheimer and Theodor Adorno, "The Culture Industry: Enlightenment as Mass Deception," *The Dialectic of Enlightenment* (New York: Continuum, 1972), 123–71; and Leo Lowenthal, "The Triumph of Mass Idols," *Literature, Popular Culture and Society* (1944; Palo Alto: Pacific, 1961), 109–40. For excellent histories of celebrity, see Leo Braudy, *The Frenzy of Renown: Fame and Its History* (New York: Oxford University Press, 1986); Joshua Gamson, *Claims to Fame: Celebrity in Contemporary America* (Berkeley: University of California Press, 1994); and P. David Marshall, *Celebrity and Power: Fame in Contemporary Culture* (Minneapolis: University of Minnesota Press, 1997). For histories of film stardom, see especially, Richard Dyer, *Stars* (London: BFI, 1979), and Richard de Cordova, *Picture Personalities: The Emergence of the Star System in America* (Champagne: University of Illinois Press, 1981).

86. BIFI, FIF 967. Letter from Rupert Allan to Robert Favre Le Bret, April 3, 1959.

87. *Le Figaro littéraire*, April 25, 1953.

88. *UniFrance Film infos*, October 1952, n. 20, p. 22

89. François Truffaut, *Arts* 619 (15–21 mai 1957).

90. BIFI, FIF 954. Letter to Raoul Lévy from Favre Le Bret, April 8, 1958.

91. Emmanuelle Decaix and Bruno Viller, "Interview of Maurice Bessy," *Cinématographe*, n. 58 (1980): 4–8.

92. See André Bazin, "The Entomology of the Pin-Up," in *What Is Cinema?* ed. and trans. Hugh Gray (Berkeley: University of California Press, 1971).

93. *Variety*, May 13, 1959.

94. Toni Howard, "Whindig of the Movie Queens."

95. *Life* 52, June 15, 1962.

96. They also offer another look at French film culture that is different from the cinephilic discourse of the *Cahiers du cinéma*. The shows are not accessible in their entire run and if made available would afford an excellent set of documents to study. I would like to thank Christine Barbier-Bouvet of the Inathèque for helping me gain access to the Chalais materials.

97. BIFI, FIF 1040, CA, June 13, 1967.

98. BIFI, FIF 919, May 10, 1955.

99. See Elihu Katz and Daniel Dayan, *Media Events: The Live Broadcasting of History* (Cambridge: Harvard University Press, 1992).

100. *Reflets de Cannes*, interview with Sophia Loren, s.d., from *C comme cinéma, Cannes, Chalais* (1997) documentary produced by Mei Chen Chalais and Rémy Grumbach, Inathèque.

101. *Reflets de Cannes*, interview with Brigitte Bardot, s.d. (probably 1955) from *C comme cinéma, Cannes, Chalais*

102. Interview with Signoret, *Reflets de Cannes*, May 2, 1959; interview with Fonda, 1963, from *C comme cinéma, Cannes, Chalais*.

103. BIFI, FIF 855, Sept. 17, 1939.

104. See Jacques Portes, "Les origines de la légende noire des accords Blum-Byrnes sur le cinéma," *Revue d'histoire moderne et contemporaine* 33 (April–June 1986): 314–29, and Jens-Ulff Moeller. *Hollywood's Film Wars with France.*

105. BIFI, FIF 914. Letter from Abel Green to Favre Le Bret, March 2, 1954.

106. BIFI, FIF 863. Message from Eric Johnson to the Festival, 1946.

107. NARA, RG 59 511.51/5–1551; Letter from Viola Ilma to Dwight Eisenhower, April 27, 1951.

108. Herrick Library, Cannes Files, 1952, "Report of the Academy Executive Secretary."

109. FIF 926, March 25, 1955.

110. FIF 945, April 18, 1957.

111. BIFI, FIF 914. Letter from Favre Le Bret to Madame Georges Bidault, MAE, November 18, 1953.

112. BIFI, FIF, 919, Notes sur le 5ème festival (1955).

113. Hughes owned RKO until 1955 when he sold it to Desilu. I do not know if Favre Le Bret visited him after the sale of the studio.

114. See, for example, BIFI, FIF 906, 1953. List of contacts and visit for Favre Le Bret's trip to the United States.

115. BIFI, FIF 945. Letter from Allan to Favre Le Bret, March 25, 1957.

116. BIFI, FIF 978. March 18, 1960.

117. BIFI, FIF 936. Letter from Rupert Allan to Robert Favre Le Bret, March 11, 1956.

118. BIFI, FIF 1040, CA, March 23, 1967.

119. Claude-Jean Philippe, *Cannes : Le festival* (Paris: Editions Nathan, SIPA, 1987), p. 46.

120. CAC 760010/40. Extrait du *Film Français*, "Rendements de 1ère exclusivité à Paris des grands prix des 10 derniers festivals de Cannes," s.d. Also in MAE, Nantes, ADEA, n. 930.

121. Brian Mackenzie, *Remaking France.*

122. BIFI, FIF 1024, CA, March 25, 1965.

123. MAE, Nantes, ADEA, n. 930. "Note sur le festival" to Malraux's cabinet, February 24, 1959.

124. MAE, Nantes, ADEA, n. 930.

125. BIFI, FIF 881. Simone Dubreuilh in *Libération*, August 9, 1951.

126. BIFI, IDHEC, Fes. 180. Georges Sadoul in *Les Lettres françaises*, September 15, 1949.

127. Bazin cited in *Cannes: 45 Years: Festival International du Film* (New York: Universal MOMA, 1992), p. 9.

128. BIFI, IDHEC, Fes. n. 238. Roger Vadim, "Cannes peut sauver le cinéma," *Arts* (May 14–20, 1960).

129. BIFI, FIF 894. Letter from Favre Le Bret to John McCarthy, March 14, 1952.

130. BIFI, FIF 1033. February 8, 1966.

131. BIFI, FIF 1032. July 13, 1966.

132. BIFI, FIF 869. July 1948.

133. Herrick Library, Cannes File. Report from the Executive Secretary AMPAAS, 1952.

134. FIF, CA, June 11, 1953 in CAC 960010128 (CNC 1689); *Nice-Matin* (April 17, 1956); MAE, Nantes, ADEA, n. 930, 1958, "Note sur l'administration du festival."

135. *Newsweek*, May 30, 1966, 84–85.

136. On Miramax, see Peter Biskind, *Down and Dirty Pictures: Miramax, Sundance, and the Rise of Independent Film* (New York: Simon and Schuster, 2004), p. 78. On Lévy, see Jean-Dominique Barby, *Raoul Lévy: Un aventurier du cinéma* (Paris: Jean-Clause de Lattès, 1995). For Carlo Ponti and other Italians, see Moritz de Hdealn and Stefano Della Casa, *Capitani coraggiosi: Produttori italiani* (Milan: Electa, 2003), and Barbara Corsi, *Con qualque dollaro in meno* (Rome: Editori riuniti, 2001).

137. BIFI, FIF 944. "Rapport sur le 9ème festival" (1956).

138. Michèle Manceaux, *L'Express*, May 2, 1958.

139. BIFI, FIF 867, CA, June 9, 1947, and FIF 864, "Rapport de 1947," respectively.

140. BIFI, FIF 972. Nathan Golden, "Report on the XIIth International Film Festival," June 19, 1959.

141. Archives Municipales de Cannes, letter to FIF from Assoc. Commerciale, Industrielle et Artisanale du Canton de Cannes, s.d.

142. Edgar Morin, "Notes pour une sociologie du festival de Cannes," *Les Temps modernes*, n. 114–15 (Juin–Juillet 1955): 2273–84; 2279.

143. Novais Texeira, *O Globo*, May 7, 1951.

CHAPTER THREE

1. Richard Ivan Jobs, *Riding the New Wave: Youth and the Rejuvenation of France after World War II* (Ph.D. diss., Rutgers, 2002).

2. Susan Weiner, *Enfants Terribles: Youth and Femininity in the Mass Media in France, 1945–1968* (Baltimore: Johns Hopkins University Press, 2001).

3. James B. Twitchell, *Living It Up: America's Love Affair with Luxury* (New York: Simon and Schuster, 2003). This use of populuxe defines the term as a form of luxury product designed for mass consumption. The term refers to an aesthetic style associated with Southern Californian–inspired futuristic "Googie" architecture.

4. Charles Rearick, *The French in Love and War* (New Haven: Yale University Press, 1997), pp. 131–38.

5. Simone de Beauvoir, *Brigitte Bardot and the Lolita Syndrome* foreword by George Amberg (New York: Arno Press and New York Times, 1972), p. 6. Article originally published in *Esquire Magazine* 52, n. 2 (August 1959): 32–38. Translated by Bernard Fretchman. Citations are from the *Esquire* article.

6. Bardot lived several public lives. I concentrate on her film career but she also had an important run as a recording artist in France and later as an animal rights activist. See Chantal Nadeau, "BB and the Beasts: Brigitte Bardot and the Canadian Seal Controversy," *Screen: The Journal of the Society for Education in Film and Television* 37, n. 3 (1996): 240–50; and Ginette Vincendeau, *Stars and Stardom in French Cinema* (London and New York: Continuum, 2000).

7. See Ginette Vincendeau, "Hollywood Babel: The Coming of Sound and the Multiple-Language Version" in Higson and Maltby, eds., *"Film Europe" and "Film America,"* pp. 207–24; and Nataša Ďurovičová, "France: An Alien Ally" in Martin Barnier and Raphaelle Moine, eds., *France/Hollywood: Echanges cinématographiques et identités nationales* (Paris: L'Harmattan, 2002), pp. 39–60. See also Douglas Gomery, *Shared Pleasures: A History of Movie Presentation in the United States* (London: BFI, 1992). The problem with Gomery's explanation for the early base for foreign film in the United States being immigrants is that French people made up a very small immigrant group and yet French films have always been among the most popular foreign films with American audiences. See John Higham, *Strangers in the Land: Patterns of American Nativism, 1860-1925*, 4th ed. (1955; New Brunswick: Rutgers University Press, 1998); and John Bodnar, *The Transplanted: A History of Immigrants in Urban America* (Bloomington: Indiana University Press, 1985).

8. Barbara Wilinksy, *Sure Seaters: The Emergence of Art House Cinema* (Minneapolis: University of Minnesota Press, 2001).

9. BYU, MSS 2441. Lillian and Philip Gerard Collection, Box 1 from article in *American Film,* May 1976, "The Ascendance of Lina Wetmuller" by Lillian Gerard.

10. Dudley Andrew, *Popular front Paris and the Poetics of Realism* (Cambridge Mass: Harvard University Press, 2005).

11. BYU, MSS 2441. Lillian and Philip Gerard Collection, Box 1.

12. *Motion Picture Herald*, July 15, 1950.

13. *New York Sun*, Eileen Creelman, "Picture Plays and Players," December 29, 1948.

14. BYU, MSS 1491. Bosley Crowther Collection, Box 16. Draft of article on best foreign films; c. 1952.

15. Tino Balio, *United Artists: The Company that Changed the Film Industry* (Madison: University of Wisconsin Press, 1987), p. 63; and Barbara Wilinksy, *Sure Seaters*; and Frank Walsh, *Sin and Censorship: The Catholic Church and the Motion Picture Industry* (New Haven: Yale University Press, 1996), pp. 241–61. See excellent archival materials in BYU, MSS 2441 Lillian Gerard Collection, Box 7, and Bosley Crowther Collection, MSS 1491, Box 18.

16. CAC, 760010/0072 CNC, Davis letter to Cravenne, May 7, 1954.

17. Al Hine, "What Has Happened to French Films?" *Holiday*, October 1954.

18. CAC 760010/0073 CNC. Distribution Materials.

19. BYU, NATO, MSS 1446 Box 41, folder 11; Reade quoted in TOA Convention Handbook, 1958.

20. Various advertising materials, found in Herrick Library, *And God Created Woman* PCA File.

21. Higson and Maltby, *"Film Europe" and "Film America."*

22. BYU, NATO, MSS 1446, Box 40, folder 5, TOA on Sept 24, 1948.

23. Richard Maltby, *Hollywood Cinema* (Oxford: Blackwell, 1995), p. 72.

24. Jon Belton, *Widescreen Cinema* (Cambridge: Harvard University Press, 1992).

25. BYU, NATO, MSS 1446, Box 41, folder 11. Report by Walter Reade, head of TOA Foreign Film Committee, published in Convention Handbook, October 1958.

26. BYU, NATO, MSS 1446, Box 41, folder 10. Progress Report of the 1956 TOA Convention and Trade Show, NYC, September 20–24, 1956.

27. BYU, NATO, MSS 1446, Box 41, folders 11 and 12.

28. BYU, NATO, MSS 1446, Box 41, folder 11. Report by Walter Reade, head of TOA Foreign Film Committee published in Convention Handbook, October 1958.

29. BYU, NATO, MSS 1446, Box 43, folder 2. Press release, Oct 26, 1955, "Comments made to Union Internationale de l'Exploitation Cinematographique," from Myron Blank, president , TOA in Rome.

30. BYU, NATO, MSS 1446, Box 43, folder 2. Press release, Oct 26, 1955, "Comments made to Union Internationale de l'Exploitation Cinematographique," from Myron Blank, president, TOA in Rome.

31. CAC 901625, 175, s.d., c. 1964–65, James Meunier, Rapport: Voyage d'études: "Le Film français en Amérique."

32. Herrick Library, MPAA Annual Report, 1953, p. 20.

33. Herrick Library, MPEA Annual Report, 1955.

34. CAC 760010/0072. Brochure from AUFF.

35. Herrick Library, MPAA Annual Report, 1951.

36. Herrick Library, MPAA, press release, February 21, 1951, Microfilm 15. Advisory Unit Materials.

37. CAC 760010/101, UFF, Procès Verbaux, January 25, 1950.

38. CAC 760010/0072, UFF from Meyer Beck, May 26, 1950.

39. CAC 760010/0073, UFF February 2, 1950, "A Response to the Set-up of the Kreisler Organization," by Jacques Chabrier to Robert Cravenne.

40. L'objectif 289, n. 109, February 1, 1958.

41. MAE, Quai d'Orsay, Relations Culturelles, 1945–59, Echanges Culturelles, 126 NY. December 16, 1949. From the Conseiller Culturel près l'ambassade de France aux EU (Réné Messières) to MAE, Dir. gen des rels cults.

42. MAE, Quai d'Orsay, Relations Culturelles, 1945–59, Echanges Culturelles, 126 NY. December 16, 1949. From the Conseiller Culturel près l'ambassade de France aux EU (Réné Messières) to MAE, Dir. gen des rels cults.

43. See Balio, United Artists, and Wilinsky, Sure Seaters.

44. CNC, Bulletin d'information, n.17, January–April, 1951.

45. Robert Cravenne, Le Tour du monde du cinéma français (Paris: Dixit, 1995), p. 93.

46. CAC 760010/0072, UFF from Meyer Beck, May 26, 1950.

47. CAC 760010/0073, Compte rendu de mission aux USA du Délégation Général, April 6, 1953; no signature, probably Cravenne.

48. CAC, CNC 1733, memo dated July 24, 1953 prepared by Henry Kaufman to UFF Film in Paris.

49. CAC, CNC 1733, UFF, March 1954. Note on a discussion with Eric Johnston of the MPAA.

50. Ibid.

51. CAC, CNC 1733, UFF, April 15, 1955, "Le Film français aux Etats-Unis."

52. Variety, October 5, 1955.

53. CAC, CNC 1733. Report from Maternati to UFF, 1956.

54. CAC, CNC 1733. Maternati to Cravenne, December 29, 1955.

55. "A Boost for French Films," Business Week, June 30, 1956, p. 103–4; Herrick Library, MPEA press release, December 17, 1956.

56. CAC, CNC 1733, 1956. Report from the FFO to the CNC.

57. CAC 910625/172. Report on French Films in the USA.

58. CAC CNC 760010/0002, 1955. Rapport Moral UFF and CAC, CNC 1733. Report from Maternati to UFF, 1956 for number of newsletters.

59. CAC 910625/172. Letter from La Badie to Cravenne, January 22, 1957.

60. CAC 760010/1022. Letter from Flaud to Maternati, February 3, 1959.

61. Herrick Library, Oral History 106, Robert Vogel, p. 298.

62. *Variety*, November 13, 1957 and May 2, 1963.

63. CAC, CNC 1733. Rapport from Maternati, November 13, 1957.

64. *Variety*, November 13, 1957.

65. Bosley Crowther, *New York Times*, August 4, 1957; and Fred Hift in *Variety* as cited in CAC, CNC 1733, letter from Maternati to Flaud October 15, 1957.

66. CAC, CNC 1733. FFO memo, s.d. In fact, according to Jacques Flaud, in 1956, 40 percent of the film industry's business came from profits on export. He makes this claim in an interview with André Bazin and Doniol-Valcroze in *Les Cahiers du cinéma* 12 (May 1957): 4–15, 7.

67. BYU, MSS 2441, Lillian and Philip Gerard Collection, Box 4. MOMA catalog, "Sixty Years of French Cinema," May 29–Sept. 30, 1957.

68. BYU, NATO, MSS 144, Box 44, Annual Report of the TOA Foreign Film Committee, October 21, 1958. Walter Reade.

69. Richard Kuisel, "The French Fifties," *Yale French Studies*, n. 98 (2000): 119–34.

70. Ginnette Vincendeau, *Stars and Stardom in French Cinema* (London: Continuum, 2000), pp. 82–109, 84.

71. François Nourissier, *Brigitte Bardot* (Torino: Grasset, 1960), p. 24.

72. *UniFrance film infos*, n. 36 (August–September 1955): 6–9.

73. Home movies by Louis Bardot as shown in documentary film, *Brigitte Bardot: Take One* (1996).

74. *LA Times Magazine*, October 26, 1952.

75. *Le Figaro littéraire*, April 25, 1953.

76. On such photography, see Elizabeth Willis-Tropea, "Hollywood Glamour" (Ph.D. diss., History Department, USC, 2007).

77. From *Paparazzi*, directed by Jacques Rozier, bonus materials, *Le Mépris* DVD.

78. See Kirse Granat May, *Golden State, Golden Youth: The California Image in Popular Culture, 1955 1966* (Chapel Hill: University of North Carolina Press, 2002).

79. Leo Braudy, *The World in a Frame*, and Joshua Gamson, *Claims to Fame*.

80. *UniFrance film infos*, n. 38 (January–February 1956), and *UniFrance film infos* n. 39 (March–April 1956).

81. CAC 910625/172, Spring 1956. Letter from Maternati to Cravenne.

82. CAC 901625/172, July 12 1956 from Maternati to Courau at UniFrance Film.

83. *Cahiers du cinéma*, n. 71 (May 1957): 65–67.

84. BIFI, *Franc-Tireur*, s.d., December 1956, likely.

85. According to an article in *Variety* (May 2, 1963) that listed the top box office films in first-run Paris theaters between 1952 and 1960, the film was not even among the top sixty-five best grossing films.

86. Robert Chazal, *Paris presse*, January 12, 1956.

87. See Weiner, *Enfants Terribles*, and Kristin Ross, *Fast Cars, Clean Bodies* (Cambridge: MIT Press, 1995).

88. François Truffaut, *Arts* 619 (May 15–21, 1957).

89. Claude de Givray, "Nouveau Traité de Bardot," *Les Cahiers du cinéma* 12, n. 71 (May 1957).

90. The dream ballet as a device is the major achievement of *An American in Paris* and was used

in other musicals on film since it had been used on the stage in *Oklahoma* in 1943. Other references to musicals include a gym setting and nightclub number with men in tuxedoes from *Gentlemen Prefer Blondes*, pirate ship out of *The Pirate*, and a *pas de deux* against a stylized backdrop of balloons that is a pale invocation of Kelly and Caron.

91. "BB: France's MM," *Esquire* 48, n. 3 (September 1957): pp. 55–58.

92. *Variety*, January 23, 1957.

93. *New York Times*, October 22, 1957.

94. CAC 910625/172, Maternati to Cravenne, October 24, 1957.

95. CAC 760010/0074, November 13, 1957. Report from Maternati to Cravenne. In this report, he notes that the film is a huge success, doing $20,000 a week at many theaters; playing in Boston in a 1340-seat theater and with increasing ticket sales in the second and third weeks. For example, the dubbed version in Boston brought in $13,000 first week, $22,000 the second week.

96. Reports from FFO, Maternati to Cravenne in various reports found in CAC 760010/0074 and CAC 910625/172.

97. *Variety*, April 2. 1958.

98. Herrick Library, Production Code Administration, Report of the Legion of Decency, "And God Created Woman."

99. *Variety*, April 2, 1958.

100. CAC, CNC 910625/172. March 10, 1958, Maternati to Cravenne.

101. Dick Williams, *LA Mirror News*, June 6, 1958.

102. Toni Howard, "Bad Little Bad Girl," *Saturday Evening Post*, June 14, 1958.

103. *Time*, November 11, 1957.

104. *Variety*, October 30, 1957.

105. Marc Mancini, "So Who Created Vadim?" *Film Comment* 24, n. 2 (March–April 1988): 18–23.

106. Dick Williams, *LA Mirror News*, February 5, 1958.

107. Simone de Beauvoir, "Brigitte Bardot and the Lolita Syndrome," translated by Bernard Fretchman, *Esquire* 52, n. 2 (August 1959): 32–38, 32. All subsequent citations in this section will cited in text.

108. André Maurois, "BB: The Sex Kitten Grows Up," *Playboy* 11, n. 7 (1964): 84–93, 134–35.

109. Roger Vadim, *Bardot, Deneuve, Fonda*, trans. Melinda Camber Porter (New York: Simon and Schuster, 1986).

110. *Life* 44, n. 26 (November 1957): 50–57.

111. Claude de Givray, "Nouveau traité de Bardot, " *Les Cahiers du cinéma* 12, n. 71 (Mai 1957).

112. Herrick Library, Bardot Clippings File. *LA Herald Express*, April 28, 1959. Her segment was recorded in their Eiffel Tower studio but never broadcast.

113. *Hollywood Reporter*, February 3, 1958.

114. CAC, CNC 760010/0074.

115. BYU, Bosley Crowther Collection. MSS 1491, Box 15, folder 4, July 7, 1958.

116. MAE, Quai d'Orsay, Amérique, Etats-Unis 542, Jacques Baeyens, consul général, New York to Hervé Alphand, French ambassador to the United States, December 9, 1957.

117. MAE, Quai d'Orsay, Amérique, Etats-Unis 542, Jacques Baeyens to Hervé Alphand, December 9, 1957.

118. CAC, CNC 910625/172, April 22, 1958, Maternati to Cravenne.

119. *Hollywood Citizen News*, June 14, 1960.

120. *France soir*, February 15, 1961.

121. It is remarkable how little attention has been paid to the popular French cinema of the era. Ginette Vincendeau has pointed this out in Richard Dyer and Vincendeau, eds. *Popular European Cinema* (London: Routledge, 1992), and her own book on French stars, *Stars and Stardom in French Cinema* (London: Continuum, 2000), is one of the few studies like it.

122. See Anotine de Baecque, *La Cinéphilie* (Paris: Fayard, 2003).

123. De Baecque, *La Nouvelle Vague*, Weiner, *Enfants Terribles*. Richard Neupert, *A History of the French New Wave Cinema* (Madison: University of Wisconsin Press, 2002) is an excellent synthesis that introduces a more cultural historical approach while still rehearsing some of the more internal and formal aspects of the New Wave.

124. A good revision that underlines this is Michel Marie, *The French New Wave, An Artistic School*, trans. Richard Neupert (Malden, MA: Blackwell, 2003). First published in France, 1997.

125. De Baecque, *La Nouvelle Vague*, Weiner, *Enfants Terribles*. Richard Neupert, *A History of the French New Wave Cinema*. Richard Neupert, for example, has expanded the definition by looking at its development in its own time, ultimately defining it as the messy constellation it actually was. In addition, Antoine de Baecque and Susan Weiner, most notably, have made more general attempts to situate the New Wave in the cultural history of the postwar period by contextualizing it as part of a broader youth culture in France.

126. Lynn Higgins, *New Novel, New Wave, New Politics* (Lincoln: University of Nebraska Press, 1996).

127. Louis Menand, "Paris, Texas: How Hollywood Brought the Cinema Back from France," *New Yorker*, February 17, 2003, 168–74.

128. Neupert, *A History of the French New Wave Cinema*, p. 38–39.

129. David Schoenbrun, "Paris In the Sixties: The Great Upsurge," *Esquire* 57, n. 2 (February 1962): 82–84, 134–35.

130. Ibid.

131. Laurence Alfonsi, *L'Aventure américaine de l'oeuvre de François Truffaut* (Paris: Haramattan, 2000).

132. Hollis Alpert, "Are Foreign Films Better?" *Saturday Review*, December 24, 1960, 43–53, 44.

133. BYU, MSS 2441, Lillian and Philip Gerard Collection, Box 2. *Letter from France* 3, n. 17 (June–August 1959). This should make more complex Michel Marie's notion that UFF orchestrated "La Nouvelle Vague." See his *The French New Wave*, p. 9.

134. Robert Cravenne, *Le Tour du monde du cinéma français* (Paris: DIXIT, 1995), p. 241, citing an UniFrance Annual Report, 1965.

135. CAC 901625/175, s.d., c. 1964-65, James Meunier, Rapport: Voyage d'études: "Le Film français en Amérique." p. 15.

136. BYU, MSS 2441, Lillian and Philip Gerard, Box 2. Letter from Griffith to Gerard, September 29, 1968; letters to follow from same location.

137. On the Malle film, see Pierre Billard, *Louis Malle: Le rebelle solitaire* (Paris: Plon, 2003), esp. pp. 204-9. The film was Bardot's weakest at the box office until Godard's *Le Mépris*.

138. Susan Hayward, in *French National Cinema* (London: Routledge, 1993), argues that the film is more about the death of the cinema than Bardot herself (239).

139. Herrick Library, clippings files, "Brigitte Bardot," studio press release, 1965.

CHAPTER FOUR

1. Herrick Library, MPAA Annual Report, March 25, 1946, p. 7–8.
2. Thomas Guback, *The International Film Industry* (Bloomington: Indiana University Press, 1969), p. 178.
3. Ibid., p. 199.
4. Dimitris Eleftheriotiotis, *Popular Cinemas of Europe: Studies of Texts, Contexts and Frameworks* (New York: Continuum, 2001), p. 11. Carrière quoted in early 1990s as president of the Foundation for Audiovisual Professions, FEMIS, France from *Conflict or Cooperation in European Film and Television* (Manchester: European Institute for the Media, 1992), p. 25.
5. Jean-Claude Batz, *A Propos de la crise de l'industrie du cinéma: Etudes du Centre National de Sociologie du Travail* (Brussels: Editions de l'Institut de Sociologie Université Libre de Bruxelles), p. 72.
6. Ian Cameron in *Cinéma hebdomadaire*, supplément, May 6, 1968, clipping found, FIF P 239, A 293, Box 10, French press on 1968.
7. Peter Lev, *The Euro-American Cinema* (Austin: University of Texas Press, 1993). See also Pierre Berthomieu, "Tactiques hollywoodiennes: Studios américains et pays européens dans les Années Cinquante," in Jean-Pierre Bertin-Maghit, ed., *Les cinémas européens des années cinquante* (Paris: AFRHC, 2000), pp. 11–17.
8. Herrick Library, MPAA Annual Report 1953.
9. See Nataša Ďurovičová, "Translating America: The Hollywood Multilinguals, 1929–1933," in Rick Altman, ed., *Sound Theory/Sound Practice* (New York: Routledge, 1992), 138–53; Andrew Higson and Richard Maltby, eds., *Film Europe and Film America: Cinema, Commerce and Cultural Exchange, 1920–1939* (Exeter: University of Exeter Press, 1999), especially Ginnette Vincendeau, "Hollywood Babel: The Coming of Sound and the Multiple-Language Version," pp. 207–24.
10. Walter Wanger, "Donald Duck and Diplomacy" in *Public Opinion Quarterly* (Fall 1950): 443–52, 444.
11. Wanger, "Donald Duck and Diplomacy," p. 445.
12. "A Program by the MPAA to Improve Public Attitudes towards the American Motion Picture at Home and Abroad," 1962, p. 3 in MPAA Files, Herrick Library.
13. BYU, Bosley Crowther Collection, MSS 1491, Box 15, folder 5, from Crowther to Lester, March 18, 1960.
14. *Motion Picture Exhibitor*, August 12, 1964, Herrick Library.
15. BYU, NATO, MSS 1446, Box 41, folder 16, 1963. Meeting in Miami Beach, p. 3.
16. BYU, Bosley Crowther Collection, MSS 1491, Box 16, folder 19, n.d., c. 1961.
17. BYU, Bosley Crowther Collection, MSS 1491, Box 16, folder 19, n.d., probably 1965–66.
18. Brian Taves and Stephen Michaulk, Jr., eds. *The Jules Verne Encyclopedia* (Lanham: Scarecrow Press, 1996), p. 211.
19. Michael Todd, Jr., and Susan McCarthy Todd, *A Valuable Property: The Life Story of Michael Todd* (New York: Arbor House, 1983), p. 267.
20. For biographical information, see Michael Todd, Jr., and Susan McCarthy Todd, *A Valuable Property: The Life Story of Michael Todd* (New York: Arbor House, 1983).
21. Radio interview, Mike Todd with Tex and Jinx McCreary, March 7, 1956, Mike Todd Clippings File, p. 7, Herrick Library.
22. Todd, Jr., and Todd, *A Valuable Property*, pp. 134–35.

23. Jon Belton, *Widescreen Cinema* (Cambridge: Harvard University Press, 1992). I am indebted to Belton's excellent study for much of the material on the history of widescreen in the next several pages.

24. Steven C. Caton, *Lawrence of Arabia: A Film's Anthropology* (Berkeley: University of California Press, 1999), pp. 109–10.

25. Todd, Jr., and Todd, *A Valuable Property*, p. 212.

26. Ibid., p. 239.

27. For an excellent volume that summarizes this literature, see Jeffrey Ruoff, ed., *Virtual Voyages: Cinema and Travel* (Durham: Duke University Press, 2006).

28. Jon Belton, *Widescreen Cinema* (Cambridge: Harvard University Press, 1992), p. 92.

29. Belton, *Widescreen Cinema*, p. 114.

30. Todd, Jr., and Todd, *A Valuable Property*, p. 245.

31. Art Cohn, *The Nine Lives of Mike Todd* (New York: Random House, 1958), p. 375.

32. *Variety*, December 2, 1953.

33. According to his son, he paid only $100,000 and according to the *Hollywood Reporter* (September 22, 1954) he paid $130,000 for the rights.

34. Stephen Silverman, *Dancing on the Ceiling* (New York: Knopf, 1996), pp. 98–99.

35. William Wyler Collection, Herrick Library, Box 52, folder 687, Paramount memo to William Wyler from John Mock, April 3, 1953.

36. Robert Bingham, *Hollywood Reporter*, January 27, 1957.

37. These figures are notoriously slippery. We know that *Variety* listed it as the second largest grossing film domestically at $16.2 million in 1957, after the $18 million of *Ten Commandments*. We also know that in 1977, *Variety* listed it as the fortieth all-time high grosser in unadjusted dollars in domestic release. Both of these numbers are published in Cobbett Steinberg, *Reel Facts* (New York: Vintage, 1978). The larger of the two comes from Brian Taves and Stephen Michaulk, Jr., *The Jules Verne Encyclopedia*, p. 225.

38. "Mike Todd at Harvard", p. 4, n.d., c. spring 1957. Mike Todd Clippings File, Herrick Library.

39. "My Exhibitor Beef," probably a press release, c. 1956. Herrick Library, Mike Todd Clippings.

40. Ibid.

41. The DeMille film had some Egyptian locations (when in Egypt DeMille had a heart attack). It is mostly a studio special effects extravaganza.

42. Art Cohn, ed., *Around the World in Eighty Days Alamanach* (New York: Random House, 1956), p. 42.

43. Todd, Jr., and Todd, *A Valuable Property*, p. 302.

44. Michael Wood, *America in the Movies* (New York: Columbia University Press, 1975).

45. Radio interview, Mike Todd with Tex and Jinx McCreary, March 7, 1956, pp. 47, 49, 56, Mike Todd Clippings File, Herrick Library.

46. "Mike Todd at Harvard," p. 20, Mike Todd Clippings File, Herrick Library.

47. Art Cohn, *The Nine Lives of Mike Todd*, p. 379.

48. *Los Angeles Times*, October 31, 1956.

49. Fred Hift, *Variety*, October 18, 1956.

50. Radio interview, Mike Todd with Tex and Jinx McCreary, March 7, 1956, p. 47 and 49, Mike Todd Clippings File, Herrick Library.

51. Jeffrey M. Pilcher, *Cantínflas and the Chaos of Mexican Modernity* (Wilmington: Scholarly Resources, 2001), p. 163.

52. John Huston Papers, Herrick Library, letter from Ernest Anderson to John Huston, April 30, probably 1955. The letter also says that the film was to be directed by Carol Reed, from a script by Wolfe Mankowitz and would star Alec Guinness, Fernandel, Robert Morley, and Gina Lollobrigida.

53. In fact, Verne's success as a science fiction writer seems so entirely disconnected for his national origin, that in the course of writing this book, many of my own friends have been surprised to learn that Verne was French.

54. Jules Verne, *Le Tour du monde en 80 jours* (1873; reprint Paris: Livre de Poche, 2000), p. 86.

55. Harry Kurnitz "The Antic Arts: Movies," *Holiday*, October 1956, 77, 112.

56. *Newsweek*, October 29, 1956.

57. *Newsweek*, November 5, 1956.

58. *France-Observateur*, May 30, 1957.

59. Philip Hartung, *Commonweal*, November 9, 1956.

60. Art Cohn, ed., *Around the World in Eighty Days Almanack* (New York: Random House, 1956).

61. Radio interview, Mike Todd with Tex and Jinx McCreary, March 7, 1956, p. 16, Mike Todd Clippings File, Herrick Library.

62. "An Open Interview with Mike Todd," c. 1957, p. 3, Mike Todd Clippings File, Herrick Library.

63. Todd, Jr., and Todd, *A Valuable Property*, pp. 281–82.

64. Robert Hatch, *Nation* 183, November 10, 1956, p. 417.

65. *The Ten Commandments* features a notorious prologue of DeMille describing the battle between freedom and tyranny, for example. Road show musicals often had overtures.

66. Alan Nadel, *Containment Culture: American Narratives, Postmodernism and the Atomic Age* (Durham: Duke University Press, 1995), esp. ch. 4.

67. Radio interview, Mike Todd with Tex and Jinx McCreary, March 7, 1956, p. 7, Mike Todd Clippings File, Herrick Library.

68. There is a book of the exhibit, *The Family of Man* (New York: Simon and Schuster for MOMA, 1955). See also Eric Sandeen, *Picturing an Exhibition: The Family of Man and 1950's America* (Albuquerque: University of New Mexico Press, 1995).

69. Blake Stimson, *The Pivot of the World: Photography and Its Nation* (Cambridge: MIT Press, 2006), p. 67. Oddly, his book does not at all mention film, despite its allied function. Even in relation to the exhibit, its caption-writer, Dorothy Norman noted that it was "more related to the motion picture tradition than to that of Stieglitz." In a sense, this consideration of Todd can be read fruitfully in relation to Stimson on photography.

70. This information is according to Todd and Todd, Jr., *A Valuable Property*, pp. 307–8. Tino Balio has a different account. He says UA put up $2 million and that the film played on a two a day basis in the initial run. See Tino Balio, *United Artists: The Company That Changed the Film Industry* (Madison: University of Wisconsin Press, 1987), pp. 129–32.

71. Information found in George Stevens Collection, Herrick Library. Stevens studied the grosses of several epic blockbusters as he prepared to distribute *The Greatest Story Ever Told*.

72. As listed in Cobbett Steinberg, *Reel Facts* (New York: Vintage, 1978).

73. Brian Taves and Stephen Michaulk, Jr., *The Jules Verne Encyclopedia* (Lanham: Scarecrow Press, 1996), p. 225.

74. *Variety*, June 16, 1982.

75. The other nominations were for best director, art direction, set direction, and costume design.

76. Mason Wiley and Damien Bona, *Inside Oscar: The Unofficial History of the Academy Awards,* ed. Gail MacColl (1986; New York: Ballantine Books, 1996), p. 276 and 278.

77. Natasha Fraser-Cavassoni, *Sam Spiegel* (New York: Simon and Schuster 2003), p. 2.

78. Louis Berg, "Movies on the Move," *This Week,* August 16, 1953.

79. Natasha Fraser-Cavassoni, *Sam Spiegel.* Taylor not only started using her British passport in this period, but she had two contracts, one as a star being paid $125,000 while another for her role as "co producer" under the emblem of her Swiss company, Camp Films, in which she received $375,000 and a 10 percent gross on receipts in excess of $5 million (206).

80. Irving Bernstein, *Hollywood at the Crossroads: An Economic Study of the Motion Picture Industry,* prepared for the Hollywood AFL Film Council December 1957, p. 48. He used columns in the *Hollywood Reporter* that noted where films were being shot. This is imperfect data but is characteristic of what people thought was going on in the period.

81. See Natasha Fraser-Cavassoni, *Sam Spiegel,* and Jean-Dominique Barby, *Raoul Lévy, Un Aventurier du cinéma* (Paris: Jean-Claude de Lattès, 1995).

82. Omar Sharif with Marie-Thérèse Guinchard, *L'Eternel masculin* (Paris: Stock, 1976), p. 136. Caton also discusses Sharif's career.

83. Sharif, *L'éternel masculin,* p. 76.

84. A. Weiler, *New York Times,* June 24, 1965.

85. Sharif, *L'éternel masculin,* p. 29.

86. Pascal Brienne in *Les Lettres françaises,* October 22, 1964.

87. *Bundy: An Oral History of Andrew Marton,* interviewed by Joanne d'Antonio, ed. Adele Field (Los Angeles: Director's Guild, 1980), p. 183–84.

88. I want to thank my colleague Phil Ethington for sharing his knowledge and research about theses films. For *Trader Horn,* see William Stull, "In Africa with Trader Horn," *American Cinematographer* 10, n. 10 (January 1930): 8–9, 26; Ray Cabana, Jr., "Concerning Trader Horn," and Jon Tuska, "Trader Horn: A Cinematograph," both in *Views and Reviews* 3, n. 1 (1930): 34–58. On the 1950 *King Solomon's Mines* see especially Rudy Behlmer, "King's Solomon's Mines" in two parts in *American Cinematographer* 70, n. 5 (May 1989): 38–44, and n. 6 (June 1989): 38–46. For his own use of these materials, see his forthcoming book, *Ghost Metropolis.*

89. It also seems apparent that after *Around the World* all the big budget location films had crews also filming the making of the movie. The author used DVD Bonus Materials to verify some of the production information. The material now used as the bonus materials on DVDs include featurettes (shorts about the location shoot, for example, that may well have screened on television).

90. In some instances, such as *King Solomon's Mines* (1950), the codirector Andrew Marton said they never watched anything they were shooting during production. That film was made, of course, prior to wide jet availability.

91. Fraser-Cavassoni, *Sam Spiegel,* p. 233.

92. James Chapman, *License to Thrill* (New York: Columbia University Press, 2000), pp. 75–76.

93. Steven C. Caton, *Lawrence of Arabia: A Film's Anthropology* (Berkeley: University of California Press, 1999) See especially his discussion in chapters 4 and 5.

CONCLUSION

1. Stephen Rebello, "All That Baz," *Movieline*, June 2001, 63–67.

2. *New York Times Magazine*, November 14, 2004.

3. Sean Cubbitt, *The Cinema Effect* (Cambridge: MIT Press, 2004), 356.

4. Charles Acland, *Screen Traffic: Movies, Multiplexes, and Global Culture* (Durham: Duke University Press, 2005).

5. Philip H. Gordon and Sophie Meunier, *The French Challenge: Adapting to Globalization* (Washington, D.C.: Brookings Institute Press, 2001), 11. See also Grantham, *Some Big Bourgeois Brothel. Contexts for France's Culture Wars with Hollywood* (Lutton: University of Lutton Press, 2000).

Bibliography

ARCHIVAL SOURCES AND SPECIAL COLLECTIONS

Academy of Motion Picture Arts and Sciences, Margaret Herrick Library
Core Collection
John Huston Collection
Oral History Project: Lela Simone and Robert Vogel
Production Code Administration (PCA) Files
Stills Collection
Vincente Minnelli Collection
William Wyler Collection

Archives Municipales de Cannes
2R65, 2R66, 93 W 18

Bibliothèque du Film (BIFI), Paris
Archives of the Cannes Film Festival, BIFI, FIF. References cite the original internal
    festival organization rather than new BIFI reorganization of materials not completed
    at the time of publication.
IDHEC Files, festivals and individual film files by title

Bibliothèque National de France, Arsenal
Rondel Collection
UniFrance infos Newsletters

Brigham Young University, L. Tom Perry, Special Collections Library
Bosley Crowther Collection, MSS 1191
Lillian and Philip Gerard Collection, MSS 2441
National Association of Theater Owners Collection, MSS 1446

Centre d'Archives Contemporaines (CAC), French National Archives, Fontainebleau
Centre National de la Cinématographie (CNC): 760009, 760010/072; 760010/073; 910625
    /172; especially materials of UniFrance Film. Original CNC archival box references are
    numbered 1347–1733, etc.

Inathèque
Cinépanorama
Reflets de Cannes, 1951–68 (all materials available at Tolbiac; many reproduced expressly
    for this research).

Ministère des Affaires Etrangères, Nantes
Archives des Echanges Artistiques

Ministère des Affaires Etrangères, Quai d'Orsay
Relations Culturelles, 1945–59, Echanges Culturels
Amérique, Etats-Unis

National Archives, College Park, MD
Record Group, 59 and 84

University of Southern California, Special Collections
MGM Collection, Freed Archive.

FILMOGRAPHY

Act of Love, dir. Anatole Litvak, UA, 1953.
The Agony and the Ecstasy, dir. Carol Reed, Twentieth Century Fox, 1965.
An American in Paris, dir. Vincente Minnelli, MGM, 1951.
April in Paris, dir. David Butler, Warner Bros., 1952.
Around the World in Eighty Days, dir. Michael Anderson, UA, 1956.
Around the World in Eighty Days, dir. Frank Coraci, Walt Disney Pictures, 2004.
Le Ballon rouge, dir. Albert Lamorisse, Montsouris, 1956.
Les Bijoutiers du clair de lune, dir. Roger Vadim, CEIAD/Kingsley-International, 1958.
Black Tights, dir. Terence Young, Talma Films, 1960.
Bonjour tristesse, dir. Otto Preminger, Columbia, 1958.
Bridge on the River Kwai, dir. David Lean, Columbia, 1957.
*Brigitte Bardot: Take One***,** dir. Alain Bourgrain-Dubourg, TF1**,** 1996.
C comme cinéma, Cannes, Chalais, dir. Rémy Grumbach, Inathèque, 1997.
Can-Can, dir. Walter Lang, Twentieth Century Fox, 1960.
Cette sacrée gamine, dir. Michel Boisrond, Lutetia, 1956.
Charade, dir. Stanley Donen, UA, 1963.
Daddy Long Legs, dir. Jean Negulesco, Twentieth Century Fox, 1955.
Dear Brigitte, dir. Henry Koster, Twentieth Century Fox, 1965.
Doctor No, dir. Terence Young, UA, 1962.
Doctor Zhivago, dir. David Lean, MGM, 1965.

Du Rififi chez les hommes, dir. Jules Dassin, Indus, 1954.

En Cas de malheur, dir. Claude Autant-Lara, Incom/Kinglsey-International, 1958.

En Effeuillant la marguerite, dir. Marc Allégret, Films EGE, 1956.

Et Dieu créa la femme, dir. Roger Vadim, Columbia, 1956.

Exodus, dir. Otto Preminger, UA, 1960.

Fall of the Roman Empire, dir. Anthony Mann, Bronston, 1964.

Folies bergère, dir. Henri Decoin, Sirius Films, 1956.

French Can-Can, dir. Jean Renoir, Franco-London Films, 1954.

From Russia with Love, dir. Terence Young, UA, 1963.

Gigi, dir. Jacqueline Audry, Codo Cinema, 1949.

Gigi, dir. Vincente Minnelli, MGM, 1958.

Goldfinger, dir. Guy Hamilton, UA, 1964.

Les Grandes manoeuvres, dir. René Clair, Filmsonor, 1955.

Helen of Troy, dir. Robert Wise, Warner Bros., 1956.

Irma La Douce, dir. Billy Wilder, UA, 1963.

King of Kings, dir. Nicholas Ray, Bronston, 1961.

Lawrence of Arabia, dir. David Lean, Columbia, 1962.

Lili, dir. Charles Walters, MGM, 1953.

La lumière d'en face, dir. Georges Lacombe, CGC, 1955.

Lust for Life, dir. Vincente Minnelli, MGM, 1956.

La Mariée est trop belle, dir. Pierre Gaspard-Huit, Générale de Film, 1956.

Le Mépris, dir. Jean-Luc Godard, Rome-Paris Films/Embassy, 1963.

Les Girls, dir. George Cukor, MGM, 1957.

Moulin Rouge, dir. John Huston, Romulus Films/UA, 1952.

Moulin Rouge! dir. Baz Luhrmann, Twentieth Century Fox, 2001.

Never on Sunday, dir. Jules Dassin, Lopert/Melina Films, 1960.

Orfeu negro, dir. Marcel Camus, Dispat, 1959.

Paparazzi, dir. Jacques Rozier, Films du Colisée, 1964.

Paris Holiday, dir. Gerd Oswald, UA, 1958.

Une Parisienne, dir. Michel Boisrond, Filmsonor/UA, 1957.

The Pink Panther, dir. Blake Edwards, UA, 1963.

The Red Shoes, dir. Michael Powell and Emeric Pressberger, Eagle-Lion, 1948.

Le Repos du guerrier, dir. Roger Vadim, Cocinor, 1962.

Sabrina, dir. Billy Wilder, Paramount, 1954.

Si Versailles m'était conté, dir. Sacha Guitry, Cocinor, 1954.

Silk Stockings, dir. Rouben Mamoulian, MGM, 1957.

Summertime, dir. David Lean, UA, 1955.

Three Coins in a Fountain, dir. Jean Negulesco, Twentieh Century Fox, 1954.

Vie privée, dir. Louis Malle, CIPRA/MGM, 1962.

Viva María, dir. Louis Malle, UA, 1965.

NONARCHIVAL PRIMARY SOURCES

Alpert, Hollis. "Show of Strength Abroad in Are Foreign Films Better." *Saturday Review* (December 24, 1960): 13–53.

Batz, Jean-Claude. *A propos de la crise de l'industrie du cinéma: Etudes du Centre National de Sociologie du Travail*. Brussels: Editions de l'Institut de Sociologie Unversité Libre de Bruxelles, 1963.

Berg, Louis. "Movies on the Move." *This Week*, August 16, 1953.

Bernstein, Irving. *Hollywood at the Crossroads: An Economic Study of the Motion Picture Industry*. Prepared for the Hollywood AFL Film Council. December 1957.

Bitsch, Charles, and Jean Domachi. "Entretien avec Vincente Minnelli." *Les Cahiers du cinéma*, n. 74 (Août/septembre 1957): 4–18.

Cameron, Ian. *Cinéma Hebdomadaire*, supplément, May 6, 1968.

Centre National de la Cinématographie, Bulletin d'information (1947–1968).

Cohn, Art, ed. *Michael Todd's Around the World in 80 Days Almanac*. New York: Random House, 1956.

———. *The Nine Lives of Mike Todd*. New York: Random House, 1958.

Creelman, Eileen. "Picture Plays and Players." *New York Sun*, December 29, 1948.

Decaix, Emmanuelle, and Bruno Viller. "Interview of Maurice Bessy." *Cinématographe*, n. 58, (1980): 4–8.

Domarchi, Jean, and Jean Douchet. "Rencontre avec Vincente Minnelli," *Les Cahiers du Cinéma*, n. 128 (February 1962): 3–13.

The Family of Man. Exhibition catalog. New York: Simon and Schuster for MOMA, 1955.

Harcourt-Smith, Simon. "Vincente Minnelli." *Sight and Sound* 21, n. 3 (March 1952): 115–19.

Hine, Al. "Paris in the '90's." *Holiday*. April 1953.

———. "What Has Happened to French Films?" *Holiday*. October 1954.

Howard, Toni. "Whindig of the Movie Queens." *Saturday Evening Post*, May 18, 1956.

Huth, Hans. "Impressionism Comes to America." *Gazette des beaux arts* 29, series 6 (April 1946): 225–52.

Jeanne, René, and Charles Ford. "Grandeur et décadence du 7e art." *Mercure de France*, August 1960.

Kurnitz, Harry. "The Antic Arts: Movies." *Holiday*. October 1956.

Maurois, André. "BB: The Sex Kitten Grows Up." *Playboy* 11, n. 7 (1964): 84–93, 134–35.

Minnelli, Vincente, and Hector Arce. *I Remember It Well*. Garden City: Doubleday, 1974.

Morin, Edgar. "Notes pour une sociologie du Festival de Cannes," *Les Temps modernes* (June–July 1955): 2273–84.

Moussinac, Léon. "Une ère nouvelle commence," *L'écran Français*. September 18, 1946.

Nourissier, François. *Brigitte Bardot*. Torino: Grasset, 1960.

Renoir, Jean. *Ecrits, 1926–1971*. Paris: Editions Belfond, 1974.

Wanger, Walter. "Donald Duck and Diplomacy." *Public Opinion Quarterly* (Fall 1950): 443–452.

Secondary Sources

Abel, Richard. *The Red Rooster Scare: Making Cinema American, 1900–1910*. Berkeley: University of California Press, 1999.

Acland, Charles R. *Screen Traffic: Movies, Multiplexes and Global Culture*. Durham: Duke University Press, 2003.

Alfonsi, Laurence. *L'Aventure Américaine de l'oeuvre de François Truffaut*. Paris: Haramattan, 2000.

Altman, Rick. *The American Film Musical*. Bloomington: Indiana University Press, 1987.

Amar, Pierre-Jean. *Le Photojournalisme*. Paris: Nathan Université, 2000.

Andrew, Dudley, and Steven Ungar. *Popular Front Paris and the Poetics of Culture*. Cambridge: Harvard University Press, 2005.

Appadurai, Arjun. *Modernity at Large: Cultural Dimensions of Globalization*. Minneapolis: University of Minnesota Press, 1996.

Auslander, Leora. *Taste and Power: Furnishing Modern France*. Berkeley: University of California Press, 1996.

Bakker, Gerben. "Entertainment Industrialized: The Emergence of the International Film Industry, 1890–1940." *Enterprise and Society* 4, n. 4 (2003): 579–85.

———. "Selling French Films on Foreign Markets: The International Strategy of a Medium-Sized Film Company." *Enterprise and Society* 5, n. 1 (March 2004): 45–75.

Balio, Tino, ed. *The American Film Industry*. Madison: University of Wisconsin Press, second edition 1985.

———. *United Artists: The Company that Changed the Film Industry*. Madison: University of Wisconsin Press, 1987.

Baranowski, Shelly, and Ellen Furlough, eds. *Being Elsewhere: Tourism, Consumer Culture, and Identity in Modern Europe and North America*. Ann Arbor: University of Michigan Press, 2001.

Barby, Jean Dominique. *Raoul Lévy: Un aventurier du cinéma*. Paris: Jean-Clause de Lattès, 1995.

Beale, Marjorie. *French Elites and the Threat of Modernity, 1900–1940*. Stanford: Stanford University Press, 1999.

Beauchamp, Cari, and Henri Béhar. *Hollywood on the Riviera: The Inside Story of the Cannes Film Festival*. New York: William Morrow, 1992.

Belton, Jon. *Widescreen Cinema*. Cambridge: Harvard University Press, 1992.

Bergstrom, Janet. "Jean Renoir's Return to France." In *Exile and Creativity: Signposts, Travelers, Outsiders and Backward Glances*, edited by Susan Rubin Suleiman. Durham: Duke University Press, 1998.

Berthomieu, Pierre. "Tactiques Hollywoodiennes: Studios américains et pays européens dans les années cinquante." In *Les cinémas européens des années cinquante*, ed. Jean-Pierre Bertin-Maghit. Paris: AFRHC, 2000.

Bertin-Maghit, Jean-Pierre. *Le Cinéma français sous Vichy: Les Films français de 1940 à 1944*. Paris: Revue du Cinéma/Albatros, 1980.

Bertrand, Jean-Caude and Francis Bordat. *Les Medias français aux Etats-Unis*. Nancy: Presse Universitaire de la France, 1994.

Bess, Michael. *The Light-Green Society: Ecology and Technological Modernity in France, 1960–2000*. Chicago: University of Chicago Press, 2003.

Bigsby, C. W. E. *Superculture*. Bowling Green: Bowling Green University Press, 1975.

Billard, Pierre. *D'or et de palmes. Le Festival de Cannes*. Paris: Découvertes Gallimard, 1997.

———. *Louis Malle: Le rebelle solitaire*. Paris: Plon, 2003.

Biskind, Peter. *Down and Dirty Pictures: Miramax, Sundance, and the Rise of Independent Film*. New York: Simon and Schuster, 2004.

Bloch, Marc. *Strange Defeat*. New York: Norton, 1968.

Bodnar, John. *The Transplanted: A History of Immigrants in Urban America*. Bloomington: Indiana University Press, 1985.

Boorstin, Daniel. *The Image: A Guide to Pseudo-events in America*. New York: Vintage Books, 1992.

Braudy, Leo. *The World in a Frame: What We See in Films*. Chicago : University of Chicago Press, 2002.

Brunetta, Gian Piero. *Storia del cinema italiano dal 1945 agli anni ottanta*. Roma: Editori Riuniti, 1982.

Brunette, Peter. *Roberto Rossellini*. New York: Oxford University Press, 1987.

Butsch, Richard. *The Making of American Audiences: From Stage to Television, 1750–1990*. Cambridge: Cambridge University Press, 2000.

Cannes cinema, cinquante ans de Festival vus par Traverso. Textes de Serge Toubiana avec Thierry Jousse et Joël Magny. Paris: Les Cahiers du cinema, 1997.

Cannes 45 Years: Festival International de Film. New York: MOMA, 1992.

Cannes: Trente-cinq ans. De Maurice Bessy, Ginette Billard and Roger Régent. Paris: Festival de Cannes, 1982.

Cary, John and John Kobal. *Spectacular! The Story of Epic Films*. London: Hamlyn: 1974.

Casanova, Pascale. *The World Republic of Letters*. Translated by M. B. DeVoise. Cambridge: Harvard University Press, 1999; 2004.

Casper, Joseph Andrew. *Vincente Minnelli and the Film Musical*. South Brunswick and New York: A. S. Barnes and Company, 1977.

Cate, Phillip Dennis, et al. *Color Revolution: Color Lithography in France, 1890–1900*. Santa Barbara: Peregrine Smith, 1978.

Caton, Steven C. *Lawrence of Arabia: A Film's Anthropology*. Berkeley: University of California Press, 1999.

Caute, David. *The Dancer Defects: The Struggle for Cultural Supremacy during the Cold War*. Oxford: Oxford University Press, 2003.

Chalais, François. *Les Chocolats de l'entreacte*. Paris: Stock, 1972.

Chapin, Mary Weaver. "Henri de Toulouse-Lautrec and the Café-Concert: Print-Making, Publicity, and Celebrity in Fin-de-Siècle Paris." Ph.D. dissertation, Art History, New York University, 2002.

Chapman, James. *License to Thrill*. New York: Columbia University Press, 2000.

Charney, Leo, and Vanessa R. Schwartz, eds. *Cinema and the Invention of Modern Life* Berkeley: University of California Press, 1995.

Chartier, Roger. "Texts, Symbols and Frenchness." *Journal of Modern History* 57, n. 4. (1985): 682–95.

Chessel, Marie-Emmanuelle. *La Publicité: naissance d'une profession. 1900–1940*. Paris: CNRS Editions, 1998.

Chew, William J. III, ed. *National Stereotypes in Perspective: Americans in France, Frenchmen in America*. Amsterdam: Rodopi, 2001.

Clark, T. J. *The Painting of Modern Life: Paris in the Art of Manet and His Followers*. Princeton: Princeton University Press, 1985.

Cohen, Lizabeth. *A Consumer's Republic: The Politics of Mass Consumption in Post-War America*. New York: Knopf, 2003.

Cohen, Margaret and Carolyn Dever, eds. *The Literary Channel: The Inter-National Invention of the Novel*. Princeton: Princeton University Press, 2002.

Cohen-Solal, Annie. *"Un Jour, ils auront des peintres": L'avènement des peintres américains. Paris 1867–New York 1948*. Paris: Gallimard, 2000.

Condemi, Concetta. *Les cafés-concerts: histoire d'un divertissement*. Paris: Quai Voltaire, 1992.

Corsi, Barbara. *Con qualque dollaro in meno*. Rome: Editori Riuniti, 2001.

Costigliola, Frank. *France and the United States: The Cold Alliance since World War II*. New York: Twayne, 1992.

———. "The Nuclear Family: Tropes of Gender and Pathology in the Western Alliance." *Diplomatic History* 21, n. 2 (Spring 1997): 163–83.

Crary, Jonathan. *Suspensions of Perception: Attention, Spectacle, and Modern Culture*. Cambridge: MIT Press, 1999.

Crary, Jonathan. *Techniques of the Observer: On Vision and Modernity in the Nineteenth Century*. Cambridge: MIT Press, 1990.

Cravenne, Robert. *Le tour du monde du cinéma français*. Paris: Dixit, 1995.

Crawley, Tony. *Bébé. The Films of Brigitte Bardot*. London: LSP Books, 1975.

Crisp, Colin. *The Classic French Cinema, 1930–1960*. Bloomington: Indiana University Press, 1997.

Cubbit, Sean. *The Cinema Effect*. Cambridge: MIT Press, 2004.

Dalle Vacche, Angela. *Cinema and Painting: How Art Is Used in Film*. Austin: University Texas Press, 1996.

———. "A Painter in Hollywood: Vincente Minnelli's An American in Paris" *Cinema Journal* 32, n. 1 (Fall 1992): 63–83.

Darnton, Robert. *The Great Cat Massacre*. New York: Basic Books, 1984.

Darnton, Robert. "The Symbolic Element in History," *Journal of Modern History* 58, n. 1 (1986): 218–34.

De Baecque, Antoine. *La cinéphile: invention d'un regard, histoire d'une culture, 1944–1968*. Paris: Fayard, 2003.

———. *La Nouvelle Vague*. Paris: Flammarion, 1998.

De Beauvoir, Simone. Foreword by George Amberg. *Brigitte Bardot and the Lolita Syndrome*. New York: Arno Press and New York Times, 1972.

De Grazia, Victoria. *Irresistible Empire: America's Advance through Twentieth-Century Europe*. Cambridge: Harvard University Press, 2005.

De Jean, Joan. *The Essence of Style: How the French Invented High Fashion, Fine Food, Chic Cafés, Style, Sophistication and Glamour*. New York: Free Press, 2005.

De la Motte, Dean, and Jeannene Przyblyski. *Making the News: Modernity and the Mass Press in Nineteenth-Century France*. Amherst: University of Massachusetts Press, 1999.

Delage, Christian. *La Vision nazie du cinéma*. Lausanne: L'age d'Homme, 1989.

Della Casa, Stefano. *Capitani coraggiosi: produttori italiani*. Milan: Electa, 2003.

Dimendberg, Ed. *Film Noir and the Spaces of Modernity*. Cambridge: Harvard University Press, 2004.

Dulles, Foster Rhea. *Americans Abroad: Two Centuries of American Travel*. Ann Arbor: University of Michigan Press, 1964.

Dunant, Caroline. "Visions of Paris." *Sight and Sound* 60, n. 1 (Winter 1990–91): 42–47.

Durgnat, Raymond. *Jean Renoir*. Berkeley: University of California Press, 1974.

Durovičová, Nataša. "France: An Alien Ally." In *France/Hollywood: Echanges Cinématographiques et Identités Nationales*, edited by Martin Barnier and Raphaelle Moine, 39–60. Paris: L'Harmattan, 2002.

Dyer, Richard. *Stars*. London: British Film Institute, 1979.

Dyer, Richard and Ginette Vincendeau, eds. *Popular European Cinema*. London: Routledge, 1992.

Eleftheriotis, Dimitris. *Popular Cinemas of Europe. Studies of Texts, Contexts and Frameworks*. New York: Continuum, 2001.

Ellwood, Dave W. and Rob Kroes, eds. *Hollywood in Europe: Experiences of a Cultural Hegemony*. Amsterdam: Vrije Universiteit Press, 1994.

Elsaesser, Thomas. "Two Decades in Another Country: Hollywood and the Cinéphiles." In *Superculture*, edited by C. W. E. Bigsby. Bowling Green: Bowling Green University Press, 1975.

———. *Weimar Cinema and After: Germany's Historical Imaginary*. Routledge: New York, 2000.

Endy, Christopher. *Cold War Holidays: American Tourists in France*. Chapel Hill: University of North Carolina Press, 2004.

Ethington, Philip and Vanessa Schwartz, eds. "Urban Icons." Special issue. *Urban History* 33, n. 1 (May 2006).

Ethis, Emmanuel. *Aux marches du palais: Le festival sous le regard des sciences sociales*. Paris: La Documentation Française, 2001.

Feenberg, Andrew. *Alternative Modernity: The Technical Turn in Philosophy and Social Theory*. Berkeley: University of California Press, 1995.

Fehrenbach, Heide. *Cinema in Democratizing Germany: Reconstructing National Identity after Hitler*. Chapel Hill: University of North Carolina Press, 1995.

Fehrenbach, Heide, and Uta G. Poiger, eds. *Transactions, Transgressions, Transformations: American Culture in Western Europe and Japan*. New York: Berghahn Books, 2000.

Fernandez, James. "Historians Tell Tales of Cartesian Cats and Gallic Cockfights." *Journal of Modern History* 60, n. 1 (1988): 113–27.

Field, Adele, ed. *Bundy: An Oral History of Andrew Marton*. Interviews by Joanne d'Antonio. Los Angeles: Director's Guild, 1980.

Fierro, Annette. *The Glass State: The Technology of the Spectacle, Paris, 1981–1998*. Cambridge: MIT Press, 2004.

Fordin, Hugh. *MGM's Greatest Musicals: The Arthur Freed Unit*. New York: Da Capo Press, 1996.

Forgacs, David, and Sarah Lutton, eds. *Roberto Rossellini: Magician of the Real*. London: British Film Institute, 2000.

Fraser-Cavassoni, Natasha. *Sam Spiegel*. New York: Simon and Schuster, 2003.

Frelinghuysen, Alice Cooney. *La Collection Havemeyer: Quand l'Amérique découvrait l'Impressionisme*. Paris: Réunion des Musées Nationaux, 1997.

———. *Splendid Legacy: The Havemeyer Collection*. New York: The Metropolitan Musuem, 1993.

Frémaux, Thierry. "L'aventure cinéphilique de Positif." *Vingtième Siècle* 23 (1989): 21–33.

Friedman, Thomas. *The Lexus and the Olive Tree*. 2nd ed. New York: Anchor Books, 2000.

Gamson, Joshua. *Claims to Fame: Celebrity in Contemporary America*. Berkeley: University of California Press, 1994.

Garelick, Rhonda K. *Rising Star: Dandyism, Gender, and Performance in the Fin de Siècle*. Princeton: Princeton University Press, 1998.

Gilroy, Paul. *The Black Atlantic*. Cambridge: Harvard University Press, 1993.

Gomery, Douglas. *Shared Pleasures: A History of Movie Presentation in the United States*. Madison: University of Wisconsin Press, 1992.

Gordon, Philip H., and Sophie Meunier. *The French Challenge: Adapting to Globalization*. Washington, D.C.: Brookings Institute Press, 2001.

Gottlieb, Sidney, ed. *Roberto Rossellini: Rome Open City*. New York: Cambridge University Press, 2004.

Grantham, Bill. *Some Big Bourgeois Brothel: Contexts for France's Culture Wars with Hollywood*. Luton: University of Luton Press, 2000.

Guback, Thomas. *The International Film Industry: Western Europe and America since 1945*. Bloomington: Indiana University Press, 1969.

Guback, Thomas. "Non-market Factors in the International Distribution of American Films." *Current Research in Film: Audiences, Economics, and Law* 1 (1985): 111–26.

Guilbault, Serge. *How New York Stole the Idea of Modern Art*. Chicago: University of Chicago Press, 1983.

Gundle, Stephen. *Between Hollywood and Moscow: The Italian Communists and the Challenge of Mass Culture*. Durham: Duke University Press, 2000.

Guy, Kolleen. *When Champagne Became French: Wine and the Making of a National Identity*. Baltimore: Johns Hopkins University Press, 2003.

Handyside, Fiona. "'Paris isn't for changing planes; it's for changing your outlook': Audrey Hepburn as European star in 1950s France." *French Cultural Studies* 14, n. 3 (2003): 288–98.

Hansen, Miriam. *Babel and Babylon: Spectatorship in American Silent Film*. Cambridge: Harvard University Press, 1991.

———. "The Mass Production of the Senses: Classical Cinema as Vernacular Modernism." *Modernism/Modernity* 6, n. 2 (1999): 59–77.

Harris, Neil. *Cultural Excursions: Marketing Appetites and Cultural Tastes in Modern America*. Chicago: University of Chicago Press, 1990.

Harvey, Stephen. *Directed by Vincente Minnelli*. Foreword by Liza Minnelli. New York: MOMA; Harper and Row, 1989.

Harvey, Sylvia. *May '68 and Film Culture*. London: British Film Institute, 1978.

Hecht, Gabrielle. *The Radiance of France: Nuclear Power and National Identity after World War II*. Cambridge: MIT Press, 1998.

Held, David, and Anthony McGrew, eds. *The Global Transformations Reader: An Introduction to the Globalization Debate*. 2nd ed. Cambridge, UK: Polity Press, 2003.

Herbert, Robert L. *Impressionism: Art, Leisure and Parisian Society*. New Haven: Yale University Press, 1988.

Heyman, Danièle and Jean-Pierre Dufreigne. *Le Roman de Cannes: 50 ans de Festival*. Paris: TF1 Editions, 1996.

Higashi, Sumiko. *Cecil B. DeMille and American Culture: The Silent Era*. Berkeley: University of California Press, 1994.

Higham, John. *Strangers in the Land: Patterns of American Nativism, 1860–1925*. 4th ed. New Brunswick: Rutgers University Press, 1955; 1998.

Higonnet, Patrice. *Sister Republics. The Origin of French and American Republicanism*. Cambridge: Harvard University Press, 1988.

————. *Sister Revolution: French Lightening, American Light*. Faber and Faber: New York, 1999.

Higson, Andrew, and Richard Matby, eds. *"Film Europe" and "Film America": Cinema, Commerce and Cultural Exchange, 1920–1939*. Exeter: University of Exeter Press, 1999.

Hjort, Mette, and Scott Mackenzie, eds. *Cinema and Nation*. London: Routledge, 2000.

Hubert-Lacombe, Patricia. *Le Cinéma français dans la guerre froide (1946–56)*. Paris: Harmattan, 1996.

Iriye, Akira. *Global Community: The Role of International Organization in the Making of the Contemporary World*. Berkeley: University of California Press, 2002.

Jacquemelle, Guy. *Citizen Cannes*. Paris: Editions du Mécène, 1997.

Jeancolas, Jean-Pierre. *15 Ans des années trentes: Le Cinéma français, 1929–1944*. Paris: Stock 1983.

Jeancolas, Jean-Pierre. "L'arrangement Blum-Byrnes à l'épreuve des faits. Les relations cinématographiques franco-américaines de 1944 à 1948" *1895*, n.13 (1993): 3–49.

Jobs, Richard Ivan. "Riding the New Wave: Youth and the Rejuvenation of France after World War II." Ph.D. dissertation, Rutgers, 2002.

Jouhad, Christian. "La 'Belle Epoque' et le cinéma." *Le mouvement social*, n. 139 (avril-juin 1987): 106–11.

Judt, Tony. *Past Imperfect: French Intellectuals, 1944–56*. Berkeley: University of California Press, 1994.

————. *Postwar: A History of Europe since 1945*. New York: Penguin, 2005.

Kalifa, Dominique. *La culture de masse en France, 1860–1930*. Paris: Editions La Découverte, 2001.

Keylor, William. "'How They Advertised France': The French Propaganda Campaign in the United States During the Break-Up of the French-American Entente, 1918–23." *Diplomatic History* 17, n. 3 (Summer 1993): 351–73.

King, Anthony D. *Culture, Globalization and the World-System*. Minneapolis: University of Minnesota Press, 1997.

Kracauer, Siegfried. *From Caligari to Hitler*. Princeton: Princeton University Press, 1947.

Kroes, Rob. "American Empire and Cultural Imperialism: A View from the Receiving End." *Diplomatic History* 23, n. 3 (Summer 1999): 463–77.

Kuisel, Richard. "Americanization for Historians," *Diplomatic History* 24, n. 3 (Summer 2000): 509–15.

————. "The Fernandel Factor: The Rivalry between the French and American Cinema in the 1950s," *Yale French Studies*, n. 98 (2000).

————. *Seducing the French*. Berkeley: University of California Press, 1994.

LaCapra, Dominic. "Chartier, Darnton and the Great Symbols Massacre." *Journal of Modern History* 60, n. 1 (1988): 95–112.

Latil, Loredana. *Le Festival de Cannes sur la scène internationale*. Paris: Nouveau Monde Editions, 2005.

Le Clézio, Jean-Marie, and Robert Chazal. *Les Années Cannes: 40 ans de festival*. Paris: Hatier, 1987.

Lebovics, Herman. *Mona Lisa's Escort: André Malraux and the Reinvention of French Culture*. Ithaca: Cornell University Press, 1999.

Lebovics, Herman. *True France: The War over Cultural Identity, 1940–1945*. Ithaca: Cornell University Press, 1994.

LeBrun, Dominique. *Paris-Hollywood. Les français et le cinema américain*. Paris: Hazan, 1987.

Lebrun, Michel. *Le Rendez-vous de Cannes*. Paris: Editions Jean-Claude Latthès, 1986.

Lev, Peter. *The Euro-American Cinema*. Austin: University of Texas Press, 1993.

Levenstein, Harvey. *Seductive Journeys: American Tourists in France from Jefferson to the Jazz Age*. Chicago: University of Chicago Press, 2000.

———. *We'll Always Have Paris: American Tourists in France since 1930*. Chicago: University of Chicago Press, 2004.

Loyer, Emanuelle. "Hollywood au pays des cinés-club (1947–1954)." *Vigntième siècle* (January–March 1992): 45–55.

Mackenzie, Brian. *Remaking France: Americanization, Public Diplomacy and the Marshall Plan*. New York: Berghan Books, 2005.

Malkki, Lisa. "Citizens of Humanity: Internationalism and the Imagined Community of Nations" in *Diaspora* 3, n. 1 (1994): 41–68.

Maltby, Richard. *Hollywood Cinema*. London: Blackwell, 2000.

Mancini, Marc. "So Who Created Vadim?" *Film Comment* 24, n. 2 (March–April 1988): 18–23.

Marie, Michel. *The French New Wave, An Artistic School*. Translated by Richard Neupert. Malden, MA: Blackwell Publishing, 2003.

Marling, Karal Ann. *As Seen on TV: The Visual Culture of Everyday Life in the 1950s*. Cambridge: Harvard University Press, 1994.

Mathy, Jean-Philippe. *Extreme-Occident: French Intellectuals and America*. Chicago: University of Chicago Press, 1993.

May, Kirse Granat. *Golden State, Golden Youth: The California Image in Popular Culture, 1955–1966*. Chapel Hill: University of North Carolina Press, 2002.

May, Lary. *Screening Out the Past: The Birth of Mass Culture and the Motion Picture Industry*. Chicago, University of Chicago Press, 1980.

McCauley, Elizabeth Anne. *Industrial Madness: Commercial Photography in Paris, 1848–1871*. New Haven: Yale University Press, 1994.

Menand, Louis. "Paris, Texas: How Hollywood Brought the Cinema Back from France." *New Yorker* (February 17, 2003): 168–174.

Merck, Mandy. *Perversions. Deviant Readings*. New York: Routledge, 1993.

Miller, Toby, ed. *Global Hollywood*. London: BFI, 2001.

Mollier, Jean-Yves. *Le camelot et la rue: politique et démocratie au tournant des XIX et XX Siècles*. Paris: Fayard, 2004.

Moretti, Franco. *Atlas of the European Novel, 1800–1900*. London: Verso Press, 1999.

Musser, Charles. *Before the Nickelodeon: Edwin S. Porter and the Edison Manufacturing Company*. Berkeley, University of California Press, 1991.

Nadel, Alan. *Containment Culture: American Narratives, Postmodernism and the Atomic Age*. Durham: Duke University Press, 1995.

Naremore, James. *The Films of Vincente Minnelli*. Cambridge, UK: Cambridge University Press, 1993.

Nasaw, Davis. *Going Out: The Rise of Public Amusement*. New York: Basic Books, 1993.

Neale, Steve. "Art Cinema as Institution." *Screen* 22, n. 1 (1981): 11–39

Neupert, Richard. "'Dead Champagne': *Variety*'s 'New Wave.'" *Film History* 10 (1998): 219–30.

Neupert, Richard. *A History of the French New Wave Cinema*. Madison: University of Wisconsin Press, 2002.

Nichols, Bill. "Global Image Consumption in the Age of Late Capitalism." *East-West Film Journal* 8, n. 1 (January 1994): 68–85.

Nolan, Mary. *Visions of Modernity: American Business and the Modernization of Germany*. Oxford: Oxford University Press, 1994.

Nowell-Smith, Geoffrey, and Steven Ricci, eds. *Hollywood and Europe: Economics, Culture, National Identity, 1945–1995*. London: British Film Institute, 1998.

Pagden, Anthony. "The Genesis of 'Governance' and Enlightenment Conceptions of the Cosmopolitan World Order." *International Social Science Journal*, n. 155 (March 1998): 7–15.

Palmer, R. R. *Age of the Democratic Revolution: A Political History of Europe and America, 1760–1800*. Princeton: Princeton University Press, 1969.

Pascal, Michel. *Cannes: Cris et chuchotements*. Paris: NIL, 1997.

Pells, Richard. *Not Like Us: How Europeans Have Loved, Hated and Transformed American Culture since World War Two*. New York: Basic Books, 1998.

Philippe, Claude-Jean. *Cannes: Le festival*. Paris: Editions Nathan, SIPA, 1987.

Pilcher, Jeffrey M. *Cantínflas and the Chaos of Mexican Modernity*. Wilmington: Scholarly Resources, 2001.

Planel, Alomée. *Quarante ans de Festival*. Paris: Londreys, 1987.

Poiger, Uta G. *Jazz, Rock and Rebel: Cold War Politics and American Culture in a Divided Germany*. Berkeley: University of California Press, 2000.

Portes, Jacques. "A l'origine de la légende noire des accords Blum-Byrnes sur le cinéma," *Revue d'histoire moderne et contemporaine* 33 (avril-juin 1986): 314–29.

———. *Fascination and Misgivings: The United States in French Opinion, 1870–1914*. Translated by Elborg Forster. Cambridge: Cambridge University Press, 2000.

———. "Hollywood's French Topics (1925–1956): A Strange Definition of Identity." Unpublished paper. 2001.

Powell, Michael. *A Life in the Movies*. New York: Knopf, 1986.

Rabinowitz, Lauren. *For the Love of Pleasure: Women, Movies, and Culture in Turn-of-the-Century Chicago*. New Brunswick: Rutgers University Press, 1998.

Rearick, Charles. *Pleasures of the Belle Epoque: Entertainment and Festivity in Turn-of-the-Century France*. New Haven: Yale University Press, 1985.

———. *The French in Love and War: Popular Culture in the Era of the World Wars*. New Haven: Yale University Press, 1997.

Rentschler, Eric. *The Ministry of Illusion: Nazi Cinema and Its Afterlife*. Cambridge: Harvard University Press, 1996.

Rifkin, Adrian. *Street Noises: Parisian Pleasure, 1900–1940*. Manchester: Manchester University Press, 1993.

Rihoit, Catherine. *Brigitte Bardot: Un myth français*. Paris: Livre de Poche, 1986.

Rioux, Jean-Pierre, and Jean-François Sirinelli. *La culture de masse en France de la Belle Epoque à nos jours*. Paris: Fayard, 2002.

Robbins, Bruce. *Feeling Global: Internationalism in Distress.* New York: New York University Press, 1999.

Robinson, Edward G., with Leonard Spigelgass. *All My Yesterdays: An Autobiography.* New York: Hawthorn Books, 1973.

Robinson, Jeffrey. *Bardot: An Intimate Portrait.* New York: Donald Fine, 1994.

Roger, Philippe. *The American Enemy: The History of French Anti-Americanism.* Translated by Sharon Bowman. Chicago: University of Chicago Press, 2005.

Rosello, Mireille. *Declining the Stereotype: Ethnicity and Representation in French Cultures.* Hanover: University Press of New England, 1998.

Ross, Kristin. *Fast Cars, Clean Bodies: Decolonization and the Reordering of French Culture.* Cambridge: MIT Press, 1995.

Rupnik, Jacques, Denis Licorne, and Marie-France Toinet. *The Rise and Fall of French Anti-Americanism.* Translated by Gerry Turner. New York: St. Martin's Press, 1990.

Rydell, Robert W. and Rob Kroes. *Buffalo Bill in Bologna. The Americanization of the World, 1869-1922.* Chicago: University of Chicago Press, 2005.

Samuels, Maurice. *The Spectacular Past: Popular History and the Novel in Nineteenth-Century France.* Ithaca: Cornell University Press, 2004.

Sandeen, Eric. *Picturing an Exhibition: The Family of Man and 1950s America.* Albuquerque: University of New Mexico Press, 1995.

Saunders, Frances Stonor. *The Cultural Cold War: The CIA and the World of Arts and Letters.* New York: New Press, 2000.

Saunders, Thomas. *Hollywood in Berlin: American Cinema and Weimar Germany.* Berkeley: University of California Press, 1994.

Scott, Allen J. *On Hollywood: The Place, The Industry.* Princeton: Princeton University Press, 2005.

Schwartz, Vanessa R. "The Eiffel Tower." In *Urban Icons: Multi-media Companion to Urban History* 33, n. 1 (May 2006). www.journals.cambridge.org/urbanicons

———. *Spectacular Realities: Early Mass Culture in Fin-de-siècle France.* Berkeley: University of California Press, 1998.

Sekula, Alan. "Paparazzo Notes." In *Photography Against the Grain: Essays and Photowork, 1973-1983,* pp. 23–31. Nova Scotia: Press of the Nova Scotia College of Art and Design, 1984.

Sellier, Geneviève and Ginette Vincendeau. "La nouvelle vague et le cinéma populaire: Brigitte Bardot dans *Vie privée* et *Le mépris.*" *Iris* (Fall 1998): 115–30.

Servel, Alain. *Frenchie Goes to Hollywood: La France et les français dans le cinema américaine de 1929 à nos jours.* Paris: Henri Veyrier: 1987.

Sharif, Omar, and Marie-Thèrese Guinchard. *L'eternel masculin.* Paris: Stock, 1976.

Sherzer, Dina. "The New Wave and Its Franco-American Intersections: An Essay in Cultural Pointillism." *Contemporary French Civilization* 15, n. 1 (1991): 52–69.

Silver, Kenneth. *Making Paradise: Art, Modernity and the Myth of the French Riviera.* Cambridge, MIT Press, 2001.

Silverman, Stephen. *Dancing on the Ceiling: Stanley Donen and His Movies.* New York: Knopf, 1996.

Sklar, Robert. *Movie-Made America: A Cultural History of American Movies.* New York: Vintage [1975] 1994.

Smith, Dina M. "Global Cinderella: *Sabrina* (1954), Hollywood and Postwar Inter-nationalism." *Cinema Journal* 42, n. 4 (Summer 2002): 27–50.

Sorlin, Pierre. "1957: A Divided Europe. European Cinema at the Time of the Rome Treaty." *Contemporary European History* 8, n. 3 (1999): 411–24.

Spigel, Lynn. *Make Room for TV: Television and the Family Ideal in Postwar America.* Chicago, University of Chicago Press, 1992.

Starr, Kevin. *Americans and the California Dream, 1850–1915.* New York: Oxford University Press, 1973.

Steinberg, Cobbett. *Reel Facts: The Movie Book of Records.* New York: Vintage, 1978.

Stokes, Melvyn, and Richard Malthy, eds. *Hollywood Abroad: Audiences and Cultural Exchange.* London: British Film Institute, 2004.

Strauss, David. "The Rise of Anti-Americanism in France: French Intellectuals and the American Film Industry, 1927–1932." *Journal of Popular Culture* 10, n. 4 (Spring 1977): 752–59.

Studlar, Gaylyn. "'Chi-Chi Cinderella': Audrey Hepburn as Couture Countermodel." In *Hollywood Goes Shopping*, edited by David Desser and Garth S. Jowett, 159–78. Minneapolis: University of Minnesota Press, 2000.

Swann, Paul. "The Little State Department: Hollywood and the State Department in the Postwar World." *American Studies International* 29, n. 1 (April 1991): 1–19.

Sweeney, Regina. *Singing Our Way to Victory: French Cultural Politics and Music during World War I.* Wesleyan: Wesleyan University Press, 2001.

Taves, Brian, and Stephen Michaulk, Jr., eds. *The Jules Verne Encyclopedia.* Lanham: Scarecrow Press, 1996.

Terrio, Susan J. *Crafting the Culture and History of French Chocolate.* Berkeley: University of California Press, 2000.

Thompson, Kristin. *Exporting Entertainment: American in the World Film Market, 1907–1934.* London: British Film Institute, 1985.

Thomson, Richard, Philip Dennis Cate, and Mary Weaver Chapin. *Toulouse-Lautrec and Montmartre.* Washington, D.C.: National Gallery of Art, 2005.

Tiersten, Lisa. *Marianne in the Market: Envisioning Consumer Society in Fin-de-siècle France.* Berkeley: University of California Press, 2001.

Todd, Michael, Jr., and Susan McCarthy Todd. *A Valuable Property: The Life Story of Michael Todd.* New York: Arbor House, 1983.

Tomlinson, John. *Globalization and Culture.* Chicago: University of Chicago Press, 1999.

Toscan du Plantier, Daniel. *Cinquante ans du Festival de Cannes.* Paris: Ramsay, 1997.

Troy, Nancy J. *Couture Culture: A Study in Modern Art and Fashion.* Cambridge, MA: MIT Press, 2003.

Trumpbour, John. *Selling Hollywood to the World: U.S. and European Struggles for Mastery of the Global Film Industry.* Cambridge, UK: Cambridge University Press, 2002.

Turan, Kenneth. *From Sundance to Sarajevo: Film Festivals and the World They Made.* Berkeley: University of California Press, 2002.

Twitchell, James B. *Living It Up: America's Love Affair with Luxury.* New York: Simon and Schuster, 2003.

Ulf-Moeller, Jens. *Hollywood's Film Wars with France: Film Trade Diplomacy and the Emergence of the French Film Quota Policy.* Rochester: University of Rochester Press, 2001.

Vadim, Roger. *Bardot, Deneuve, Fonda*. Translated by Melinda Camber Porter. New York: Simon and Schuster, 1986.

Variety editors. *Cannes: Fifty Years of Sun, Sex and Celluloid*. Foreword by Clint Eastwood. Los Angeles: Hyperion. Miramax Books, 1997.

Vasey, Ruth. *The World According to Hollywood, 1918–1939*. Exeter: University of Exeter Press, 1997.

Verdaguer, Pierre. "Hollywood's Frenchness: Representations of the French in American Films." *Contemporary French and Francophone Studies* 8, n. 4 (2004): 441–51.

Vincendeau, Ginette. "France, 1945–1965 and Hollywood: The Policier as Inter-national Text." *Screen* 33, n. 1 (Spring 1992): 50–80.

———. "Hollywood Babel: The Coming of Sound and the Multiple-Language Version." In *"Film Europe" and "Film America:" Cinema, Commerce and Cultural Exchange, 1920–1939*, edited by Andrew Higson and Richard Maltby. Exeter: University of Exeter Press, 1999.

———. *Stars and Stardom in French Cinema*. London: Continuum, 2000.

Wagnleitner, Reinhold, and Elaine Tyler May, eds. *"Here, There and Everywhere": The Foreign Politics of American Popular Culture*. Hanover, NH: University of New England Press, 2000.

Waldman, Diane. "The Childish, the Insane and the Ugly: The Representation of Modern Art in Popular Films and Fictions of the Forties." *Wide Angle* 5, n. 2 (1983): 52–65.

Wall, Irwin. *The United States and the Making of Postwar France, 1945–1954*. New York: Cambridge University Press, 1991.

Walsh, Frank. *Sin and Censorship: The Catholic Church and the Motion Picture Industry*. New Haven: Yale University Press, 1996.

Walsh, Michael. "National Cinema, National Imaginary." *Film History* 8 (1996): 5–17.

Walton, Whitney. "Internationalism and the Junior Year Abroad: American Students in France in the 1920s and 1930s." *Diplomatic History* 29, n. 2 (April 2005): 255–78.

Wasson, Haidee. *Museum Movies: The Museum of Modern Art and the Birth of Art Cinema*. Berkeley: University of California Press, 2005.

Weiner, Susan. *Enfants Terribles: Youth and Femininity in the Mass Media in France, 1945–1968*. Baltimore: Johns Hopkins University Press, 2001.

Wiley, Mason, and Damien Bona. *Inside Oscar: The Unofficial History of the Academy Awards*, edited by Gail MacColl. New York: Ballantine Books, 1996.

Wilinsky, Barbara. *Sure Seaters: The Emergence of Art House Cinema*. Minneapolis: University of Minnesota Press, 2001.

Wollen, Peter, and Joe Kerr, eds. *Autopia: Cars and Culture*. London: Reaktion Books, 2002.

Wood, Michael. *America in the Movies*. New York: Columbia University Press, 1975.

Young, Robert. *Marketing Marianne: French Propaganda in America, 1900–1940*. New Brunswick: Rutgers University Press, 2004.

Index